THE
ANOINTING

PAUL RIGBY

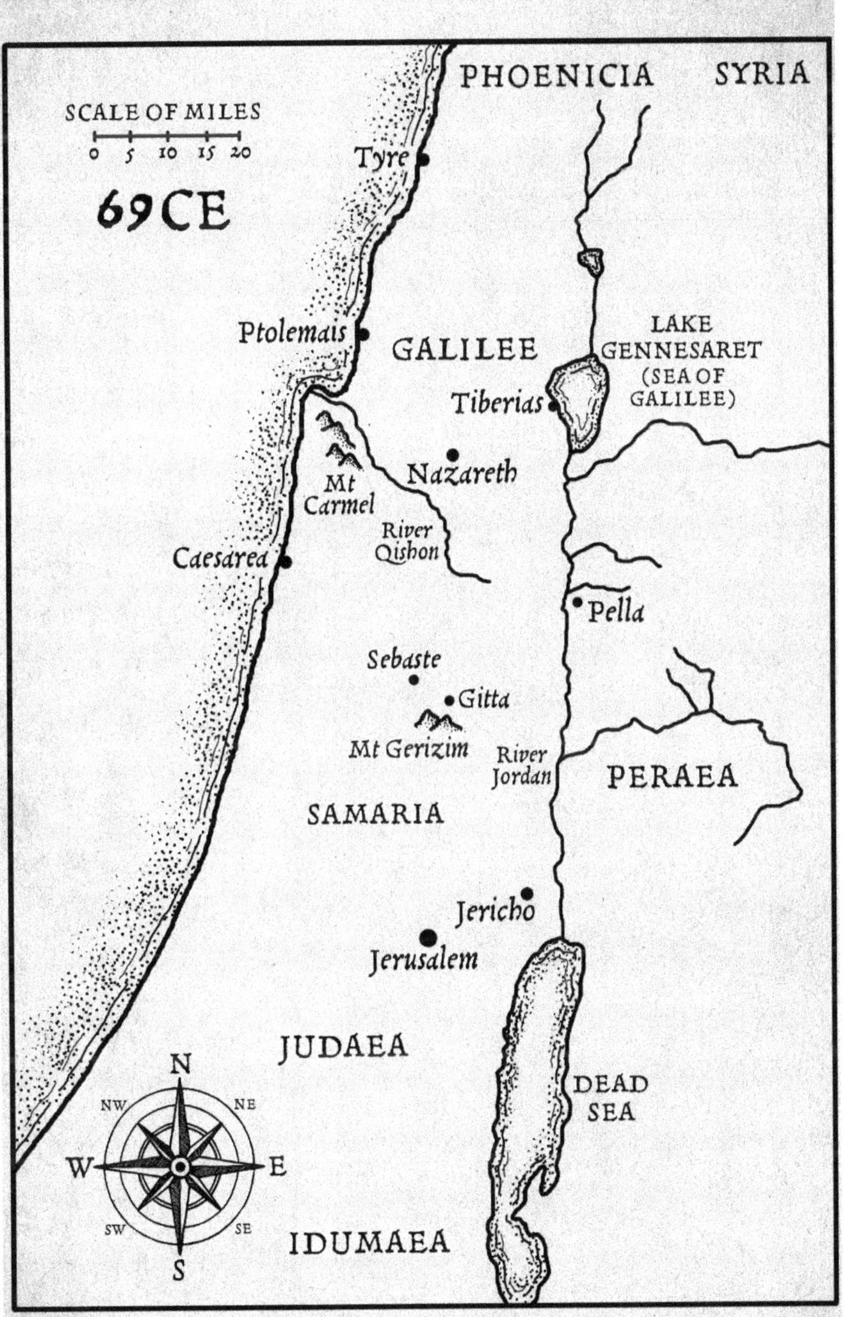

SCALE OF MILES
0 5 10 15 20
69 CE
PHOENICIA
SYRIA
Tyre
Ptolemais
GALILEE
LAKE GENNESARET (SEA OF GALILEE)
Tiberias
Nazareth
Mt Carmel
River Qishon
Caesarea
Pella
Sebaste
Gitta
Mt Gerizim
River Jordan
PERAEA
SAMARIA
Jericho
Jerusalem
JUDAEA
DEAD SEA
N
NW
NE
W
E
SW
SE
S
IDUMAEA

AUTHOR'S NOTE

This tale includes many details from 'history'. History however is not a fixed entity. The record can include many things other than objective truth. We might correctly parrot dates in school, yet who could deny history's subjective experience, knowing that each culture and generation interprets history in the light of its own understanding—and there may be several competing versions. Napoleon Bonaparte upheld the view that history was a set of lies agreed upon not as the record is being made but after the fact, once opposing parties had been eliminated.

We each see the world not only through our eyes but more importantly through our attitudes. Should I change my mood, my underlying sense of what is real changes too. In this way I invent the world I see.

Does that argument seem fanciful and unscientific? Blame it on our fixation with outmoded Newtonian concepts. Isaac was a great man, yet science has moved on. The Copenhagen interpretation of quantum mechanics (though that particular explanation is not the only one) says the appearance of reality that we perceive is a construction of our own minds. This applies not only to history books but also to our individual lives. If I invent the world I see, the world of the present, then surely my past and future will be formulated in the same way. It opens the possibility that according to my degree of wisdom and resilience, I might take up a position of assuming life has only appropriate things in store for me even while my experiences may appear both 'good' and 'bad'. I could come to an understanding that this process will be most successfully accomplished through my acquiescence and without my interference.

Being creative with the past is not at all off the table. The discoveries of physics suggest that time is purely relative; another theory from quantum mechanics says there could be an indefinite number of co-existing universes—and all events exist concurrently. Co-existing universes allow us to think in terms of 'probable realities' or simultaneous alternative outcomes of a single situation. If there are many branching roads along the way and we appear to take a 'wrong' turn, why should we not go back and change direction?

There is even the question of time's very existence. One point of view says there is neither past nor future. Instead, there is only NOW —the ever-present moment, which is also eternity. We then habitually solidify those moments depending on our personality preferences, and this helps to determine for us what is 'real'. (Our beliefs about the flow of time from past to present to future may prevent us from contemplating this proposal.)

Whatever way we deal with it, history is not clear-cut. I suggest imagination has a respectable role. Albert Einstein, a re-definer of our worldview, believed 'Imagination is more important than knowledge'.

And so to the story. I wrote the first draft a long time ago but might have guessed that stories have a habit of rebelling against their author and insisting on their independence, this certainly happened to me. There is some sort of historical foundation with a few well-known characters and agreed-upon exits and entrances. But rather than adhere rigidly to the historical script (which in any case is smudged and torn in vital places) I have taken some good lines and let others write themselves.

One of the most significant influences on the development of Western civilisation was the growth of the Christian religion. Yet the Jesus story as it has come down to us is an interpretation of a number of reports of a probable past reality. There have been of course many interpretations but historically the most persuasive has been that of the Church of Rome.

However, Rome is neither the hero nor villain of the piece. Christianity was created by men - men trying to come to terms with the message and the inspiration of Jesus. The idea that all is interconnected (Bell's theorem from back in 1964 and still not disproved forces us to consider there is no such thing as 'separate parts') is an excellent basis for the Christian virtues of tolerance and forgiveness. Humanity is from one perspective a single organism straddling 'time' and 'space'. I am not disconnected even from the members of the various tribunals known as the Holy Inquisition of centuries past who might have burned this book and its author.

A modern attempt to discover the 'real story' of Jesus sparked tremendous study and application; *The Five Gospels*, sub-titled The Search for the Authentic Words of Jesus, published in the 1990s. This work applied rigorous rules as to methodology, rules that were specified to make the result independent of any particular ecclesiastical or political leaning. It focussed on the Gospels of Mark, Matthew, Luke, John and Thomas.

One description of the intended result was 'to unlock doors too long bolted shut by a combination of elitism and technical jargon'. Twenty-four scholars, fellows of The Jesus Seminar, worked for six years, firstly inventorying all the surviving ancient texts for works attributed to Jesus. (Later they produced their own translation of the gospels. Appropriately that was known as The Scholars Version and was published as part of *The Complete Gospels* under the editorship of Robert J. Miller in 2010.)

This project acted to uncover and sometimes discredit the possibly poetic yet otherwise often unnatural and outdated language of older bibles. The attitude taken by the scholars was that Jesus was a man of the people who communicated in the straightforward language of the people. He was most likely not a writer but an orator who spoke short, provocative and memorable words and stories. The Scholars Version was determined to bring this Jesus fully alive while at the same time doing its very best to evade statements, appearing in existing bibles, that the authors believed were almost certainly not made by Jesus. This was especially true when they saw credible evidence of teachings developed and inserted by Christian evangelists and clergy during much later years of the development of the new religion. Among other indications they applied the following rule: 'Only sayings and parables that can be traced back to the oral period, 30 - 50 CE, can possibly have originated with Jesus'.

Another thing the scholars didn't like was any reference by Jesus that tended to support his intentional martyrdom. Such utterances were likely considered a later 'Christianisation' of the real Jesus. A characteristic regarded more favourably was where Jesus spoke against the haughty righteousness of the conservative religious authorities such as the Sadducees and Pharisees, supplanting their way of operating with his own direct, pithy statements.

For me the rigorous nature of *The Five Gospels* produced the strong impression of a study whose time had come. Particularly because biblical stories tend to be dished out when one is young and impressionable. It never occurred to me in my childhood days that the gospels might have been subjected to or even designed with a whole raft of 'additions' or 'improvements' over the centuries. But then it wasn't hard to imagine: should you wish to promote a particular line of what's right or wrong, why not ascribe your ideas, your anecdotes, to Jesus?

Yet how much simpler and better it was to focus on the most straightforward utterances, the most simple and forthright actions of a man who walked, spoke and acted across Palestine in order to uplift humanity.

None of this means that Jesus, beyond the actual words he spoke and the direct actions that went with them, was not a highly advanced soul with depths few of his disciples or chroniclers could grasp in their entirety if at all. The attempts to dig down into those depths made over the centuries have produced a wide range of ideas, inspirations and opinions. We will try not to complicate those attempts.

Christianity is possibly not as familiar to many of us as we might think. For example, many traditional bible versions agree that 'a word spoken against the Holy Spirit is not forgivable'. There were a couple of implications here. It was hard to find a valid and arresting explanation for this Holy Spirit, apart from its important inclusion in the Trinity. Here are two possible descriptions that still leave plenty of room for further investigation: 'A channel of power from and into the deeper energies that created and sustain us' and: 'The voice for (not of) God'.

Forgiveness of sins is a well-known and standard element of most Christian teachings such as the Nicene Creed retained in similar form by Roman Catholic, Orthodox, Anglican, and major Protestant churches. I found one recent Christian teaching deeply focussed on forgiveness, but not about God forgiving us. Rather, it made a strong case that forgiveness was only intended for humans to release each other. The explanation was simple—God *did not* forgive, simply because He/She/the Nameless would never condemn their own creations, thus 'forgiving' those creations was redundant. Rather than focussing on the subject of 'sin', forgiveness was about us forgiving our neighbours as we would like to be forgiven ourselves. This was confirmed by the apostles Matthew and Luke quoting Christ: Don't pass judgement so you won't be judged.

And what should we make of the Gospel of John with its deep themes concerning the nature of God including our access to Him or lack thereof and the sonship of Jesus? This approach is mostly rather different from Mark, Luke and Matthew and even from Thomas. Jesus was not much inclined—except particularly in John—to refer to himself and his mission, although John also reported Jesus speaking clearly on people needing to love one another.

The Five Gospels saw in John suggestive evidence of early Christian internal debates and controversies about Jesus' identity: 'Focus on the historical Jesus has been displaced by speculation regarding the mythic redeemer figure.'

In thinking about the ways in which Mankind has used and misused the ideas and beliefs around Jesus and all the errors and horrors they have helped introduce to every corner of civilisation, I was happy to discover that not too many years ago a dedicated group of academic specialists worked diligently to discover the actual meanings spoken by the real Jesus of Nazareth.

A very obvious problem with Christianity, but by no means limited to that religion, is the exclusivity principle. When my understanding of what is true has to do battle against what others believe is true; when I demand my truth has to be accepted in every detail without question; when I am not only right but superior in spirit, then we are ready to sink without trace. Jesus never initiated such behaviour.

Now is a good time to treat the entire subject of Christ's mission with less surface emotion and much more depth. (A task that is surely too important to be left to theologians and church authorities alone.) Then we might discover more value in it.

We live with increasingly difficult global conditions. Almost everything we may have once felt we knew as bedrock is breaking around us. But in such times, there is the (admittedly difficult) opportunity for renewal.

Jesus did not live a life of ease. Yes, he and his message were welcomed by some, but he was also misunderstood or attacked by many. He was betrayed and then suffered a worse death than most of us can imagine. Despite all that he carried out his function diligently to the end.

If we could be more deeply perceptive about Jesus and his lifework - in other words, if we chose to view the phenomenon anew with an active/receptive, higher-inspired attitude - we might begin to change things, both within and without. We might even assist the beginnings of a shift in the foundations of a large part of our culture. In changing the view of our past, we could offer ourselves the chance of freeing our present and the better hope of a meaningful future.

1
THE SETUP

THE CAVE WAS small and dusty. Dull shards of pottery showed that the place had sheltered people before, but Mark was not impressed by this historical vote of confidence. The smell of something dead coming from deep within the narrowing shadows, contrasted with the perfect sunset outside. More importantly, the hideout was inconspicuous, the entrance veiled by acacia branches and nearby there was spring water trickling over rocks.

The hour of evening prayers approached yet he could think only of the soreness in his feet and leg muscles. God would surely forgive a lapse. He was after all on God's business while everywhere in the land the works of the ungodly prospered. The bread was all gone and hunger distracted him. He took out his pen, ink and a torn scrap of papyrus. Others recommended the practice of unceasing prayer, but he had no habit of it any more than he had spent so much as a day with Barnabas and Paul in deliberately fasting—these were both practices some 'holy men' insisted on yet they didn't appeal. Especially as Jesus was heard to have said (Mark recorded it from more than one source) that it didn't matter what went into a person's mouth, so much as what came out of it. Writing was akin to speaking but with the possible benefit of editing before anyone else saw it.

Writing was civilised, holding out hope of control over fate and unruly emotions. Orange and pink-dyed clouds billowing over the forests of Samaria reminded him of the majesty of God which could never be erased by the ignorant disputations of men. Give me strength Master; watch over my journey into the unknown; keep my faith strong; keep your sacred words safe. There, he was praying despite himself.

Mark began to scribble and the activity soothed him. Not a living soul knew where he was and even if they did, what difference would it make? For once in his life he was glad to be a virtual nobody.

After he had finished writing he splashed his face with water, backed into the cave and curled up in his cloak, falling into the fitful sleep of the physically exhausted.

Mark might not have slept at all had he been aware that in Sebaste, barely a dozen miles distant by the flight of the crow, commander Barius the third most senior officer of the Fifth (Macedonian) legion was completing an interview with a Judaean warrior.

Barius, resplendent in full battledress, waved toward the brimming wine cup on the table between them. 'Not drinking tonight, Benjamin?'

Benjamin sat in the shadows of the room and this seemed to fit his nature. 'I'm here on business, praefect' he muttered through his thick red beard. 'No need for false pleasantries. Find this Mark for us and we'll do our part.'

The commander knew he was taking a risk dealing with a known zealot like Benjamin. In theory - and very likely in practice - this was a man with Roman blood on his hands. Yet Barius was willing to stretch a point to arrest a highly prominent follower of the seditious Nazorene sect.

Barius drummed his fingers on the table then forced his hands into his lap. These Jews were so intense and unbending that he couldn't wait for the military campaign to come to its inexorable conclusion. 'Sometimes a relaxed mind remembers more' he said reasonably. 'We're looking for one pebble on the beach of Palestine. You have to help us with all the information you can think of, however trivial.'

A Sicarii warrior who held to hard-line beliefs, Benjamin regarded the rabbi Jesus as a useful symbol of Jewish independence. If his group could interrogate this Mark and demand he spill the beans about other Christian Jewish groups and their locations, they could be infiltrated and perhaps turned. He most certainly hadn't considered turning the other cheek.

Benjamin stood. 'He's here. Bound to be. Last reported heading north-west from Jericho. He'll have scrolls and they're important to him. He's a learned man but not a fighter. He'll make mistakes, count on it! All you have to do is keep your ear to the ground. Got enough spies, haven't you?'

Anger flared in Barius' eyes. He had to play along with these insolent bastards for a little longer but as soon as Jerusalem was tamed...

The praefect did not rise. He crooked a finger at the guard and switched from Aramaic to Latin. 'Show this ah, gentleman out. Give him a pouch of incense so he may pay his respects at Caesar's altar.' The Jew Benjamin, born and bred under the Roman yoke, would understand the words and the studied insult they were intended to convey.

The Judaean took the incense and tucked it in the folds of his robe. 'We shall give Caesar the tribute he deserves' he said ambiguously, 'and burn this in honour of the One who came to lead us out of dishonour. Fetch Mark to us and we can both celebrate on the altars of our choice.' Benjamin almost stopped at the doorway; there were more double-edged statements begging to be voiced. But deciding against such a dangerous gambit, he vanished into the night.

◆

Perhaps as Mark slept some intimation of this conversation reached him because nearing midnight he awoke in a sweat.

Since early childhood he had been accustomed to vivid dreams. The trouble was that they were never prophetic, only upsetting. He tried to ignore the senseless hallucinations. Even the insistent memory of a voice repeating, 'He's coming. He's not far away now, and he's coming.'

Mark turned over, trying to find a position of least discomfort on the sandy floor of the cave. 'He's coming.' Oh quiet, he thought, I need my sleep.

Even fewer miles from Mark than Barius, a man and a woman were sitting up in bed while nodding to each other in satisfaction. 'Close' said the man. 'Won't be long. Perhaps this week. He's coming, alright.'

'Take watch on the hill road then' she said. 'And you must...'

'I'll be careful. The big knife.'

'Tell the others?'

'Not yet.'

'What sort of man?'

'Mm. Scholar, I'd say.'

The couple continued to nod like puppets in a child's show but they used no more words.

Eventually each moved into the other's arms, moonlight flooding through the window revealing their naked bodies entwined together as one. Only when this grotesque, beautiful creature had rocked and shuddered itself to a standstill did Mark's dreams fade. The prying moon illuminated him sleeping spreadeagled and snoring in his rocky crevice, giving the uncanny impression of an innocent awaiting his fate.

2

THE BACKGROUND

THIS IS IN large part my story, so I should tell you something of myself. My name is John Mark. Or simply Mark. Although it's a Latin name, I am a Jew and in the precinct of Jerusalem where I was born, they like to call me Menahem—the Comforter—because I was always drawn to the path of service.

But don't associate me with the Menahem who started the revolt against Rome! All Jews are not the same. People have strange ideas about us Jews, they weave weird stories about our clannishness and I agree there are many facts to support this idea. But we're not all reactionaries and we're not all warriors either. Many of us understand that despite our present troubles, history is breaking us free of the fetters of the past and helping us see ourselves in a new light.

And if I live through this, that's the message I'll be spreading. It's exciting to be a citizen of the world, as I call myself now. And who might I ask you has swept the cobwebs away from the old inward-looking, narrow sense of tribe and religion if it's not our brothers the Greeks?

I realise that xenophobic Jews - especially the stricter Pharisees and Essenes and for different reasons some of the bolder Levites and more self-righteous of the discredited Sanhedrists (who murdered the Master's brother) and those patriotic terrorists the Sicarii - the knife-toting zealots - might call me a traitor.

Yes, I know. It's hard to forget the Greek pogroms against the Jews of Alexandria a quarter of a century ago. But don't tar all Greeks with the same brush. A nasty squabble between Jews and Greeks in Caesarea - seat of imperial administration in Judaea - signalled the beginning of this war. And yet Florus the rapacious procurator was the real culprit. He accepted a handsome sum to settle the argument then typically pretended ignorance of the matter and left the two sides to fight it out. When Jerusalem demonstrated in protest against this and a new tax the procurator had trumped up, Florus started the massacres.

'Greeks? Not as bad as Romans' some of my fellow citizens would tell you, 'but Greeks are bad enough with their loose morals and their intellectual claptrap'.

Don't you see there's a new world, a new order now? The old rules don't apply as once they did. Would you speak to me of the Law, my kinsmen?

My Master understood that we so often overlook the spirit of the Law and favour only its dead words. Even before I came across my first wild-eyed Essene, I had met Jews living in Peraea beyond the Jordan who would not worship in the Temple, knowing that the Temple exists rather in their own hearts. Think if you will of our sacred Torah. The Torah is our law but the true translation from Hebrew is 'guidance'. It was the guidance God gave Moses, when the prophet led the Jewish people out of Egypt. It worked so well - God answered Moses and the needs of the Israelites. But what did we Jews do with that guidance? We turned it into stone; we made it a fixed Law - to be applied centuries after its usefulness had begun to decline.

That sort of Jewishness has to be changed or there are terrible things in store for my people - perhaps even worse than what they are currently suffering. Who can be sure in these days of chaos? Don't ask me to prove what I'm saying. I can't. I only know when something's hard and brittle, it breaks too easily.

Look, perhaps I shouldn't be mouthing off like this, bleeding my heart out to a stranger. And maybe I have no right to interpret the words of my Master - there'll be enough others to do that and make a mess of it - but my Master came to usher in a new age. It was to be a new time for men, a time to start fresh and see everything they think and do in a new light. He brought in a new spirit with him, a spirit of compassion - I don't care who laughs and says you can only teach folk by treating them like dogs. I tell you straight if I didn't believe all that I'm writing I wouldn't go on risking my life at a time like this when things are dangerous enough even for the most circumspect citizen. I can only say that I'm proud I was taught by the Greeks to take a wider view of life. 'Forget your grand ideas' my countrymen have told me, 'and save yourself. Don't you know that Titus has been sent by his granite-headed father, General Vespasian, to tear down the Temple stone by stone?'

They said if I must make a martyr of myself, to do it like a proper Jew and kill a few of the marauding Roman soldiers first. Now who's being impractical? Imagine me, Mark or Menahem, trading sword-blows with the grisly professionals of Trajan's Apollinaris legion (the Fifteenth). Hopeless! Mark - hardly a young man anymore - against the might of Rome? Is it too arrogant to believe that God has another task for me, and one that suits me better?

I'm a scholar of sorts. And yes, I know Rome doesn't always win. I heard the story of those savage Germans in the north-west of the Empire who destroyed two entire legions in the Teutoberg Forest. And we Jews have also shaken the Romans not a little, thanks to great courage and brilliant tactics by men like General Joseph ben Matthias of the Galilee (until he shamefully turned traitor and went over to Vespasian's side with the fancy new Roman name of Josephus Flavius). But that kind of victory isn't for me. I'm a man of letters - at least I can write my name, my eyes are clear and my wits aren't too dull.

My function is like Hermes... What's that? You don't want to hear about Hermes, about Greeks and their several gods? And now you think I must be idolatrous myself? Just wait a minute. I never bowed down to any statue and I'm never going to. But even a fool can see that Greeks like the Romans, attribute to each of their gods certain human qualities. That doesn't make them very pure deities in my eyes, but it does provide a good means of describing the differences between people. I'm the Hermes type because I watch and see what's going on and then I write it down and take the information where it is best put to use. It started when I was with Paul and Barnabas, though that's another story and now they are gone I must carry their torch.

Which brings me to why I'm here in this grubby cave writing like one possessed. Perhaps I *am* possessed as Jesus promised, possessed of the Holy Spirit. I write to a reader I know not, trying to make you understand His message. And the scroll may well be lost in the dirt with no-one to read it after I am dead.

But that reminds me. The Master proved that death was not the end; it's a fake disaster that need not touch us. I could explain this but not now. I don't want to think about death at all.

I shall pull my cloak tighter as the sun sinks toward the horizon, its light filling this valley with purples, turning the forest trees into strong dark shapes that will watch over me as I write while ever there is light to see by. I like writing.

I *must* write, whether you read this or not.

◆

Did you like Mark's forthright approach? His physical strength and courage could be in doubt, but he might well have made a diligent journalist, considering that the best of them want to suss a thing out for their own satisfaction and not just put it in the news. Nevertheless, Mark's bodily form is long gone. Perhaps he discovered something special concerning that Master of his but is there any point after so many dreary centuries, in reviving the story, unless... Unless it has meaning for today.

The latter part of the First Century CE was a time of unusual emotional and political unrest. 'Things'—comets, eclipses and meteors, as well as others less readily identifiable—were regularly seen in the sky. There was no shortage of prophets of doom, or people to listen to them. The many leaders who started personality cults seemed rather less credible, probably because of the very high levels of taxation which they imposed. In Asia, several cities were destroyed by earthquakes. Volcanoes became more active. The contemporary writer Seneca warned, 'The world itself is being shaken to pieces and there is universal consternation'.

No-one had heard then of global warming or enormous levels of industrial pollution, our seas filling up with plastic. Neither had anyone come across internet scams, tremendous species extinction nor rampant human over-population. But there was widespread awareness then as now that the world was on a collision course with destiny. Perhaps we have more in common with that era than we might think. In our day, billionaires proliferate and hundreds of millions of people are displaced and/or dispossessed, as would-be emperors make war with their neighbours or turn against and exploit their own people.

In Palestine, the most obvious outward expression of trouble was the tightening grip of Roman rule. Eventually the tension exploded into war. It was preposterous - a modest vassal state on the outskirts of the Empire unilaterally declaring independence by force of arms. But such is the way of patriots. Consider the Afghan fighters 1900 years later, successfully pitting small arms and antique armour against Soviet tanks and aircraft.

War and rumour of war was a preoccupation of the Roman Empire. Such a magnificent fighting force as the legendary legions had to be put to use. The emperor, ostensibly absolute overlord, was just another jelly in the military mould. Today's national leaders are locked into a similar situation - the more they growl at each other and increase their defence budgets, the safer they hope to feel. Ever-growing, ever-debilitating conflicts sap human resilience; while almost forgotten in the background some thousands of nuclear warheads wait patiently.

The First Century Romans and their colonies had a mixed bag of rulers. Between the death of Octavian and the appointment of Vespasian, a span of 55 troubled years with a somewhat sorry succession of emperors, much innocent blood was spilled.

Tiberius might not have been such a bad fellow although reports have it that his wisdom in office took a nose-dive near the end when he became reclusive, perverted and cruel. He was in any case responsible for enabling the accession of Gaius, better known as Caligula.

Caligula suffered madness but being emperor meant he could act out his fantasies. To show his scorn for the ineffectual senators who were supposed to check the emperor's excesses, Caligula became infamous when he planned to appoint his horse Incitatus to the Senate. Yet he didn't live long enough to do so. As for listing Caligula's crimes - there is something of the mad dictator in all of us if we choose to give it rein. Suffice to say that the emperor toyed with sex and power on a grand scale, but it gave him no peace. So, he sought solace in divinity. Caligula's subjects could honour him as a god or suffer the nasty consequences.

In about 40 CE he reversed the formerly quite tolerant Roman attitude toward Jewish traditions and tried to have his own statue installed in the holy Temple at Jerusalem. The dour Jews were not, to say the least, amused. The Jewish War might have started then and there had the emperor's supposed bad karma not caught up with him. There was a palace plot and Caligula was murdered.

Claudius was the next incumbent. It's hard to separate gratuitous slander from fact but rumours blamed him for the execution of relatives, senators and knights.

Under Claudius, the emperor in whose reign Britain was invaded and London became a Roman city, the conditions in Palestine deteriorated due to a series of greedy and incompetent procurators. After Claudius was reportedly poisoned by his wife, throw-them-to-the-lions Nero took on the imperial purple. Toward the end of Nero's reign (he committed suicide to escape his enemies) was Rome's first recorded Christian persecution and in the same year Nero fiddled while the great fire of Rome raged. Under Nero the Jews revolted, and Vespasian was sent to crush them.

There was a tremendous power struggle on the death of Nero. First Galba then Otho then Vitellius gained a brief imperial ascendancy before civil war swallowed them up.

Time was in the melting pot, with the ancient world being left behind. Most prognostications were grim and many of those who could do so ate drank and were merry, for they might die tomorrow. Yet others like Mark saw in the kaleidoscope of shifting events and dangers a pattern of great hope, a joy that did not rest on the brand of emperor, procurator or rabble-rouser calling the tune. If physical death intervened, he would meet it as best he may. Meanwhile he knew his mission and would follow it to the end because he saw glimpses of another and very different world shown to him by his Master.

Today also there are single-minded eaters, drinkers and merry makers. They may suspect, though deep-seated fears may forbid them to discuss it—perhaps even be aware of it—that the modern world is headed inexorably for tumultuous times. We have wars and rumour of wars. We have eight billion humans needing food and shelter—for a range of reasons, vast numbers miss out. We have shocking injustices in many countries. We have increasingly unpredictable and destructive weather. We have global rates of species extinction not known for millions of years.

It can't be sustained. Nevertheless, for some people, none of this matters. Bad luck will strike others, never them. Nothing wrong with cheerful and determined optimism, after all.

3

THE SAMARIAN

MARK, A RATHER slight somewhat stooping figure, left the cave at sunrise. Of the dangers that faced him that morning - balmy-aired with the fullness of summer - Roman soldiers were not the worst. Bands of Jewish zealots had a habit of swooping down from the hills, killing first and asking questions later. If you were a real Jew, why weren't you living in the wilds with them, fighting to the last?

He carried his precious scrolls of papyrus at his side, taking long loping steps, determined to put such things from his mind. This was Samaria, something of a backwater compared with the bloodier war zones of Judaea and the Galilee. And he was only making this journey because the main Roman expeditionary force was temporarily out of the country. There was an uneasy lull in the fighting. The Twelfth (Fulminata) legion, remembering its early humiliating defeat by zealots in the pass of Beth-Horon - ironically perhaps emphasising the meaning of the legion's name of Thunderstruck - was staying close to Caesarea. Jewish nationalists were licking their wounds, while generals Vespasian and Titus were away in Egypt securing their political future with the help of their enthusiastic troops. Thus, what better time to travel than now?

It was no good. Despite these sophistries there was no place of safety outside - only within. Mark didn't need the ghosts of Paul and Uncle Barnabas or even of Thomas to tell him that. He ought to know it by now. The Kingdom was within, within, within..., unassailable, pristine...then why did his heart flutter when some small animal disturbed the undergrowth? Shouldn't he too, be able to heal and cast out devils in the name of Jesus the Anointed? On this holy mission how could he fear?

'Uhh.' He froze as a figure stepped from the bushes. The man wore the crimson clothes of the wealthy and a long knife (not the short dagger of the Sicarii) hung from his belt. Bearing arms was considered proof of insurrection against imperial authority. Only desperate men wore knives.

Tiny beads of sweat stood out on Mark's forehead.

'Greetings' said the man calmly. His hair was grey and his face lined. But probably that weapon, his much better size and weight gave him the confidence of complete physical superiority.

Mark stared stupidly.

'Oh, this is your problem' the stranger realised, jogging the knife with his thigh. 'The fact is one can't be too careful these days. My name is Simon. Unless you've something lethal in that bag of yours you have nothing to fear from me.'

'There's only paper in the bag,' said Mark. 'I didn't sleep too well last night. Maybe I'm jumpy.'

'On the road, are you?'

It wasn't wise to talk freely to strangers. 'From Jericho. I am Mark.'

The bigger man nodded. 'You haven't eaten too well either, I'd say. My house is in the town not far from here.' He smiled humourlessly. 'That's if you can stand the hospitality of a mere man of Samaria.'

Remembering his mission, Mark forgot caution. 'We offer brotherhood to all - even Romans - if they believe...'

Simon snorted. 'You mean you'll accept bread from anyone when you're hungry. But would you help us when we're down? You Judaeans don't have much of a reputation here.'

Mark's voice rose with excitement. 'I am a Nazorean - some call us

Christians. I'm grateful for your offer and believe me I would help you if I could. My Master told us to love our neighbours. Why, he even told a story about a Samaritan as it happens, to emphasise the point.' He rummaged in the bag for the right scroll and then remembered his mother had retained it as one of the best scriptures for her secret Nazorean meetings. He vaguely wondered if he'd ever be able to recover those precious words with the shadow of war hanging over everyone.

Simon quietened. He stepped back into the longer grass. 'It's alright' he said. 'I knew that story long before you did. Many years ago, when you were just a kid making mud pies, we had a visit from the disciples of one Jesus of Nazareth.'

The track wound down the hillside. They walked toward the town in silence. Simon was remote and thoughtful, Mark too tired to work out his next move.

Before the war plenty of Jews would disagree with or even attack the Nazoreans, and the Roman authorities saw the new sect as a threat to their rule. After three years of brutal fighting, guerrilla war, banditry and civilian massacre, the Christians were hardly in a worse situation than any others in Israel. The moderate Nazoreans of Jerusalem including Mark's family had already evacuated across the Jordan to Pella in the relative safety of the Decapolis east of Palestine. Mark had heard reports that the monastic Essenes had been killed or driven from their wilderness communities on the shores of the Dead Sea, though whether it was by one or other of the competing Jewish zealot sects or a Roman spearhead was anyone's guess. And what side were the Essenes on? Some believed Jesus was the Saviour. Mark was sure of it, but for others of that sect the Master was too down-to-earth to suit their ascetic natures. Was he down-to-earth enough for Simon?

The ground was rough and rutted. Just walking to this Samarian town, called Gitta, was enough for Mark. How many miles had he walked? How many towns in the last ten years? He couldn't stop now.

Yet when Simon's big arm barred his way he did stop. 'What's the matter?'

'Move off the road. Can't you hear that racket?' (Mark had just barely noticed the approaching sound of hooves.) 'It's a patrol from the Roman garrison.' There was a sneer in Simon's voice. 'We are a pacified city, you know.'

They crouched close together behind a stand of pine trees and watched the infantry platoon go by. A well-built decurion-major showing his helmeted head with its side-to-side officer's plume turning slowly as he searched the path, rode on horseback bringing up the rear. A junior officer, but every inch a symbol of Roman tyranny.

'What are they doing on this little track?' Mark whispered after the platoon had passed. As if in answer, he felt something odd touching his calf. He looked down. The point of Simon's scabbard had smeared a trace of blood on his flesh. Mark jerked away. 'You haven't - you didn't...'

Simon's face was expressionless. 'Surely you heard of the exploits of the brave Cerealius, top dog of the Fifth (Macedonian) legion? He murdered more than 11,000 Samaritan men just because they chose to assemble in peaceable protest on the sacred soil of Mount Gerizim. If any town resists, the women and children are sent into slavery. And you know about their crucifixions... This is war! We fight back as best we can.'

'Then you are a zealot?'

Again that hard smile. 'My parents came from Persia. They worshipped one god, but the One God of the Flame. I'm a Samarian, but not a proper Jewish Samaritan. Yet Jews don't have a monopoly on patriotism, and this is my home.'

Simon led the way to a rocky place nearer the town where he divested himself of knife and scabbard, secreting the weapon in a heap of loose stones. 'Safe until next time' he grunted.

Mark decided he'd been silent long enough and began to argue in urgent undertones as they mingled with the subdued citizens of Gitta, who nevertheless accorded Simon cautious smiles and polite greetings.

'Thou shalt not kill, eh?' Simon answered him. 'Listen my friend. Look into the depths of any man's mind - or woman's for that matter - and you find the desire to murder. It comes out one way or another. Are even priests free of it? They enjoyed condemning that Master of yours and even felt holy at the same time. I just don't pull the wool over my own eyes.'

Many arguments marshalled themselves within Mark's mind: all the conventional wisdoms about the need to preserve the social fabric and the revolutionary Nazorean precept - originating from God via Moses but like many excellent principles, fallen of late into disrepute - that one should love one's neighbour as oneself.

Yet when he did speak it was not of the wisdom of Peter and Paul, neither of the healings on Cyprus, or the trials in Rome, nor of the courageous faith of his own family. It was as if for a moment he stepped back and someone or something else spoke through him and he listened to himself in calm appreciation: 'Look carefully at your desire to attack, at your hatred. Fix it with your inner gaze long enough and you will see that it hurts you as much as anyone else. Then look deeper. Abandon your fears and hatreds to the Holy Spirit and as He takes them lovingly, see the thing you really fear. Something that terrifies even a man like you who can face Roman soldiers without a qualm.'

Simon looked at him with curiosity. 'Well?'

Mark's voice dropped to a whisper. 'Underneath it all you will find that the desire to harm another is never justified and even killing may occur without anger or intending harm to the real man within. This can be seen in some combat situations. At the end of thinking you are only love, the love of the Creator for the created. You have used what we call the world to cover and conceal your love but whatever you do you can never extinguish your true nature.'

Mark, as surprised by this revelation as Simon, fell silent again. They came to the older man's house, a large imposing structure and a servant admitted them into the walled courtyard. There was a pergola with ancient, gnarled vines, a tiled pavement, a pool with waterlilies and in the shade near the house wall was set a couch. Against the end of this couch, lying child-like on the tiles and with head in hands, black profuse hair and deep, sea-green eyes was a woman.

There was a vibrancy about her, as though in this case God was intent on proving beyond doubt that life lay not in the shell of the body but that a numinous energy could radiate through it from some other dimension, enlivening everything within reach. Mark, celibate for longer than he would like to recall, was struck by an unfamiliar turbulence.

Simon led him past the pool to the couch. 'This is Helen' he said.

4

THE DECURION-MAJOR

THE TOWN OF Gitta in Simon's day was not so different from many Near Eastern villages of the very early 20th Century. The same buildings of primitive brick, stone and wood. The dusty roads. The donkeys, flowing clothes and urchin children. The same worship of the same God.

But in 69 CE—one year of our tale—the land was not old and tired. It was mostly green and fertile and had yet to suffer the loss of trees and topsoil attributed to the ubiquitous goat and the rapacity or ignorance of the Ottoman Empire that ruled the land for four centuries until the First World War. In this earlier age, fat cattle grazed in pastures and deer ran in forests. Then, Israel could better justify the claim that it was indeed the Promised Land.

That is not to say the people of Gitta were strangers to hardship. For hundreds of years they had suffered second-class Jewish citizenship because they were Samaritans. And for some generations they had been at the mercy of the whims of Romans and their local representatives, whether client kings or governors or even the collaborating Jewish Sanhedrists.

It was hardly surprising that Samaritans had become defensive and pessimistic. When the Roman legions knocked on Gitta's door there was not enough solidarity of resolve to resist them. But this didn't mean their presence was not bitterly resented.

Gitta was ready to accept any remedy that might relieve the situation. As Mark had begun, dimly, to appreciate, Simon was a potent brew on ailing Gitta's medicine shelf.

Had he the time and mental space to reflect more deeply during his unexpected walk with this strongly confident Simon, Mark might have wondered what it was about the grey-haired man that inspired people to something better than wallowing in the grievances of an occupied town.

At the risk of intruding into a story that we are told should be left to the characters alone, Simon was a magician (they called him Magus) a gentile from the mysterious land of the Zoroastrians. To the Samaritans, his very difference suggested he was sent especially from 'out there' to assist them in their time of need. The whispered knowledge that he sometimes assassinated Roman soldiers, in defiance of the horrific retribution should he be discovered, confirmed Simon's popularity.

But no-one expected Simon to be caught. For nearly 40 years he had been the town's leading sorcerer. He healed, foretold the future by means of astrology and more obscure practices and possessed secret knowledge. The Romans had their own magic; they applied sound for lifting stone blocks and they called on the powers of the heavens to assist them in battle. Yet even though the townsfolk were dealing with the masters of most of the known world, Gitta's confidence in their local hero was too high to be easily shaken.

Mark by contrast had few admirers. Since the age of 18 he had been an itinerant travelling across land and sea in the service of his Master, helping the disciples and believers with secretarial skills. Mostly he stayed in the background while Paul, the great proselytiser; his Uncle Barnabas, Paul's close friend of the early days; and Peter, leader of the apostles, used up the available limelight. He had served them and survived them and still he was not well known.

Nevertheless Mark, quiet and of a low-profile compared to the energetic preachers he had worked with, was a man of wide knowledge and experience. In an era when many people hardly strayed from their own villages except to partake in religious pilgrimages, Mark was literally a man of the world. He had plumbed philosophical depths, was familiar with shipping and commerce, understood several languages and cultures of the Mediterranean and had even - most disapprovingly - celebrated his 30th birthday watching the games in Rome.

As Mark and Simon stood side by side on the exquisitely-patterned tiles in Simon's courtyard (glazed hexagons especially imported from Alexandria) they represented an historical intersection point. Separately, both had already been instrumental in changing their world to an extraordinary degree. Together, their futures promised even more developments. A third factor was necessary though, to act as catalyst in this further process. Time paused; the air was still. Sounds from the marketplace became distant; birds in the evergreen shrubs, beaks poised to consume tiny insects, seemed to sleep for a second.

Then it was done. The triangle of destiny was completed by the woman who sprawled appealingly at their feet.

◆

Helen looked up at the two men from her place on the floor. Yet in the subtle politics of human interaction, it was more as if she were above them and peering down.

'What an interesting visitor you've brought' she said, rewarding Simon with an elusively brief smile and then turning to fix cat eyes on Mark.

The Judaean suddenly felt naked. Rather than risk some inappropriate remark, he gave a slight bow and waited for Simon to rescue him.

'He is Mark from Jericho, but not an ordinary Jew. I found him on the hill track before a patrol arrived and because he's a Christian, it struck me as neighbourly to help him evade our Italian masters.'

Mark immediately suspected that this was an elaborate joke. First the reference to neighbourliness - very much a Nazorean emphasis - and secondly the inference that he would probably have been arrested by the

Romans, not so much for being a Christian but for the act of terrorism just committed by Simon.

What surprised Mark was less the joke itself than his certainty that Helen understood it at once. She had propped herself up on one elbow displaying her figure in the flimsy robe to best advantage. That was disturbing enough but even more noticcablc was thc way in which she swung her attention onto Simon as though sucking the nuances from his mind without the intervening medium of words.

'Then you've had a busy morning' she said and looked again at Mark. 'This house has a good reputation for hospitality. Eat the midday meal with us Mark and you will see what I mean.'

They went through a curtain into a hallway, and a servant opened the door of a long dining room set up with a table and goblets in the Roman fashion. On one ornate bench embellished with bunches of wooden grapes, sat the same decurion-major Mark had seen earlier on the hillside.

Mark swallowed.

Thoughts flew through his mind in rapid succession. He must not show a flicker of recognition. They had been betrayed, or... Helen's apparently innocent mealtime invitation was another 'joke': Simon had known the decurion-major was here: Simon and Helen had an understanding that went beyond speech; he, Mark, was being played with. He was being tested.

And then came the frustrating realisation that for the moment he must keep all these speculations to himself.

The tall soldier rose and seemed to dominate the room. 'Ah, Simon. Good to see you.' The Roman spoke in halting Aramaic.

'Tarquin! Have you been properly attended to in my absence?' asked Simon in his even more halting Latin.

'Come now, use the common Greek,' said the soldier. 'The language of commerce suits us better. The wine is excellent, as always. Your business appointment went well?'

'Well enough, but the bargains I must strike in these days of war could be the death of me.'

Tarquin gave the hearty laugh of a healthy, self-assured man. 'You do very well, as I realise every time I enter your house. And who in Gitta has a wife more beautiful than Helen here? But you have a guest. I don't know him.'

Mark's patience was wearing thin. All this double-dealing, for whatever purpose, was not the way of his Master. He held his head high. 'I am Mark, a traveller from Jericho and a lowly follower of Jesus of Nazareth.' Suddenly it occurred to him that the bag of scrolls was still slung on his shoulder, but it was too late to be unobtrusive. What he had started, he must carry through with.

Tarquin came forward, frowning. 'A Nazorean, eh?' Let me tell you that Nazoreans bring trouble wherever they go. Our orders are to suppress any group that poses a threat to the Empire. The Jews have been tying up our finest armies for the last two years and only this morning there was another murder in the eastern sector. That's religious fanaticism for you, but we shall break it, as we shall soon break Jerusalem. You would be wise to keep your ideas of a heavenly king to yourself. I expect you understand me?'

'We say nothing against your emperor. We give to Caesar what is his. Our empire is not of this world but of another' said Mark evenly.

'Mm.' Tarquin frowned again. He liked things cut and dried, as he liked rich wine and adoring women. Every sensible man knew there was only one world that counted, a fact confirmed even by the gods' insistence on meddling in the affairs of men. 'Consider yourself lucky there has been no emperor firmly holding the reins for a while or your movement might have been pulled to a halt before now. Yet don't be too light-hearted, definite news will come from headquarters any day. Nero used to have Christians killed for sport; you may get a better deal this time, but don't bank on it.'

Helen coughed, a light but firm sound. 'If you would be seated, decurion-major, I shall order the meal to be served.'

The food was excellent, but Mark hardly noticed the taste of the stuffed woodpigeons, bread and fruit jelly and smooth pink wine. He refused to join the conversation about the price of grain and the problems of transporting olives in war time. His only contribution could have been a comment on the ever more scandalous level of 'tithing to the emperor's forces' demanded by the invaders, though he managed to stay silent. Yet the anger in him was growing and the wine helped fuel his indignation.

Tarquin leaned toward Simon. 'I can let you in on a secret. General Vespasian is on his way to Rome.' Simon nodded gravely, though this 'secret' was common talk amongst the lowliest peasants.

Tarquin spread his hands on the table. 'The soldiers in Egypt loved him! Governor Tiberius Alexander swore his unswerving support for Vespasian's nomination. It's just as I predicted, the Praetorians and the Senate will have to confirm him as our new emperor. After Vitellius and the other no-hopers we've had to put up with in the interim, it will be the only worthwhile thing those parasites have done for a long time.'

The Roman drained his goblet. 'Already there's popular feeling that the general is *Restitutor Orbis* - restorer of the world. We troops of the Fifth, the famous Macedonians, were the first to see he was the only imperial candidate worth Jupiter's arse! Why, in Alexandria, Vespasian even healed a blind man. Not only that…'

Simon interrupted. 'So, we can expect Vespasianus Flavius Caesar Augustus to recall his son and his legions from Israel and attend to more pressing matters?'

The soldier laughed unpleasantly. 'More pressing? Can we so easily forget the thousands of Romans killed by Jewish brigands? Vespasian will have to let his son fulfil the prophecies about Jerusalem. At this moment, Titus has more than 20,000 troops coming in forced march from Egypt. Not one stone of the Temple must stand upon another. That Jew Flavius told Vespasian he would be emperor - and Titus after him.'

Simon smiled. 'Ah, the wily Josephus! He escaped death when he was captured by recalling the Jewish scripture which stated the Temple would only be destroyed at the hand of a king. Then he consolidated his position by taking on the general's own surname.' (Simon always kept abreast of such intelligence; the rabbi Jesus was widely known to have forecast that Jerusalem would be destroyed and in this the religious prediction corresponded with the most recent military expectations.)

Tarquin nodded impatiently. 'And do you know what? The Hebrew prophecies of a fabulous new world ruler had nothing to do with that seditious rabbi, Jesus. They were really foretelling the accession of Vespasian.'

A goblet clattered to the floor as Mark stood up violently. 'Enough of this blasphemy.' The rush of blood to his head made it difficult to continue. 'Jesus the Anointed…you can't mention him in the same breath as Vespasian.' He stared down at the hawk nose of the decurion-major. 'I've heard about this wonderful general of yours - throwing shackled men into the Dead Sea to find out if they'd float and how long they'd last.'

Tarquin also rose but he was cold and stood several hands above Mark. His fingers moved toward his sword. 'You are a guest in the house of Simon Magus, one of the few allies of Rome in this accursed land. Yet you may not break the law. To proclaim an illegal king is a crime punishable by death. I have no alternative but to arrest you on that charge.'

They stood across the table from each other, bristling, although after the briefest pause Mark's solar plexus gave an involuntary shudder. He realised his peril. Despite his best intentions to hold fast, he looked down and away.

Helen broke into a giggle. 'You can't be serious. Arrests are for proper crimes. Not for jokes in bad taste!'

Tarquin spoke stiffly. 'Explain yourself.'

Helen shook her head and fine wisps of black hair delicately veiled the soft skin of her forehead. 'Proclaim a new king? Our Judaean is not a politician but a dreamer.' She looked at Mark in a motherly fashion. 'He could talk convincingly to his diary, but no-one in the marketplace would take any notice of him.'

'My wife is right' said Simon lightly. 'Let's face it, this Christianity has been made too much of. It's as you say, Tarquin. Rome has had internal problems of political leadership and for that reason everyone's been a bit touchy. But with Vespasian at the helm, you won't need to be concerned with such trifles.'

Tarquin turned on Simon. 'A trifle?'

'Of course' said Simon. 'No-one will remember this poverty-stricken Jesus in a few more years. It's a mountain made from a molehill.'

Mark opened his mouth, but Simon caught his eye with such a compelling glance that his need to speak evaporated. He resumed his seat.

Helen moved around the table to Tarquin. A servant poked her head into the room, noted the tension and quietly withdrew. Helen's fingers touched the soldier's arm. 'They are waiting to serve the spiced dates. I'll fill your cup.' Tarquin grunted something about preferring German barbarians to obdurate Jews and he too, sat down. Finally, the meal was over. The decurion-major ignored Mark but allowed Helen to lead him out to the courtyard pool. Some new fish had recently arrived in a glass container all the way from an Egyptian merchant at the port of Tyre. Helen stood very close to the soldier, pointing into the water. Possibly by accident, she brushed his strong torso once or twice with her breasts.

Mark waited with badly concealed chagrin, tempered by relief, in the dining room until a servant announced that Tarquin had gone. He tugged at Simon's sleeve. 'Well?' he demanded. 'What was the meaning of that performance?'

Simon stared coolly at Mark's restraining hand. 'Rather meagre gratitude from a man whose life was saved.'

'Enough games! There's some purpose behind all this. Just tell me what it is - or let me go my way.'

Simon half nodded. 'Very well. Come upstairs.' He ushered Mark up to a small room with a heavy door. Helen followed them in and closed the metal bolt. A low round table was surrounded by cushions; a window overlooked the roadway and a jug of wine stood by the wall. Simon grabbed the wine, gurgled some down his throat, took breath and shook with laughter.

'Start explaining' said Mark. He didn't like the bolted door.

'You Christians are too serious! The look on your face, when you saw that dummy Tarquin.'

'Poor Mark' said Helen. 'It's a burden, being a man of principle.' She came up and kissed him on the cheek. She had the flowing movement of a dancer. 'Before you explode with bewilderment, we'll explain it all. But we want something in return. We want to know everything about Jesus of Nazareth.'

5

JESUS, NEAR AND FAR

WHAT IS IT about Jesus of Nazareth? A man who bent to wash the feet of his disciples, who healed the sick, calmed the tempest, accepted the outcasts of society; spoke truth to power. All those churches and all that influence deployed and money collected in his name over the centuries, yet who knows him? His vision and words remain frequently obscured or at least unclear, including being 'twisted by knaves to make a trap for fools' just as Joseph Rudyard Kipling warned us against.

He hinted at life everlasting: men have interpreted this in their peculiar own ways. The inhabitants of planet Earth have wanted to kill in his name—or in the name of his Father - and be martyred, too. German soldiers wore aluminium belt buckles in the Second World War inscribed: *Gott mit uns*, God with us. My uncle brought back one from France. Thus is our urge to self-destruction sanctified. It seems we have frequently been unable or unwilling to read the message of the Nazarene.

The existence of such a strangely backward race as humanity could be a puzzle to interplanetary ethnologists. Might Earth's position on the outer perimeter of the Milky Way star system be the explanation?

Perhaps isolated from the central thrust of galactic evolution, did Earth become an outlier? Beautiful and whole in most respects but apparently flawed by its dominant mammal which nowadays seems very industrious in destroying its own life-support system. True to the tradition of double-speak, this lovable but unstable organism calls itself Homo Sapiens - *wise man*. This Sapiens has (wisely!?) developed some highly efficient methods of doing away with itself and its home. It concentrates much of its resources into gearing up for this project. Meanwhile hordes of its resource-deprived members humbly assist the process by malnourishment, preventable sickness; dying from ill-treatment by their fellows.

For those of us brought up as Christians, we may hold Jesus the Nazarene to our bosom by reflex action as if we were the proverbial drowning man clutching the straw. Often, we invite this Jesus to our marriage feasts, our births and our bodily exits. We may perhaps enjoy the upliftment of a Sunday church service. But like an influential, eccentric relative who must be humoured, we frequently prefer to keep him out of our lives the rest of the time—unless we can revise his message to suit our own particular ends, a practice that has always been popular and is hardly less so nowadays.

The name Jesus Christ may even seem to inspire a kind of archaic awe almost like remembering an authoritarian schoolmaster long after schooldays have been left behind. Yet the Nazarene didn't arrive on this planet simply to give excuse for holy war or to inaugurate a network of Sunday social clubs.

Evolution has its own imperative. When the life principle on planet Earth (and not just in the human realm) begins to collapse in on itself, a compensatory mechanism is activated.

Despite or rather because of the increasing interplay of opposing forces, a new degree of wholeness will act to manifest a new world, a new cycle of planetary existence. This will rise from the old in a kind of cosmic passion play, a living parable; offered not only to the human population. It will renew the entire planetary 'signature' from the ruins of the old.

Once more we will be faced with the question: How many varieties of life essence can there be? There is only One Life. Jesus came to point this out and to show that any other interpretation is not wicked, but merely a blurred vision.

Lost in the games of the world, some aspect of humanity still reaches for the clarity and majesty of stars. Somewhere the suspicion lurks that another way of life is our true inheritance.

Do you happen to remember how, long ago, men in faded suits used to stand on street corners earnestly proclaiming Jesus the King had come to save us from our sins? Many of us walked by uncomfortably, embarrassed or belligerent or bored. Nowadays, street preachers may be superseded by slick organisations that see benefit in embracing those who struggle to manage their own affairs and livelihoods.

Some of these groups offer unusual dogmas that are wildly different from what Jesus taught. In our ever-more complex, confusing, often downright bewildering societies, religion may either be disregarded or turned into a parody of itself. How many of us travel past churches every day, wear crosses on our breasts, perhaps consider the Christian ethics of things like contraception and abortion; decorate our homes and sing carols at Christmas? But what is it about Jesus of Nazareth? Amid the recognisable symbols, he is so often a stranger to us.

6

INTERROGATION AND ESCAPE

MOUNTED ROMAN SOLDIERS clattered through the marketplace below. A large horse carried a sonic projector. Somewhere in Palestine, an intransigent town would find its walls tested not only by the ram, by rocks and flaming projectiles from the catapult, but also by destruction-frequency sound.

Mark watched the soldiers and mused for a moment on the nature of power. Everyone wanted it. But the true power his Master offered was rarely understood, even by the gentiles who had flocked to choose Christianity when Paul held audience in the towns of Asia Minor. Of these proud new Nazoreans, breathless with the excitement Paul stirred in them, hardly a handful really understood the gift that was offered. This, Mark knew. But it was totally beyond his comprehension that the Master's message could be lost or bent into its opposite. He would have been horrified, or perhaps just disbelieving, to discover some of the purposes to which Christ's name would be put in the ensuing two millennia. In this regard, he was naïve.

Simon interrupted Mark's introspection. 'Well?' he said.

Mark slowly shook his head. 'It's too late to use the Nazarene in your schemes. He was betrayed before and now he is far beyond all your manipulations.'

Simon changed his approach. 'Don't get upset. We had to check you out somehow. Look...' He picked up a goblet from the table. 'I have some wine.'

Helen came forward, sat on a cushion at his feet. 'We'll tell you things as we see them, Mark. I'm sure you'll understand.'

Now was the time to make a stinging reply. Understand? There's not much I've understood so far. You test me as though I were a child at school, then place me in a locked room and want to make friends. How would you like the names and addresses of all Nazoreans in Israel? Go and sell the list to Tarquin for a gold talent before you chop him up and feed him to your pet fish!

Helen's manner was nothing if not cosseting. Her soft charm drew from him an impulse to be reasonable. And his Master had spoken of forgiveness. Forgive us as we - can you see me, Master? Are you watching while I attempt doing justice to your memory?

The effort showed on Mark's face. 'Yes?' he said finally. Helen sighed. 'There are greater things at stake than personal pride. This war will destroy Israel as we know it...'

'But it will be the making of Christianity' interrupted Mark with sudden insight.

'Probably' agreed Helen. 'The Nazoreans will be dispersed as will the Jews. And everywhere they go, people will listen to the stories of Jesus, despite what we said to our Roman friend.'

Simon laid a hand on the table in emphasis. 'But more important, what kind of tales will they listen to?'

Mark felt that he was on safer ground. He smoothed down the flap on his bag. 'The facts are well enough known among those who were the Master's disciples. I myself... well, people are sure to write them down and so keep alive the memory of the Saviour. But really, what has all this to do with you?'

Helen sprang up, took his hand and sat him down next to her on the cushions. Her green eyes were quite beautiful. 'Do you think that having a grand house and jumped-up visitors is enough to bring us happiness? We have certain abilities, Mark, which endowed worldly success. But what is happening in Palestine is getting beyond us. I'm sure - we're sure - Jesus held the key.' The green eyes fired. 'We want that key.'

They wanted to hear from him as though he were a prophet. He remembered the times he'd dreamed of swaying crowds the way Paul did, or of commanding the authority that was the hallmark of the outspoken Peter (even though his courage failed him to speak out at Gethsemane). Barnabas used to swig alcohol with the masses and still retain his virtue; they loved the honourable peasant in him. Always it was left to Mark to keep the books of account, pay the servants and bribe the ships' captains for a better berth. People wavering on the edge of Christianity would listen to him only because he was with the others. Neophytes sympathetic to the synagogue - and more than sympathetic to the revolutionary rabbi called Jesus - eventually made the inevitable choice, moving politely into the preferred orbit of Paul and Peter and his uncle. Now it could all be different.

'In the beginning' said Mark, 'was the Word. The Word was made flesh and dwelt among us.' This teaching was from an obscure papyrus; part of a sheaf of writings he had purchased in Idumaea with his own money, believing it to be the genuine report of one or more very early Christians. Something of the poetry suggested a most daring interpretation of his Master's mission. It was hardly the mainstream Jerusalem line but at that moment it seemed fitting.

'Mm?' Simon was actually paying attention. And Helen nodded encouragingly.

'Words are power' she said.

Mark suddenly remembered his conversation with Simon on the hill track. 'But you must know the story of Jesus? His followers surely told you when they came here years ago. And has Samaria lacked converts since? The signs and wonders that attended his birth - they must be common knowledge. His life of teaching, his cruel but redeeming crucifixion when he cheated the underworld by returning to prove that death was done away with?

'Perhaps you didn't pay attention before, because you weren't ready to hear of salvation. It's hardly surprising! First you slaughter Romans and then you smile at them.' Mark's brow wrinkled earnestly. 'I guess your neighbours are proud of you yet how many go hungry, burdened by scandalous taxation while you eat more than you need?'

Helen moved away. 'Of course we've heard the story of the Anointed One you silly fellow. But most of the doctrine came from Moses, from the Essenes of the desert and even from the orthodox Pharisees, whom the gentile Nazoreans increasingly hold in contempt. We thought you were a man of sensitivity, capable of serving us with a more intelligent answer - but we are willing to revise our opinion.'

'And as for criticising us' said Simon, 'how can you say what's right and wrong? Didn't Jesus emphasise something like: be not hasty in judgement of others if you would be free of judgement on yourself?'

Mark's picture of himself as glorious preacher began to blur. 'It's true' he conceded, 'that the Master proclaimed many things which have been spoken of by others. But words are cheap enough. It was how he said them, how he demonstrated their truth, how he healed! I never met him, you understand, I was just a youngster when he was crucified, but I've been with men who walked the length of Israel to be at his side.

'There was enough fire and grace in the Master to force history to start anew. Here's what you have to understand: this world can never be the same hereafter. Something's been awakened. He truly was the Messiah! Most Jews dispute it, because he didn't fulfil their expectations of a restored monarchy in Israel. But that's the point, the point that Paul made. Despite all his high-strung, high-caste temper - and I've been at the receiving end of it - Paul could see when others were dulled by national concerns that this Messiah was not for the Jews alone but for all men everywhere.'

More horses were passing in the street below. Mark saw the gleam of sunlight from armour.

Simon and Helen regarded him and their eyes met. The grey-haired man said, 'You are broadminded, Mark, a man of vision with a sense of history too.' His gaze flickered over Mark's linen shoulder-bag and dun coloured cloak. 'There's scholarship in you. Did you ever study religion - apart from your own?'

'I understand Greek' replied Mark, 'and I have read all I could of the great philosophers. Their logic is often like a knife cutting through the muddle of gods and goddesses, powers and symbols - and thin disguises for licentious behaviour. It's like this: there is one God, originally the God of Israel. Through my Master the Father's benediction is available to all who sincerely repent their sins; striving for the higher life which means seeing and treating others as equals. And Greek logic and cosmopolitanism is the medium by which the glad tidings will reach the far corners of civilisation.'

Helen's eyes sparkled. 'That's asking a lot of logic. But what do you know of Mithras?'

Mark shrugged. 'They call him the soldier's god. In some lands he's big news. But it sounds like just another flash-in-the-pan cult to me.'

'Then let me enlighten you,' said Simon. 'The religion of Mithras came from my parents' land of Persia, half a millennium ago. His followers know him as the mediator between the One God and man. He is also called the Word, the Light and the Good Shepherd.'

'An interesting coincidence.'

'More coincidences follow. Mithras, so the story goes - and it's generations old - was born in a cave at the winter solstice while shepherds watched and a divinatory star shone in the sky. His last meal was of bread and wine; then he was called up to heaven.'

'What are you trying to say? That my Master was a fraud? Or a figment of Mithraic imagination? Or do you try to subvert me to some Persian cult of your own concoction?' Despite his hopefully confident rhetoric, Mark felt suffocated. The whole day had been a nightmare. He almost wished that the zealots had ambushed him that morning. It would have been the clean danger of sharp-edged metal, not repeated and twisted traps for the intellect and conscience.

'I'm trying to stretch your broad mind a little further,' said Simon.

'Religious themes are repeated again and again across the ages. You see—they say Mithras was born of earth and light. The lower and higher met in him. He sacrificed the sacred bull so the earth could be fertilised with its blood. The symbolism...'

There was a knocking on the door, six or seven sharp blows.

'Master Simon! Soldiers surround the house! Something evil in the air! What shall we do?'

'Silence' said Simon. He dived across the room, staying low, and peered over the windowsill. 'The curs are out there alright. But is it me they want, or you? Either way, it's time for *exeunt*. Come on.' He dragged the bolt, swung the door and moved like a cat down the stairs. Helen pulled Mark with her as she followed. Mark stubbed his toe on the stone steps, and a muffled commotion began in the direction of the courtyard. He slowed but Helen pulled at him urgently. A cellar trapdoor loomed up and he fell into darkness.

7

BEYOND BELIEF

OUTSIDE IS CONFUSION. A detachment of Roman soldiers, all streaky armour and good-natured brutality (killing the inhabitants of Israel was a respectable living for men wearing the imperial uniform) is dealing with the straggly mob that tries to defend Simon's home.

A merchant tearfully implores the captain to wait. A devout family man, seeing Gitta's last bastion of self-respect on the edge of ruin, runs up with a sword and is casually chopped down by a burly legionary from the North African colonies. A couple of Samaritan youths, kids who swore to each other the week before to join whatever zealot gang would take them, charge the captain with a spear, knock him to the ground, stab another soldier and make off across the marketplace. One trips, a javelin finds its mark between the boy's shoulder-blades and his mother, witnessing the event, screams a piteous, timeless wail.

The soldiers stream into the walled garden. Simon's servants stand aside, sensing the patrol is only interested in Simon, Helen and maybe Mark.

These three are figures of recorded history. But you might think we aren't sticking to the truth? That depends on what truth we are all looking for.

Perception is affected if not generated by our belief systems. Beliefs are confirmed by what we feel and see. The circle is closed; another perspective cannot be introduced without an impetus strong enough to break the circle. At best, the impetus is a universal force that makes what some people call enlightenment. In the Christian context, it could be called the Holy Spirit.

Then, it is possible for us radically to change our minds about the world we see. And when this happens, the world is indeed different.

Scientists attempt to explain the physical universe in many ways. For example, there has been one conjecture that it is composed of sub-nuclear particles that result from mini or micro blackholes and whiteholes that continuously blink into and out of existence. According to this theory, everything 'solid' depends upon these quantum holes, the portals through which energy enters and leaves space-time. But where does the energy come from and go to, for heaven's sake? The rather obvious answer is *beyond space-time.* And the 'beyond-ness' is not 'out there' so much as *within* everything. To complicate an already difficult idea, the concept of space-time itself, described and comprehensively proved by Einstein over 100 years ago, is still being questioned by some physicists; not to put the great scientist down but to strive for a better understanding.

Here is another way to see it:

Imagine a blank screen. This is the world. Then, from the projector of the mind, comes a ray of thought. As it strikes the material of the screen, the ray produces a reaction which gives rise to a colour, a shape, a texture, a solid. Another thought emits. More colour, additional shape, more complexity of texture on that screen.

And so I build my world, not really believing (even as I write this description) that it is a product of my own arrangement.

Here's another explanation of 'seeing': A.H. Almaas in his book *The Unfolding Now*, talks about a little-used word that speaks volumes: *reification*. He gives this explanation: 'A reification refers to something that we have experienced or thought about that has become an object in our mind, a mental construct.' An example he gives is a piece of cutlery, the humble spoon. However, he assures us: 'The spoon you are experiencing is not the real spoon'. Rather, says Almaas, 'without reifications you will see that it is light. It is a form of light with shadows and colours, stripped of its mental-image identity as a spoon. Without those reifications or mental images, everything around you would become one vast field of light shaping itself into holograms. But usually because of our reifications, we don't see the light itself, we only see the colour and shape the light takes, which we then label as this or that object.'

It seems we make up some picture shows and switch off others. There are popular themes; many tragic. The more thoughtful of us shake our heads in despair - when will they ever learn? It was impossible not to feel this as I reported the bare details of the skirmish with the Roman soldiers. There was a wave of sadness, perhaps as well as a barely noticed ancient dark feeling; the guilty pleasure of vicariously dealing out death.

Our screens often work like this, in sombre browns, dirty greens, greys and muddier greys with bloated flashes of crimson. It is the world we have made and perhaps it is a kind of reality. But it is not the ultimately real world. And because of the Holy Spirit, which is an aspect of our own Planetary Logos, we know this to be true - even if unconsciously. There is an instinct in us, maybe small but ultimately unquenchable, to turn away from the screen of the world and find out what it is that makes up darkness. Or projects the light.

8

THE NEW OUTLAWS

'DAMNED CHRISTIANS,' SAID Simon. He squatted on the pine needles and dressed Mark's wound. Mark had received a gash to the temple as he tumbled down the stairs, and it was embellished by a fat bruise. He was laid out on a rough stretcher of cloth and greenwood branches. Helen and a group of others stood about or slouched without relaxation against the bare rock that made up the rear wall of the lean-to. The forest sky was darkening.

'Thanks very much' Mark muttered, determined to show himself, his audience and his Master that an ironical sense of humour was still possible.

Simon finished the bandaging. 'Not just you. I mean those Nazorean bastards who set the Romans on to us.'

Mark blinked. Of all the men who might be sent to save his life, why had God chosen Simon? 'You're not making sense' he said, trying to sit up. 'Why would Christians do that? You don't have to look beyond your own behaviour.'

Simon's brown staring eyes rejected all reasonableness. 'What an innocent! I'm the Magus! My information's never wrong. The Italians didn't have the imagination to figure out my game. They suspected me, yes, but only when you came along with your stupid courage and your big mouth...'

'You asked me to lunch', Mark spluttered. He tried to ignore the pain in his head, because Simon was suddenly taking gulps of breath. 'What's the matter?'

Simon's complexion was a blotchy red and grey. 'I should have realised, Nazoreans are the worst omen.' He turned to the silent onlookers. 'Everything gone' he shouted. His voice was hoarse. 'The forces of darkness crowd about us. By heaven...after all these years, finished!'

Simon struggled to take off his fine linen jacket. The embroidered sleeves were torn in a few places and smudges of dirt showed where there had been none in the morning. Finally, it came off and he flung it down on the floor of the hut.

'So much for the trappings of wealth.' He stood in his long-robed shirt looking with distaste at the crumpled red jacket. He faced Mark. 'So, the Christian virtues include poverty do they not? Then welcome me into your company, Mark. No house. No servants. No wine cellar and near enough no life either.'

Mark lay bewildered; passive.

A dark girl stepped forward. 'It's alright, Uncle Simon. We're here. If we all help each other, we'll be alright.'

Simon caressed his knife scabbard—where had he got this new blade from? Mark didn't have the energy to consider it further.

'Ah yes, Rachel dear, the wisdom and boundless optimism of youth. But when you are old and grey like me you expect something more meaningful than the teasing guiles of optimism. You look for revenge!' Contemplatively, he slid out the weapon. 'Your father, Rachel, and thousands like him - every day, an atrocity mars the land of Israel, and we line up like lambs to the slaughter. Why? An eye is for an eye, a tooth for a tooth.' He barked out 'Revenge! This lamb is not for sacrifice.'

Mark broke into a sweat. The figures of those others were blurry, dreamlike, impotent to deliver him from the madman Simon. He was in the clutches of a Lucifer; too weak to resist even by using argument.

Vaguely he noticed Helen detaching herself from the wavering human images dancing before his eyes. Helen: at the house he had been unable to disassociate her from the goddess Artemis, a beautiful but hardened huntress. Then she had mocked men with her cruel chastity. Now she herself was suddenly vulnerable.

'But we always knew' she told Simon. Artemis' white silk robe was slightly rent at the shoulder in confirmation of her mortality. 'Later or sooner, we knew it would come to this.'

Simon looked away and Mark sensed the delicate bond between man and wife had broken. Then the Magus was staring at him, and he could taste fear running into his mouth.

'Damned Christians.' The knife point hovered a finger's breadth away from his throat. Mark was certain from the pit of his stomach this was no play-act. Yet even as he faced death, he couldn't stop a bursting knowledge that Simon was suffering the same brand of agony he himself had faced back at the house: events were too complex, too contradictory. Take action! Any action!

Helen stretched out her hand and spoke to Simon as if he were the decurion-major. 'That solves nothing. Short cuts made in anger lead to a harder road in the end. Give it to me.' Two other female voices murmured support.

'Shut up, you bitches' croaked Simon. His blade remained in position. Mark saw murder in Simon's eyes, but his grunt sounded more like an animal in pain. The knife almost scraped Mark's flesh, a terrifying helplessness washed over him. Then his Master appeared.

He saw a bright light without form, but Mark knew it was the Anointed. Weakness and fear were displaced by a flood of peace and certitude. It was his Master and yet... the feeling was less that of facing an exalted being and more of meeting a trusted, even intimate, friend. He smiled to himself.

'It's you' he whispered. 'At last, you came!' Mark searched the light for his Master's face. The brightness resolved into a haloed shape. It was the confused visage of Simon.

Simon threw down the knife. 'If I were a religious man, I'd say an angel told me to spare you. As I'm not...' His voice lost its intensity. 'Who knows? Let's thank whatever gods there might be that this day is nearly at an end.'

A sigh of relief swept through the group of people gathered in the twilight of the forest. Simon spread his hands to encompass them. There was Zadok, an old man with the full white beard of a patriarch, Helen and two teenage girls, a middle-aged woman and two fellows with long ragged hair. 'This is my army,' said Simon. 'A formidable force to pitch against one-and-a-half legions and a few thousand assorted zealots.'

Mark had the presence of mind to change the subject. 'How did I - we - get here?'

'Every rat should have two tunnels out of his nest' said Simon and he explained their escape from the house by way of the cellar, down a passageway under the road and into a deserted mill. Simon had run for help to the young women, daughters of a friend who'd been killed by the Romans on nearby Mount Gerizim. Rebekah had helped carry the semi-conscious Mark to the outskirts of the town, while Rachel had fetched Lydia - their mother - and Zadok.

The log hut they were in was the home of Joseph and Yigal. Who gave the appearance of twin Esaus, unwitting thespians in a city-dweller's comedy - surely coarse, fanatical and ignorant. Mark, sitting back exhausted, discovered they were instead gentle and most hospitable for men who hadn't much to share beyond a simple roof and thin bean soup. He ate a little and fell asleep.

In the morning Rebekah, a pretty girl of no more than 17 or 18 years, brought him a dawn breakfast of bread and olives.

'Feeling better? Everyone's at the stream for ablutions. The Magus was upset, very upset, yesterday. He's sure the Romans will requisition his house. But a hawk fell dead in Helen's pool less than a week ago.' She shrugged at the inevitability of the omen.

Mark didn't like her precocious dismissal of tragedy. Even if Simon had brought it down on his own head. He changed the subject, 'And I believe your father is dead?'

Her pleasant looks set into a mask. 'Murdered, yes. By the troops of that killer Cerealius. It was more than a year ago now, but we shall never forget. Mother begged him not to go up the mountain. But he was a strict man of God. He went to join the assembly fully aware that it was very dangerous.'

Mark caught a curse in mid-delivery. He noisily cleared his throat and spat. 'Is there no limit to the stupid bravery of the Jews? When will we learn…' Again, he stopped himself.

'It doesn't matter' she said coldly, but her lip quivered. 'Criticise all you want. The passion for God is only an aberration to a man who forgets his tribe because he's learned to think and live selfishly in the guise of reason.'

'Selfish?' The blood pumped into his head. 'What's selfishness if not a man leaving his family to fend for themselves while he goes off playing the hero on a mission that's doomed before it's begun?'

She twisted away so he couldn't see the state of her face. She wiped her eyes. 'He's gone. Does it matter how and why? If you don't want to honour his memory, his obedience to God, why can't you stay silent? The Magus isn't even a Jew, but at least he's kept his promise to protect us.'

Mark glared at the shoddy rustic interior, seeking a safer opponent. 'But this isn't any way to look after you.'

'It's better than being sold as a slave. And anyway' she smiled almost shyly now, miraculously dispelling the emotional murk, 'he has a Power'.

The very idea of Power, did it wield a Will of its own? When Rebekah voiced that word, he almost thought he saw it in her eyes.

'Just feel your head' she said.

He touched his bandages. The swelling was gone and it was even hard to locate where the wound had been. 'Yes, I see what you mean.' But he didn't see at all. He desperately wanted to fit Simon into a category and could not. He changed the subject. 'And what about the old man and the two who look like Essenes?'

'Friends of Simon Magus. He has many friends.'

'And what exactly are we all going to do now, my dear?' He answered his own question before Rebekah could come up with the obvious reply. 'We're going to wait for Simon to point out the way I suppose.'

The way the Magus pointed out on his return from reconnoitring, was a planned climb up the wooded slopes of Mount Gerizim. 'We'll hide right under their noses' he said cunningly. 'It's been deserted following the massacre and the one place the Romans will never think of.'

Lydia, a large honest-looking woman in a widow's headscarf, trembled. 'That place of death?'

Simon replied, 'We will turn it into a place of life. What better memorial could there be?'

Zadok glowered. 'For a holy shrine Gerizim has an evil reputation. You haven't forgotten that bloody business with the troops of procurator Pilate? Even though it was many years ago.'

'I have a long memory for the exploits of our Italian friends and their mercenaries,' said Simon. 'Pilate didn't do so well that time. The Syrian legate had him booted back to Rome.'

'Pilate lost his job' said Zadok, 'but very many Samaritans lost their lives'. He shook his head.

'The locals were shouting about a Samaritan Messiah and waving spears.' Simon spoke without emotion. 'Pilate was always heavy-handed and any talk of Messiahs made him lose his nerve. We shall be much more careful.'

Helen sat down on a rough-hewn stool next to Mark. 'You are well again.'

The tyranny of her black hair and green eyes. Artemis hunted again. In a deliberately loud voice, standing at bay, he said 'Now you can tell me what really happened in Gitta'.

Simon lay back on the pine-needles, head in hands, giving Helen the floor.

She took Mark's hand. 'We knew our fate was tied to Christianity. By some mischance the praefect of Samaritan intelligence was in town yesterday. He met Tarquin after lunch on his way home to his quarters. The decurion-major doubtless threw in an unflattering remark about you. It seems praefect Barius had been bribed by Nazorean zealots to deliver you into their tender hands. Tarquin gave Barius the information he needed for your arrest. In all it seemed his lucky day. That troop of heavy infantry and horse in the market was preparing to leave on a mission. He had a ready-made kidnapping party.'

Mark searched her face then lowered his eyes. He wanted to believe that Helen's story was wrong. But thinking of his precious scrolls he had an uneasy suspicion it was true. Christians were divided on many issues. The apostle Paul's ideas clashed with those of the Jewish Nazorean establishment; and surely no-one knew how many other Christian sects were proliferating.

Jesus was a Jew. Must those who followed him therefore satisfy all the requirements of the law of Moses? No, said Paul. Himself a properly circumcised Jew, Paul believed Jesus had brought into being a new covenant which made circumcision unnecessary; it superseded the intricate details of Jewish religious observance. Although much of Paul's oratory had a mystical quality, hard for ordinary folk to understand, his simple bottom-line message had brought the gentiles into his orbit: 'Believe in Jesus the Anointed who died to expiate your sins, and you shall have everlasting life.' After all, did not the prophet Isaiah foretell: 'He was wounded for our transgressions... All we like sheep have gone astray; we have turned every one to his own way; and the Lord hath laid on him the iniquity of us all.'

Not understanding Paul's vision, many Nazorean Jews were scandalised by his laissez-faire attitude. 'But Paul never met the Master' they would point out. Paul had a foolproof reply to this criticism: 'My authority is direct inspiration from him of whom I speak.'

Mark, who grew ever more impatient with narrow Jewish traditionalism, leaned toward Paul's interpretation of the gospels, the good news of Christ. And the scrolls carrying those interpretations were to Mark's knowledge the only written records of the movement and its Master. (And yet nothing was simple in this discussion. Thomas had recorded Jesus rejecting the label of Master, neither did Jesus readily accede to the title of Messiah or the Anointed - the Christ - even though that was how he would go on to be understood and worshipped by millions for millennia.)

But like it or not, he - Mark the secretary, Mark who moved in the shadow of great men - was now a political figure in his own right. He might well be an impediment to those Nazorean zealots who wanted the Anointed to inspire patriotic not spiritual heroism...

Simon sat up and broke into Mark's reverie. 'And so, thanks to various Nazoreans, here we are.'

'Just a moment,' said Mark. 'If you're right and this Barius is after me, why can't you just go home and let me take my chances?'

Zadok nodded. 'Sure you're not overdramatising, Simon?'

The Magus glared at Zadok. 'It's too late for that. There's more to this than meets the eye. Helen was right - as usual. The signs have been there for anyone to read: the unusual placement of the stars, the numbers of the year, new fish in the pool, a hawk's death. Tarquin has coveted my house and wine cellar for too long. He'll use this incident to pin something on me.'

Mark thought about it. His administrative knowledge came to the fore. 'I know the Romans. They can be cruel, but they have a sense of justice. If you're sure it's only a trumped-up charge, go straight to the military tribune or even the legate himself. I bet you could protest your innocence and get away with it.'

Lydia turned to Simon and had her say. 'The stars? This is no time to rely on astrology. Place your faith in God. Today should be spent in prayer and seeking His guidance.'

'And what of this good rabbi, Jesus?' demanded Rachel the younger of Lydia's daughters. 'I hear he returned from the dead and made the lame walk. We are as bad as lame here' said the 15-year-old, 'and little better than dead. Perhaps we should rather pray to Jesus.'

'Blasphemy!' roared Zadok. 'Did your father tell you nothing Rachel? There is only one God for Israel even though the Judaeans brought back the wrong picture of Him from their captivity in Babylon; that man Ezra was too impressed by his own ideas. Praying to any other than the God of the Universe is what has plunged our land into all this mess. Only us Samaritans have the true teaching, while those other Jews lord it over us. Defilers and idolaters are never far away - let's not have them in our midst as well.'

The unkempt Joseph spoke for the first time. 'Peace, friends. When a prophet of Israel speaks or heals, he is a mouthpiece of the Unspeakable Name. The rabbi of Nazareth was one such. Yigal and I have spent many weeks contemplating and fasting in the forest awaiting the true Messiah, the Saviour, whether it be Jesus resurrected or some other. But when he comes, he'll bring God's might with him and the Romans will be blown away as if they'd never stepped on our shore.'

'What pearls of wisdom' said Simon. 'I should lose my home more often.' He stood up. 'Listen carefully everyone. The deed is done; we were waiting for Mark or someone like him to arrive and for the Romans to move in. It happened quicker than we thought but we were not completely unprepared. Now is the time for us to go ahead - forgetting the past - and forge a new life for ourselves and all we hold dear.' Simon grabbed his jacket from the corner where it had lain since the day before, dusted off the embroidery and pulled it on as if it were now a suitable uniform. 'I have known for some time it's my destiny. It is your destiny to follow me and my Helen.'

'What part do I play in this epic?' asked Mark, briefly thinking of those spectators at the Roman arena during Caligula's reign who had been thrown suddenly amongst the wild beasts in the ring, just to satisfy the emperor's macabre sense of humour.

Helen squeezed Mark's fingers. 'Christianity is the key. Remember?'

He removed his hand from Helen's soft touch. 'May the Master's key open the doors of all your hearts.' Then encouraged by his own resolve, he addressed the group. 'I'm grateful for your help. I will spend today sharing with you about Jesus. But what you've told me about the Romans and the zealots makes it clear that I must leave Samaria as soon as possible. Anything you can do to assist my passage north through the Galilee is welcome.'

Helen and Simon exchanged one of their lightning glances. 'Very well,' said Helen. 'Then we had better use this time to greatest profit.'

Yigal, hair matted and eyes overhung by big tufts of eyebrows, came forward. 'We are honoured to have you as our guest Mark. So many questions need answering.

'Some declare Jesus was the Son of God, divine in his own right, not a man at all. Yet heathens say the same of Mithras. How can Jews accept such a thing? And what of the laws of Moses and the many interpretations extracted so painstakingly and held sacred by the learned Pharisees? The rabbi of Nazareth said the Kingdom of Heaven was within. Does it mean the end of all our ancient customs?'

Yigal's questions were vital ones; they had the potential to split Christianity into many fragments and alienate - though never completely divorce—the new religion from its Jewish beginnings. Mark had no wish to fall into the traps of such weighty philosophical matters. Paul of course had the capacity to deal with them in his own unique way. But to Mark it was as though he were being shepherded into an ever-narrowing gorge when all he wanted was to spread invisible wings and soar above the cliff. Could he scramble up before the terrain became too steep? He drew breath before speaking.

'This time is the end of many things - and the beginning of others. I don't doubt that the high Temple will soon be totally destroyed, just as the Master predicted. The Israel of the Pharisees is falling into tatters before their very eyes.'

This is where he would take his leap upwards.

'But don't believe in disaster - and don't get lost in details. We are all children of God; each one has the divine spark.'

He felt again the change - that sense of being an observer and of hearing himself speak.

'When I spring with joy into the arms of a friend do I care where God is? In here or out there? Or whether Jesus is mortal or divine? Or how to interpret each iota of scripture? The knowledge of God, for however brief a moment, dissolves all such questioning. We have become accustomed to using words as though they were real in themselves. But words are only symbols of things and things are but symbols of a truer reality. Let us beware lest our words are nothing but dust and smoke choking off real life.' Mark hesitated, self-conscious. Then pushed doubts aside: 'Better to be silent and let the spirit of life speak through us instead.'

There was a mellow feeling in the air, as though the bare timber of the lean-to enclosed a cloud of invisible down. Mark felt his shoulders drop in relaxation, a physical sigh.

Only Rachel's look of awe signalled caution. Yes, life was speaking through him. But did his listeners understand that this drew him closer to them, placing all on an equal footing - and didn't make him superior and set him apart? Or was it possible he'd misjudged his function? Could it be that those earlier and simpler days of looking after literature and luggage for Barnabas and Paul had been the task he was called on to accept? Was he wrong to hope for the role of joining those Nazorean actors who would be remembered down the ages?

It didn't matter. To act just as required was the acid test of discipleship. He would relinquish these mental gymnastics and simply rest back into his purpose.

9

MAGUS UNMASKED

TODAY IS THE Sabbath, the third day we have been living at the Place of Sacrifice. It is ironically named because here commander Cerealius of the Fifth legion ordered the great massacre of Samaritans barely 20 months ago. Mass graves dot the hillside below the clearing and the cypresses that surround the Offering Temple moan distressingly in the winds that almost constantly scour the summit of Mount Gerizim.

It is called an Offering Temple because this is our Jewish heritage. The Samaritans say that around two hundred years ago the temple was so magnificent it could rival that of Jerusalem; but then it was destroyed by one of the Judean warlords asserting his superiority against his neighbours. Now a replacement though much smaller synagogue resting on the lower slopes of the sacred mountain did duty for Samaritans. Since ancient days, the term 'offering' usually meant to present one's most precious item willingly and with joy. Often it had no goal beyond a desire to come closer to God, offering reverence or thanksgiving. Yet I wondered whether this and other articles of faith could possibly survive the terrible war that bears upon us now? Or is it possible the gospels of Jesus will outstrip them all?

I feel no guilt about writing on the Sabbath. Never have the Master's teachings seemed clearer than today; 'The Sabbath was made for Man, not Man for the Sabbath'. The Sabbath measured out the weeks of orderly Jewish life; a life that to my mind is gone forever. To mourn its passing as old Zadok does (he's praying in the temple at this moment) is a waste of energy that could be spent spreading the good news of the Saviour.

The fact that I can't get on with that very task is not entirely my fault. A strange lethargy, an illness of some sort, has sapped my strength since the extraordinary events in Gitta. Helen has been treating me with a herbal remedy and Simon told me this morning it was just as well that I hadn't struck north when I originally intended. His information - he appears to have an informant in every village - is that Roman patrols on the main roads were doubled in frequency after a new cohort arrived in Sebaste from the coast. Now I rest, giving thanks to God and write my journal.

We are all well enough cared for. Most of the pilgrim accommodation was destroyed by Cerealius but we discovered a little stone house set back into the forest that suits our needs. Instead of pine needles we have proper beds to sleep on, and there is a separate place for the women. Two of Simon's servants joined us yesterday, bringing a small chest of silver and gold talents which would keep us in cheese and milk from the nearby cowherds until our dying days. Not that I expect Simon intends to spend it all on food, but he is remaining secretive about his plans. He's a fascinating character and most likely I owe my life to him. But I've made it clear every day that my destination is north to the Galilee, to Tyre and then by ship to Antioch or Corinth, where the Master's words that I've written down will be safe with the brethren.

Nevertheless, the loyalty of Simon's servants - a man and a young woman - surprised me. They surely realised that the money would have set them up for life. Instead, they were content with the reward Simon gave them on their arrival. I can't help thinking of what Lydia's daughter said: 'He has a Power'. His prediction about his house was correct, also - the servants told how they were allowed to leave unmolested, but that Tarquin moved in immediately afterward, stabling his war-horse in the courtyard and his concubines in the upper room. Unable to forget Simon's mad outburst earlier in the week I confess to having been nervous when this story was delivered. But Simon listened as meekly as a lamb, nodding absent-mindedly as though the information was out-of-date.

Of course had I been a better history student I should have realised Simon's identity right from the start. But listening to history and living it isn't quite the same thing I can tell you. Uncle Barnabas used to relish narrating the tale of Phillip's missionary journey into Samaria after Stephen was stoned and the Nazoreans in Jerusalem were resisting persecution. Suddenly it all came back to me - 'A man who for some time had astounded the Samaritans with his magic... everyone in the city from all classes of society paid close attention to him... a Great Power they said.'

A Power who was none other than Simon Magus! Barnabas had explained that Simon was baptised along with many Samaritan men and women. It was one of the most successful Nazorean missions of the early days and when news reached Jerusalem that Samaria was responding to word of Jesus, Peter and John joined Phillip. To the really committed converts they offered the precious gift of the Holy Spirit through the laying on of hands.

And then came the part that Barnabas always chuckled over. 'Well, this high and mighty Simon, the darling of Samaria despite being of no Jewish denomination, saw the changes that were taking place in ordinary men and women when Peter and John touched them. He brought a serving wench to carry a little carved chest' (it was obviously the very same one I had just seen!) 'and had the gall to go straight to Peter - Peter, if you please! - and ask him to choose his own fee if he would be so obliging as to give him, the magician, the ability to grant the spirit through his hands.'

At this point, Barnabas would usually shake his head slowly and deliberately and his listeners would attend a little closer. 'I feel sorry for that magician - the blast he got from Peter! Told him to take his gold and go to hell. Told him he had no share in that work. Told him to ask forgiveness of the Lord for his presumption!'

And then my dear departed uncle would tell his audience once again how much he felt for Simon, who made a sheepish exit with his young scrvant following him aftcr closing the lid on the untouched treasure.

Yes, I must have heard the anecdote a dozen times but only when I saw the servants yesterday with the Magus' money-chest did the denarius drop. Those stories were told years ago and the end of the tale - the vision of the abashed Simon - always left the greatest impression on me. This picture hardly fits my experience of him, confident and commanding as he usually is. Unsurprising therefore that his true identity remained hidden from me until now.

I decided it was prudent to keep my revelation to myself while I considered the consequences. Helen and Simon have an appetite for Christianity, but is it because they hunger and thirst after righteousness or because they want more tricks of magic? I cannot help thinking it is the latter, but the thought brings no relief, no belief that I have found the key to the situation. I could cast Simon in the mould of yet another would-be zealot leader who looks to an aura of spiritual authority to gain ascendancy over men. Somehow, it is all too simple. My mind is clouded and slow, like my delicate body.

The sun is warm, only losing its sting as the wind threads through the mournful cypresses. A place of holiness, yet still a place of death. It is the same paradox that grips me sitting on this boulder, thinking and scribbling. The world desperately needs comfort, but can one lonely scholar be of any assistance? Am I not as pretentious as I would accuse Simon of being?

Come unto me... and I will give you rest.

I consider the Saviour; a memory stirs. Not two weeks ago after evading the military in Jericho and distancing myself from the main road, I came across a man in foreign-looking clothes who said he was from Alexandria, making a pilgrimage to the land of Jesus' birth. I was concerned for his welfare and his sanity - someone who wanted to enter the war zone, not flee from it? He was a Greek, but an odd one, even if a man of learning like me.

Before I knew it, he had pieced together my mission and insisted on writing down a contribution for me to take. I was annoyed by his intrusion and his assumption that Christians in Egypt could know things about the Anointed which Judaeans had missed!

I feel humbler now. Who is to say precisely where the truth resides, except God Himself? I will copy out the Alexandrian's gospel snippet. He claims it was from John (which John, I wonder?) and this John repeated the belief that Jesus was not really human. The Master, he said, was actually a spiritual being who adapted himself to human perception:

'Jesus joined with his disciples in Gethsemane before the end. He assembled us all and said, "Before I am delivered to them let us sing a hymn to the Father and so go to meet what lies before us".

'He told us to form a circle, holding one another's hands, and himself stood in the middle. He began to speak in a chanting voice, and after repeating every passage we answered "Amen".'

The Greek (his name was Hector, an heroic name for a man even smaller than me) explained that the circle and chant was enacted every Sunday at the love-feast of the Christians in Alexandria.

'Don't you offer the sacrament of the Last Supper as my mother in Pella does?' I inquired.

He put down his reed pen, and I could see the charcoal ink stains on his small, neat fingers. 'You have your sacrament brother and we have ours. Christians must never fall into the same trap as the Jews and argue over which colour will make the house more beautiful while the family within sleeps on the floor and eats leftovers.'

In my best Greek I reminded Hector that I was both a Christian and a Jew but did not extend the discussion. His metaphor was actually kindly and mild seeing as I knew that in Jerusalem, Jewish supporters of the Sanhedrin, Jewish Pharisees and zealots had been murdering each other for months. This civil war would make Titus' task easier to fulfil and was encouraging the Romans to claim God's intervention on their side. The siege of the holy city would be a pushover because the fervour of the Jews had turned against itself.

'Look over my shoulder as I write,' said Hector. 'The mystery and uplift of these words leaves me in no doubt that they are indeed the Master's.'

I did as I was instructed. Amazed, I watched the words appear:

To the Universe belongs the dancer.

He who does not dance does not know what happens.

Now if you follow my dance, see yourself in me who am speaking.

You who dance, consider what I do, for yours is this passion of man which I am to suffer.

For you could by no means have understood what you suffer

Unless to you as representing the Logos I had been sent by the Father.

Learn how you suffer and you shall learn how not to suffer.

Very soon afterwards the little Hector left me, singing and skipping like a child on a feast-day. I'd given him the addresses of a couple of safe houses in Jericho, but I wondered if he would ever see the Nile again. And now I sit on my rock at the Place of Sacrifice and ponder these words he left me with. There is a ring of the East to them, nothing about morality. I can't imagine what the Essenes would make of the chant, with all their emphasis on fasting and sexual abstinence and the rigid rules of hierarchy among the brotherhood. But does sobriety by itself make for goodness? Barnabas wouldn't say so. I think he would like the Saviour's dance.

10
DANCE OF LIFE

TO DANCE, OR to remain rigid? The choice presents itself again and yet again. Dancing successfully means to trust an inherent capacity which makes our steps for us. Good dancing is a flow, a process. We may learn the steps but if we deliberately execute each one through the use of conscious intellect we will no longer be dancing. Likewise, we may understand truth and live it, but too much testing - the application of controversy in an attempt to gain 'proof' - will smother its delicate actuality.

Latest in the long line of truth seekers are the physicists. Scientist David Finkelstein thought it was misleading to label as 'particles' those entities involved in the most primitive events of his quantum topology theory - the reason being he said, that these entities don't move in space or time, they carry no mass, have no charge, neither do they have energy in the usual sense of the word.

Finkelstein viewed space, time, mass and energy as being one remove away from the universe's principal events. In other words, the basic unit is a *process* that gives rise to those secondary qualities we recognise as space, time, mass and energy.

What does this tell us? It tells us that the world of nuts and bolts is not the only world. It tells us that the world of nuts and bolts requires a deeper, more powerful underpinning if it is to exist at all.

First the dance. Then the dancers. The reality of the dancers is enshrined in the dance. Without the dance, dancers have no identity and are adrift in the dark.

A cloud of inky unknowingness envelops planet Earth, and we hear the faint cries of those who have lost their way, believing themselves to be damned. The Dance Master having gone or else poised to administer retribution, they experience the worst horror of guilt, fear, loneliness.

Yet looked at differently none of this has ever happened. The dance never ends. It is just that dancers may close their eyes and for an instant see themselves in a nightmare. There is nothing to fear because only in their imagination have they forgotten their steps. They cannot lose the dance nor compete against the Dance Master. Their Conductor *is* the dance. And the dance itself created them.

11

DISCUSSION AND DANGER

THE SHADOWS LENGTHENED, impaling the gloomy pillars of the Offering Temple, and Mark walked slowly back to the house. He considered the warm sun, the mountain air and an evening meal awaiting him; yet the whole of Israel was under the heel of the invader, only counting the weeks to be crushed out of existence.

Simon's servants had left two days previously, each carrying a purse with the equivalent of ten years' Temple taxes. They declined Simon's invitation to stay, striking east for Peraea because they held to a popular contemporary belief in a great catastrophe, a second Flood—and for good reason they considered the lull in the war indicated only the calm before the storm.

At the house there was an argument about the wild boar that Simon had killed and triumphantly dragged in. Zadok was affronted; the smell of pig was bad enough he said, without having to see others eat it. Simon jeered and declaimed that Man was a natural hunter. 'Moses received his spiritual guidance on domestic matters a long time ago' Simon added.

'If he'd have talked to God this afternoon, I'm sure the Almighty would have made allowances for our changed circumstances.' Penetrating as this insight might have been, Simon's contempt for Jewish custom was poorly concealed.

The meal over, Helen told Mark, 'It's time for our Nazorean to sing for his supper'. The women sat on one side of the main living room, the men against the other wall, on mats, cushions and stools. Mark moved into the centre of the space and cleared his throat.

Helen said, 'Your reports of the Anointed have been very interesting, but they are the sort of thing a schoolteacher uses to bring his pupils to attention before the real lesson begins. Stories of kindness and healing are surely just a preparation for the details of the Nazarene's journeys east through Persia, Kashmir and Tibet?'

Mark looked down and curled his left toes around his right ankle. 'You must realise' he muttered, 'that Peter didn't like those facts to be made public. What purpose does it serve to tell everyone that Israel's greatest prophet spent over half his life in foreign countries?' He lifted his eyes with some defiance. 'So, he travelled as a young man and reached lands that are only rumours to many of us? Is that of any interest to the starving widow, or the father who sees his son taken into slavery? The ideas, the hope, the promise of salvation - what is geography compared to that?'

'But you said it yourself' exclaimed Simon. 'Christianity is for all men - all women, too. And it could be if you didn't try to gloss over Jesus' acceptance by Zoroastrians and Hindus and Buddhists as well as by Jews, Greeks and possibly Egyptians too!'

'Let me confirm that I'm hearing this right' Zadok said sarcastically. The Samaritan was still huffy about the pig. The remnants of the carcass hung in a corner by the door: Simon refused to move it outside because of the forest's jackals and wild cats.

'Simon wants all the world to have one religion. The Jews including Samaritans must conveniently forget their ancient form of civilisation, their feasts and history, their observances to their God - and embrace pagans as equals.'

Simon leaned toward Zadok, triumphantly gesticulating with an open-palmed hand. 'Not so my friend. I don't care what *religion* people have. This Anointed One, or Christ as the Greeks put it, was beyond religion. If my suspicion is right, he was telling us how to live in harmony with life. That's what I call Knowledge. Religion is a social phenomenon - something quite different.'

Zadok's astonishment at this answer was comical. His beard jutted, his mouth opened but nothing came out.

'Tell us about Jesus in those far-away places' begged Rachel. 'Were there dangers? Why did he go? Did an angel tell him?'

Mark relented. 'When Jesus was barely more than a child, he amazed all in his presence with his authoritative attitude, teaching of the One God. People came to Nazareth to hear him, first from the Galilee, then from further afield. Wealthy and noble families realised that this young boy would be a perfect catch for their daughters.'

'Mm' Rachel dreamed.

'But' said Mark, 'the first will end up last, as we say. These dynastic hopes were dashed when the young Master left his parents' house one night, made his way to Jerusalem and joined a caravan of merchants on their way to Sind.'

Joseph blinked. 'Sind? That is on the edge of the world.'

'Not by a thousand leagues it isn't. Trade routes go much further east to a place called Cathay and then north to where wise men live in the snows of the highest mountains. Even further than both of these is the destination the Master was heading toward.' He scanned the faces of the group, questioning within himself whether he should go on.

'What a storyteller Mark is,' said Simon. 'Even the right theatrical pauses.'

'Well' continued Mark with a rush, 'Jesus understood his destiny. Before he could return to his land of birth, he had to complete his own inner trials; realise his true identity as a Son of God; anchor this within the body of the Earth. And so Jesus finally reached Shamballa, an oasis of the purest Light in the bleakest coldest desert. Shamballa, where the Will of God is clearly known. Only after he had seen the glories of Shamballa was he ready to return to us.'

'What are you talking about?' It was Zadok again. He combed his beard with his fingers, a majestic gesture designed to bring his pronouncement the respect it deserved. 'Now you two, Joseph and Yigal, you'll understand me. We don't need a Messiah who goes tripping around foreign lands for all the world like some dreamy Greek. Our Messiah must be a Jew who knows how to bring back days of peace and plenty, break the pride of the Judaeans and show the people of Israel that they must once again live under the letter of God's word.'

Lydia's mouth twitched. 'Are you mad, or dreaming? What Messiah could return our young men from digging Nero's pestilent canals? Or bring back our children from the mines in Cyprus where they will live and die without ever again seeing the sunshine? How could he clear out the bodies of Jews that pollute Lake Gennesaret, let alone bring them back to life?' Her voice was muffled as she buried her face in her hands, but the bitter irony came through: 'Peace and plenty'.

In the silence that followed, Rachel nervously scratched with a twig at the mortar between the stones of the wall. Little runnels of dust cascaded to the floor.

'Stop that' snapped Simon.

She dropped the twig, but the grains still trickled down.

'And so' said Mark, trying to pick up the threads of the story, 'when Jesus returned, he was a very different man. He could have stayed with honour in any of a dozen kingdoms along the way because all peoples saw the Light shining from him and everywhere his teachings were respected. But he came back to us. Who...'

'Look' Simon whispered harshly. 'There!' All over the western wall, mortar was trembling, rupturing, crumbling and powdering: hanging in the air as fine dust.

'Down' urged Helen. 'On the floor. Cover your ears. Breathe deeply.'

As he raised hands to his head, Mark felt worms burrowing and burning into his ears. Fresh clouds of dust erupted from the wall. The worms bit deeper, fixed jaws into his skull and rattled his teeth. Pain sizzled along the bones and into his brain. Through the murk he saw the others prostrate, only Simon and Helen sitting up with their eyes closed.

After an agonising time the worms retreated. Slowly at first, then with accelerated relief. They gingerly removed hands from ears. Mark felt a background buzz and throbbing pain in his head.

Helen and Simon still sat there immobile, apparently oblivious. Rebekah got up, rubbed the dust from her eyes and it turned to streaks of mud on her face. 'It hurts' she whimpered.

Without moving his head Simon glanced quickly about the room. 'We were lucky' he said. 'They nearly got us.'

'Who nearly got us?' Mark's eyes were watering and his voice wavered.

'It was the Roman Sound,' said Lydia. 'They must know we're here. Soon it will be the soldiers.' She spoke flatly, resigned.

'But we can run' coughed Zadok. 'It's dark. We'll get away. It was by God's grace that Helen and Simon were able to keep the killing sound at bay. We're not destined to die yet.'

Simon nodded. 'Helen is maintaining our protection. I don't think they'll try again. They believe they've stunned whoever was within range. There's a camp down the slopes - I could see it. Soon as I've had a breather, I'll turn my mind to the details. Meantime, Rachel! Bring wine for everyone. We've deserved it.'

The girl stumbled off to find the wineskins, dusting down her robe.

Simon remained in cross-legged position on the floor next to Helen. 'Come closer, Mark.' The Judaean crawled over to him. Simon grunted approval. He spoke softly but directly into Mark's ear. 'This is just for you.' Mark's outraged eardrums protested but he listened.

'We have to face facts, and the facts are not good. Expect an attack at any time. If we are separated, or either one killed, we should have the benefit of each other's knowledge.'

'What knowledge?'

'It's too late to tell everything, but there are a few essentials.' His breath fanned Mark's cheek. 'If you ever get out of here alive you will have a choice. Depending on how you tell the story of the Anointed the world will lean one way - or the other.'

'A strange time for jokes' said Mark.

'An even stranger time for false modesty. Just listen carefully. I mightn't get another chance. Folk in Samaria call me the Great Power; it amused me to accept their title. Yet an infinite strength - the root of the universe - dwells in every human being and it's in you, too: this quality only requires awakening. That's number one. Number two, you're uniquely placed to gain the confidence of gentile Christians. When Jerusalem turns into a heap of rubble, you can be sure the mantle of the future will fall on Nazorean Egyptians and Greeks and' he allowed himself a short laugh, 'even bloody Romans.

'I hear there's a man in Rome - a leader of the Christians - who escaped after Nero hung his comrades on posts and burned them as substitute street-lamps. With so much pain impressed into his memory he has only one thought, to ensure that Christianity survives. He gives himself a new title, not Power or Messiah or Rabbi, but Bishop. He will demand that Nazoreans obey him and his successors, just as the Sanhedrists treated Jews. If he succeeds, no matter what the Romans do, Christianity will survive, probably taking root in the lands comprising the Empire. As the punishments devised by the Romans become harsher and crueller, hoping to stamp out the Nazorean threat to the cult of the emperors, I expect that more men and women will perversely flock to be baptised.'

Mark replied soothingly: 'Don't be cynical Simon. I know that you, too, have flocked to baptism! And while I do not belittle the sufferings of the faithful, let me suggest less gloom on that subject. No matter what I think of Vespasian, he couldn't be anywhere near as bad as that demented Nero. Have faith yourself! It's only this cursed war that makes us all fear the worst.'

'Listen!' Simon's hissed reply set Mark's ears ringing again. 'Alright, you're a hero! But I haven't time for side-track conversations. Putting it simply, if this bishop gains ascendancy among the Nazoreans, much of your Master's wisdom will be lost. Don't you see? Christianity will have a hierarchy that will regulate membership and ensure survival. But what will happen to Knowledge?

'Mighty courage and tenacity there will be - I see it in you, and when I look into the world beyond the world, I see it in the future - but that's no substitute for truth. Christians will be torn to shreds by wild animals in the Roman amphitheatres without succumbing to their captors' promises: that by cursing Christ they would be freed. Yet the cause of true freedom will suffer more.'

A fresh shower of dust came from the wall. The terrible insistent noise began again. Yigal and Joseph, who had been massaging each other's heads, clung together like lovers and rolled on the floor. Helen, who had remained sitting up with eyes closed, flinched. As the burrowing of the worms tickled Mark's ears in exquisite agony, he grabbed again at his head to fend them off.

Nazorean politics. Jewish politics. Roman politics. What did any of that matter when you were about to have the humours break free of your body in the extremity of agitation? All he dared entertain the thought of as the pain rose like a wave and carried him somewhere strangely familiar, was that his Master moved close.

Then the Anointed explained - and with infinite patience - that God being life and only life, cared nothing for the unimportant death of the body; nor could a man's true inner life ever be eclipsed by so-called unending sorrow or the supposed barren distance between Creator and Created. And Mark was further told that while not dismissing the value of all the other denizens of planet Earth, he must never forget that Mankind had been created expressly in His image.

12

A SOUND ARGUMENT

FROM STORIES DOING the rounds in Jerusalem and Jericho, Mark had gleaned something about the Roman sound.

Did we say the 'Roman' Sound? It's like this: Somewhere around a century before our story began, another Mark, Mark Anthony, started his fateful affair with Egypt's Queen Cleopatra. As a young army commander, Anthony had won important victories for Rome in Palestine and Egypt. Cleopatra was a noble of Greek ethnicity, like Alexander the Great who annexed Egypt without bloodshed in 332BCE. (This move was cleverly contrived by Alexander, because Egyptians welcomed Grecian rule as liberation from the oppressive Persians).

It was said that Anthony, having become besotted with the accomplished and clever Cleopatra, took up all things Egyptian, including learning the deep secrets of sound from the priests of Heliopolis. (How else could they have cut and placed huge stone blocks finished as if with lasers and displaying the results to all who cared to glance at their millimetre-precision joins in the mighty pyramids of Giza?) Then after Anthony was brought down by his rival Octavian (later to become Emperor Augustus) the Roman war machine appropriated the esoteric knowledge of sound. Unsurprisingly, the legions considered it no less than their due for assuming military leadership of the Western world.

Now what's that you say? This is fantasy? Perhaps, but which part? It is not the writer's part to answer the question. We should however re-emphasise the *pyramid* fantasy—that the 2.3 *million* or more blocks of limestone and granite, laid to build the Great Pyramid, could be cut and transported then finely cement-joined along perfectly angled and flat planes fashioned using only the relatively soft copper tools of the era. Really? Then each of those blocks had to be placed so precisely that the finished building would end up with its apex positioned exactly over its base. Further, the four faces are aligned to the four cardinal points with a deviation from true less than 0.015 percent. You might think that at least the pyramid was built on a nice smooth area of desert sand? No, the chosen area incorporated a large and irregular chunk of rock; around and on top of which the monument was established. There's much more to it; but talk to a structural engineer about the extreme difficulty of achieving those aspects just mentioned.

The 'Sound' was used mainly for lifting stone to complete Rome's more grandiose building projects. The grapevine had it that the method was now adapted for military use although most of the wise men who supervised manufacture of the equipment were in short supply. They'd fled Rome to escape the latest civil unrest.

Three years previously, Nero had demanded that the stiff-necked Jews be the first to experience the ravages of this secret weapon and his Macedonian legion went to Palestine with five lightweight sonic projectors in its baggage.

Excellent results were obtained in the campaign against the hardy fighters of the Galilee. Not only stone but also flesh and bone succumbed. Sound was poised to take a major role in the Jewish War. Yet trained, effective operators were at a premium. Adjustment of the weapons was a tricky procedure and the risk of a backfire always present. Many officers viewed the projectors with suspicion for this reason— as well as because their natural professional soldiers' sense of fair play was affronted.

Morale dropped when men proud of their physical prowess had to stand aside and wait while initiates fiddled with metal plates. 'The Sound' dropped out of the major engagements and sieges in Palestine and within a few years, the requisite skills sank below surface in the stream of history.

But when praefect Barius chanced upon a projector and a competent operator from the garrison at Gitta, and when he considered his reward from the Nazorean zealots on the one hand and most likely from commander Cerealius or even Titus on the other, the gods seemed to have smiled on his plan to round up the Nazorean ringleader John Mark and the suspect, wealthy magician Simon.

Barius' investigations led him to expect difficulties in locating Simon. Not so! Shadowing the Magus' servants was a piece of cake and the irony of the forest hiding place was the final serendipity. 'Cerealius' old stamping ground' Barius told decurion-major Tarquin. 'Would you care to join me on the slopes of Mount Gerizim and help teach these amateur rebels a lesson in guerilla tactics? Find the magician and I'll wager we'll find this Mark. You can recognise them both, and there'd be something in it for you.'

Ten picked men, a *contubernium* of eight soldiers together with two Sound specialists, made their way independently to a prearranged spot below Gerizim's summit where the officers joined them. 'I don't believe all the superstitious nonsense I hear about Simon' Barius explained to Tarquin, 'but the man's ability to gather information appears remarkably thorough and accurate. There's no reason to give our magician even the slightest chance of slipping the noose we've got ready for him.'

And when the sonic operator assured Barius that the first blast should stun and perhaps kill anyone in the supposedly deserted stone house, the praefect felt instinctively that a second, longer attack was necessary.

The praefect's gut feeling was on target. Simon's talent for gathering military intelligence was remarkable. Of course, he had contacts throughout Samaria. But more importantly, the Magus could project his mind to a distant place or person and simply listen. As for surviving sonic attack, Simon and Helen couldn't withstand the Roman Sound for long. But when in the right state of awareness, they were able to shield themselves and others near to them.

Many centuries before, when the Egyptian pyramids at Giza were still awesomely costumed in fresh-dressed white limestone that reflected the sun far out to sea, such skills would hardly have merited extraordinary interest. But numerous secrets of the mind had since fallen into disuse, and now it would take more than another two millennia to revive them.

Barius was satisfied with the extended second blast. He ordered the sonic to cease fire. The two Sound operators set up camp with their equipment and horses while the others prepared to climb the mountain. 'Stay for two nights and then unless we return and tell you otherwise, take your gear back to Sebaste' the praefect told the operators. To the others, 'Take your positions, men - nice and easy.' The soldiers chose their paths carefully through trees that creaked in the wind. They carried small torches that alternately flared and smoked. When the house came into view all was still. But the flicker of a lamp showed through the window shutters.

The Romans fanned out to surround the building. Barius, sword in hand, banged on the door. It creaked open to reveal an empty room, but he noticed something behind the door. Though middle-aged, the praefect was agile and fit. He slashed savagely as he turned. His reward was a nice leg of pork.

13

DEATH ON THE MOUNTAIN

TORCHLIGHT AND NOISES in the undergrowth told them the Romans were getting closer. He had to keep bamboozling them as best he could. Simon held out his hands to break the scratching rush through the forest. 'Into the trees' he hissed.

The two hermits, the girls and their mother, aided by a natural flow of adrenalin, were agile enough in clambering up the pines. The problem was Zadok.

Simon went to his assistance, lifting his leg while the old man flustered, tangling himself in his robe.

'D'you want us all killed?' growled the Magus under his breath. 'Hop to it.'

The winking torches showed through the branches. Simon swung up last, climbing like a monkey.

Tarquin's detachment stopped just short of the foliage where the outlaws were hiding. 'Attention!' he barked. 'We retire to the higher slopes, men - otherwise we could be piddling around here all night.

First duty is to check with the guard at that house. Next, we search the Offering Temple itself. Keep swords drawn, and no stragglers.'

In the second or two that the soldiers needed to re-orient themselves, Simon was on them. As he dropped, his knife flashed. His victim collapsed. The Magus grabbed the soldier's torch and used it to whack another legionary amidships. Taken by surprise, the soldiers cried out and backed off, giving Simon the chance to attack a third legionary who managed to inflict a flesh wound before the Magus struck him too.

'Damn you, there's only one of them,' shouted Tarquin. Yigal jumped down next to the decurion-major and swung a heavy branch at his face. Tarquin dodged, lunged and struck the long-haired man a powerful blow. Simon made off with two soldiers in pursuit, until Tarquin bellowed, 'Stay here, you fools! Men! Make a circle. Face outwards. Melas - attend the wounded.' The decurion-major called out to the German legionary nicknamed Bear: 'You and Paulus, take a good look into those trees. One of the brigands fell on us from there.'

Bear and Paulus cautiously went out of the circle of their comrades, poked torches among the cypress fronds. Bear pushed back his helmet and cackled. 'By Wotan! We are menaced by three women!'

Tarquin only relaxed a fraction. 'Get them down—quickly. Then keep searching.'

They soon found Joseph. He descended quietly and stood looking in disbelief at his prone companion. 'Yigal...'

Now the decurion-major was happier. 'We have your friends, Magus!' he shouted into the trees. 'Any funny business and they get the chop.'

Tarquin's squad retreated toward open ground, carrying their wounded and goading the prisoners to keep up. Yigal, motionless and covered in blood, was abandoned. 'Didn't you know the price of war against Rome?' sneered Tarquin in answer to Joseph's pleading. Lydia and her daughters knew, if Joseph did not. They walked without hope and pulled him with them, saving him from a beating.

At a suitably darkened distance, Simon hobbled after the soldiers, grasping the wound on his leg. Concentrating on the retreating light of the torches, he stumbled over Yigal's body, and a steadying hand gripped his shoulder. It was Zadok. 'He's dead,' said the old man.

The torches bobbed on their way to the Place of Sacrifice. Yigal was gone and the others taken. It was only a matter of time before Mark and Helen were caught. Zadok held the glowing remains of a discarded torch. He could see the blood glistening on Simon's leg. Simon's face, too, was injured. Then Zadok realised that the wetness he saw there was tears.

14

A VICTORY OF SORTS

THE SHUFFLING PROGRESS of the soldiers halted while Bear tied the wrists of the prisoners. He allowed some play in the rough leather thongs, partly out of pity. He couldn't help thinking of his family and his own forests in Bavaria. Under the camouflage of darkness Rebekah and Rachel brought to mind a homelier image than the ragged whores of Ptolemais, the sad seaport hags who'd been his first impression of the Chosen People. The young Jewish sisters reminded him somewhat of flaxen-haired cousins he had played with in more innocent days.

But the big German's leniency, it must be said, was more motivated by disdain. He'd fought against zealots in the Galilee. They'd tear you apart with their bare limbs and teeth like the hounds of Hecate if they were given the chance - as vicious and unforgiving as that God they prayed to. Yet this sorry mob...obviously not of the same calibre.

Melas, almost as broad and even taller than Bear, used his strength to help his two wounded comrades through the undergrowth. Varus was in a bad way. Simon's knife had pierced his neck near the collarbone, and his tunic was soaked with blood. Melas bandaged him up as best he could in the dark. Varus had absorbed all the mythology about soldiers' honour and being a man, but the pain was too much. Intermittently, he sobbed like a baby, stifling the shameful noise with clenched teeth.

Legionary Demetrius, formerly a slave from Athens, held onto Melas' shoulder to steady his progress. Congealing blood stuck his fingers together, but Demetrius was not unhappy. He counted himself fortunate to be a Roman soldier. Regular food, status and protection, with only shallow wounds to the left arm and leg marking today's duty.

Bear took the lead with Curtis, the damage to whose leather coat (branded when Simon attacked him with the torch) could be smelled if not seen.

Then came the prisoners. After them, pushing branches aside, were Melas and his two charges, flanked by Paulus and a second German, a young protege' of Bear's who was inevitably nicknamed Cub.

Tarquin brought up the rear. He scowled. It was sheer carelessness, the way he'd accepted Barius' judgement about everything. So much for the magic Sound! And then, when they had seen evidence of only a small outlaw group at the house and were encouraged by the fresh food scraps and the hot embers of a fire, he had allowed Barius to order him into giving chase through the trees. Meanwhile, the praefect was taking it easy, guarding the little house with the rest of the troops.

For all Tarquin knew, a hundred bandits were ready to spring from the shadows to Simon's aid. Why had he given in to his stupid soldier's pride and come along tonight in the first place? There was no point for wangling the house in Gitta, if he was going to die on the slopes of this Samaritan sand-heap. And then there was the other problem waiting back at Gitta. Those women! It had seemed a good idea at the time to bring all three, but now they were ensconced in his new accommodation they fought like cats. He thought the Jewish obsession for cleanliness would be a safe bet. But loose women were the same everywhere and if that Beruriah turned out to have the pox…

'Light ahead' said Bear, not bothering about 'sir'.

'Identify' rapped out Tarquin.

'Could be one of our lot near the Offering Temple. We're close to the clearing, I'll wager.'

Not close enough, Tarquin fretted. 'Get a move on. Curtis, help Melas.' Curtis turned, let his sword drop. Simon's vision was very sharp, and the brief glimmer of torchlight reflected off iron told him all he needed to know.

'By Juno.' It was the last words Curtis would speak. In a move worthy of the fastest Judaean dagger-men, Simon's blade slid between the Roman's ribs. The Magus melted away into the shadows as the soldier's body fell.

'Is that you, Tarquin?' Barius bellowed from somewhere neither near nor far.

'It's an attack' shouted Tarquin instinctively, without seeing what had happened to Curtis.

'Over here, you men!' The praefect's voice carried through the forest. Sandals kicked up dust across the Place of Sacrifice as the troops on guard raced in Barius' direction. 'Kill the prisoners' ordered Tarquin.

'Me?' asked Bear, grabbing Lydia. 'Too bad for Curtis, but they're my ticket out of here.'

Tarquin hesitated. He'd settle with the German later. 'Barius! To me! Reinforcements!'

The praefect ran into the forest ahead of his soldiers, brandishing a light and heading for the others' torches. This was an easy target for Simon. He took his time intersecting the praefect's path. Barius blundered on. The Magus rose up like an avenging angel - and was knocked sideways as Zadok, eager to prove his worth after last time, charged out at Barius. The Roman sidestepped the worst of the off-balanced Samaritan's club. Before either Zadok or Simon could sort themselves out they were surrounded.

'Don't spike them.' Barius wasn't so winded that he forgot to protect a possible source of income. A minute later, Tarquin and his party appeared. The Romans could hardly credit that just one lightly armed man - even if the famous Magus of Gitta - was responsible for their losses. Bear's knots were tied in earnest this time. The Romans assembled in the Place of Sacrifice and, too late to assist either side, the moon rose.

Tarquin adjusted his helmet and drew himself up to full height. 'So, the great magician is just a common brigand.' The Magus said nothing, but his mocking eyes suggested: 'There, doesn't that make you feel better?'

Cub punched Simon in the groin and the Magus jack-knifed and fell. 'You'll stop smirking when we crucify you,' said the soldier. It wasn't just the bravado of the newly victorious. He realised Simon's knife could so easily have struck him instead of Curtis.

'Where's the Nazorean?' demanded Barius. No-one answered but Varus, who lay on the ground, coughed blood. 'Hang on old chap' said Melas gruffly to his dying comrade, 'we'll have you fixed in no time when we get you back to camp'.

'Alright' said the praefect, answering the unspoken request, 'that's enough for tonight. We'll put up in the temple. Bear and Melas, keep first watch. Take those shawls from the women to make fresh bandages for Varus.' He glanced meaningfully at Tarquin. 'I'll interrogate the prisoners in the morning, so I expect them to stay alive.' Barius turned to Cub. 'Go and collect some firewood.'

'Yes sir' said the youth, the tension draining. 'And maybe a skin of wine and some pig from that house?'

15
THE LOWLIEST ALTAR

'JUST SETTLE DOWN' ordered Helen very softly. She pulled the heavy curtain shut, cutting off the silhouette of the altar and the pale starlight spilling in through the main door.

'I don't like this' said Mark, almost coughing in his attempt to sound authoritative. 'If they find us, we're cornered like rats. Why here, of all places? And what did Simon want us to split up for?' Bodily weakness took the bite out of his words. Mark was vaguely aware of how churlish he sounded. He tried to make himself comfortable in the cramped space. Here behind the altar and against the wall of the Offering Temple it was inky dark and the stone was bruising.

'Quiet' Helen whispered. 'If you give me a chance I can weave us some protection. And you know why we split up - so as to allow everyone a better chance. Be grateful you weren't sent out to fight. Now' she breathed, 'I am going to make us invisible. By that I just mean the Romans will be oblivious to us.'

'Pity you didn't do that when we were having supper' muttered Mark. But his complaint lacked conviction. It seemed certain to him she had saved their lives by her meditations when the killing Sound came. And what evidence proved that Helen *couldn't* make them invisible?

'I hope you remember what Simon told you,' said Helen presently.

'Uh?' He was more than half asleep.

'By all that's mighty, keep your wits about you tonight! You don't really understand how important you are, do you?'

The Nazorean smiled thinly in the gloom. He tried to keep his voice down though it wasn't easy. 'Since I met you and your husband, I've been finding a lot of things hard to understand. Why do you insist on making everything so complicated? If I get out alive, I spread the gospel of my Master. And that's about it.'

He could see her eyes barely as points of light against the background of the night. 'Mark' she said, and he was surprised at the feeling in her gentle voice, 'you could be used to create and promote a religion that the rabbi Jesus never taught. For example, there might well be a push to distance the Nazoreans from the Jews—and to build up ill-feeling that will likely come to a head when this war is finally lost. Your stories could show Jesus making fun of Pharisaic legalism, without balancing the account by explaining his own leanings toward much of the teachings of the Pharisees.' She whispered almost musically: 'Think of it. You could make out that the Jews *as a nation* sent your Master to an ill-timed death, even though thousands of devout Jews loved him. You could suggest, by the way you described Pilate's part, that the Romans were just innocent bystanders to the crime of the century. You could use the name of Jesus to support particular morals and social codes; and suppress the principle of personal revelation in favour of an authoritative organisation.' Her words grew softly urgent. 'You could erase from your stories certain indications of individual responsibility that would be disliked by a religious hierarchy bent on retaining control of the wider community. For instance, there would be Jesus' knowledge of the wheel of births and deaths.'

Mark replied slowly, 'I think I see what you mean...'

She retained the whisper, but now the irritation was clear. 'Your mind's stopped functioning! I must have made too strong a medicine for you tonight.'

He felt her arm against his. Physical contact somehow gave him to understand. 'You've been sedating me!' he hissed 'You didn't want me to leave here. You kept me prisoner so I might never see Asia or Rome again. You two and your tricks! Peter was right, those years ago - you have no part in our work. You're clever, both of you, but unworthy to tell *me* about the Anointed.'

'Wait, Mark!' Her voice was even gentler now. No, it had to be another device to subvert him. 'Don't try denying what I know is true' he said coldly.

'You're right. We did try to keep you with us, but only for the best reasons. And yes, Simon did try to purchase the power of delivering the Holy Spirit by the laying on of hands. He was younger then. Must a man pay forever for one mistake?'

He could imagine what his Master would say to that. And practically speaking, it hardly mattered whether he forgave Helen or not. Neither of them could go anywhere or do anything at this moment. They were stuck with each other. 'Suppose I believe you' he breathed. You have told me how the Nazorean teachings might be corrupted; what shouldn't be emphasised. No doubt you have it all worked out what I *am* supposed to record about the Master - though how you'd know better than me, I can't imagine.' He said what was front of mind, no matter if it was somewhat indulgent or even whining.

But then, despite the dark or perhaps because of it, he could sense honesty in her reply: 'Haven't you realised yet? It's the very reason why we needed you to come along. We appreciated only too well how politics could contaminate this pure teaching. Simon knows that because truth is ageless, he already understands a great deal of the Nazarene's message. Nevertheless, as you explained earlier tonight, Jesus initiated something new. That's the vital part - the part that complements the world's existing wisdom. Simon and I were missing that part. But you, Mark - you have it! Now will you blame me for keeping you here?'

She was so quietly animated, he was reminded of the moment he first set eyes on her. Once again, he could feel the glow of her skin, the subtle and mostly natural perfume of it; the vitality of her blood finding a sure response in his own.

'So you need me' he said. 'And I suppose to complete this work, I also need you.'

'The force of the Saviour is with you' she said, taking his hands in hers. It was so simple, he had never thought of it like that before. Man, woman and understanding existed in a timeless state of high potential. Then everything started to happen.

Hands that were on hands suddenly reached for calves, thighs, breasts. Lips found lips. A fear, an exhilaration swept Mark along. While other lives hung in the balance. In the *Offering Temple*? And what of Simon Magus who could 'see' through walls - and what of Roman soldiers ready to kill without compunction? But the body spoke a different language and swiftly, silently, inexorably it tried to have its way.

Talk of eternity? Not the kind of eternity that stood looking at itself but joined its own celebration. Tumbled into its own maelstrom. He could hardly see her green eyes even now, but he remembered. He recalled the many occasions when those eyes had flaunted their superiority. A masculine archetype—some ancient, now welcomed stranger - called for revenge. The drug-induced lethargy fell away.

But the promised synchronisation with her was demolished by its own desire. Reaching deeper into barely known reserves, he found raw sex; to be delivered as nature intended. It was cut off by Helen as rapidly as it had begun. She regained her cool reserve and murmured: 'No. Not like that.' She twisted away.

He was left without either dignity or piety, transcendence or tenderness - not even physical release. He silently cowered under the weight of humiliation, yet the silence saved them. Only minutes later he heard the faint sound of someone outside, near the wall vent closest to where he and Helen lay.

Against the quiet of the night, he discerned the very softest clink of armour and a funny, liquid murmur. On cue, a Roman soldier had come to add his own insult to the profaned pride of Samaria, the Offering Temple.

INTERLUDE

HUMANS ARE OPINIONATED. They are quite likely to feel that they know, understand and must announce to their world a fulsome exposition and judgement on any situation, person, idea, or event that crosses their mind. This is especially probable when they are in fact quite unable even to grasp correctly the matter in hand. It's all too easy to erase the question-marks relating to a favoured topic, and then to write in whatever answer or answers might fit the need (*our* need) of the moment. The whole process seems to go with an allied characteristic, which is the very popular belief that we (unlike many or most others) are pretty much always and absolutely *right*.

This strategy can have, putting it mildly, unwanted consequences.

Take decurion-major Tarquin as an example. Boorish, selfish, proud and cruel. Yet that was only one side of his soul. There was another, unlikely as it might seem from how he has behaved during our brief acquaintance. But these as yet unforeseen aspects in Tarquin should not be discounted, if we wish to avoid an over-simplified opinion of humankind.

We could instead push our cherished points of view aside and look wider and deeper. For instance, the ancient Egyptians, during at least some of their thousands of years of history and pre-history, had many useful ideas. An important idea was that one should not reach for perfection but rather, for balance.

There are elements of life that uplift, yet these elements cannot stand alone. There must be challenges, difficulties, including things we may even choose to call evil. Only because of the twin effects can life evolve and here we use the word 'evolve' in its most essential sense.

In Egypt, Amon-Ra the Sun god, representing all things good, existed alongside Seth, the master of storms, disorder and warfare. Seth killed his brother, the revered and mighty Osiris, yet also gave his name to Seti 1, the Pharaoh who worked most diligently and successfully to improve the Egyptian state. Seti's temple at Abydos still breathes of the dignity, reverence and significance of his reign.

In real life there is always the plus and the minus, the easy and difficult, strengths and weaknesses, applying to every situation and person. While we might prefer to rid ourselves of these events, whether slightly annoying, shockingly tumultuous, or anything in between, unfortunately they offer the only way that our souls will develop as they can and should.

To attain health in body or mind it might be better to reach for a balance point rather than trying to completely eradicate all the negatives we perceive—that latter task will in any case prove futile.

Once in a while, the balance point when it comes could be cause for amazement.

Enough of discussion and theory. Let's watch what happens.

16
ONE DOOR CLOSES

THE SMOKY GLARE of two braziers illuminated the temple. The heavy smell of pork was mixed with the lesser odours of sweat, human blood, a sweet ointment (smeared ineffectually on Varus' deep neck wound) and behind the altar, a lingering trace of the rose-water that Helen always applied to her face and arms.

Both Helen and Mark were acutely aware that now they were trapped and had to stay hidden - silent and unmoving behind the altar curtain - despite their recent clumsy antics.

Mark's muscles ached. His knees were sore, his mind in turmoil. There was no way to get comfortable, no way to ignore Helen crouched next to him, no way to forget Rebekah's cries when one of the soldiers took her into the vestibule, no way to ignore Simon's defensive failure, no way to believe he himself would get out of this alive. He used his bag of scrolls as a cushion - there was little else it could be good for now.

He thought of Paul talking his way out of trouble with the authorities in Asia Minor and of his mother exhorting him to simple faith while virtual genocide took place around her. But these examples of inspiration failed to reach him. He was like a man tensing - and knowing the futility of tensing - as he falls from a high cliff.

Helen was lost in her own world. Simon captured. Mark free but a liability rather than an asset. Her emotions were cloudy, her direction unsure. For the third or fourth time she prepared to go into meditation. Surely this time she would reach Simon?

At the other end of the building, Barius was worrying about possible repercussions. He would have to construct his report rather carefully. The secret Sound had turned out a failure, and two good men had been lost. (Varus couldn't hold out much longer.) There was no evidence at least until he got the hot irons on Simon, whether the Nazorean Mark was up here on the mountain at all. If he didn't keep sweet with the Nazorean zealots, would they renege on their promises and join up with the other freedom fighters in Jerusalem? And if Titus got to hear about that...

Tarquin dozed morosely, wondering how he might ensure that Simon was despatched as soon as possible on that short but significant journey across the river Styx. Like Barius he didn't believe a half of what he'd heard about Simon, but it would be tidier to have him killed. The gods alone knew what yarns he might spin under interrogation. How about a convenient 'escape attempt'? Who'd be the best one to bribe? Not Melas. Demetrius? Paulus? Or Cub? Dribbling slightly (the wine had taken effect) Tarquin slept on it.

Rachel was comforting her sister. Wrists still bound she stroked Rebekah's cheek with her own. Rebekah sobbed almost soundlessly, staring into the darkest corner of the temple. Lydia stood over them both - an emotionally drained woman, a Samaritan, an outcast amongst the Jews, the often-outcast race. (Even before the war, when they comprised over a tenth of the population of the Roman Empire and enjoyed certain privileges, Jews had never truly been accepted as equal citizens.) Yet Lydia's fierce gaze was enough to keep the soldiers away after Kerios, the legionary who'd raped Rebekah, complained to his comrades that the girl 'laid there like a jelly-fish - no spirit at all'.

Varus was mercifully in a coma. His attacker lay next to him immobilised by the simple expedient of having his wrists and ankles tied to a heavy pine log. Simon's face gave the impression of one who has all the answers, awaiting only the right moment to use them.

Zadok, by contrast, had defeat written all over him: guilty because he had aborted Simon's attack, outraged at the Romans, ashamed that the crunch had come and he had barely summoned up a whisper of his usual strident faith in the One God of Israel.

Who could have guessed that Simon's state of mind was almost identical to Zadok's? Maybe only Helen, whose probing consciousness kept running up against a wall of self-pity and destructive anguish beneath that calm exterior.

Joseph looked down on Varus and Simon. Foe and friend but now they didn't appear so different, both vulnerable to the exigencies of the world. There used to be himself and Yigal to confront that world, but… the righteous were smitten, the ungodly prospered. It was more than mere humanity could understand. Somewhere there had to be a higher authority, a high court that was able to judge truly. Under his breath, Joseph hummed a funeral hymn in memory of his friend who'd been left to the scavenging cats and jackals.

The braziers burned lower; the watch changed to Cub and Tarquin. Most of the soldiers gave up eating, drinking and ogling the girls, and slept.

Mark, experiencing a kind of delirium, mentally called on the name of Jesus and tried to forget his shameful rush of passion, his jumbled thoughts and feelings, his short periods of mental blanketing. Helen continued to meditate hoping to prevent Simon from spiralling into catatonic depression. Bear dreamed of hunting his namesakes across pure white snowfields. Joseph stared sleeplessly at Tarquin. Tarquin sliced his finger with his sword edge to stay awake.

Demetrius was kept awake by his injuries. He eyed the prone Rebekah and thought listlessly that now she'd been oiled up, she wouldn't make so much fuss if he had his go. Barius had drunk a belly full of wine, but his mind refused to switch off; running across his eyelids was an action replay of last week's mass crucifixion of rebels in Sebaste. Demetrius groaned as his arm began to fester. And Varus died.

A gentle roseate glow in the doorway began to vie with the shrinking light of the braziers.

17
THE MAGIC SHOW

'HERE, BOY!' SAID Tarquin, jerking alert and prodding Cub. 'Do you see that?'

The young soldier made a show of alertness. But it was safer not to admit to anything. The area adjacent to the main doors was certainly brighter and a funny colour too. 'What, decurion-major?' he played for time.

Tarquin was agitated. 'Don't be ridiculous, I mean that light.' He pointed with his sword at the offending cloud of brightness.

Joseph was watching it too. Throwing aside caution, he burst out: 'Angels look like that!'

The hermit kept the rest of it to himself - remember when Peter, the apostle of the Nazoreans, was rescued from prison? An angel saved him and perhaps 0 blessed Father whose Name may not be voiced, it will be our turn now...

The light appeared to flow in from under the temple door. A thought occurred to Tarquin. He stepped over to where Simon lay trussed up and kicked the magician's blooded leg.

'Okay, trickster. You can turn off the magic show now.' Simon, who had finally relaxed a little and drifted off into a light sleep, awakened with a grunt.

'On his left sir' urged Cub. 'Varus doesn't look too good.'

Tarquin bent over Varus' body. He'd seen enough dead in his time. 'Soldier' he announced to Cub, 'this brigand's killed a comrade. He ought to get what's coming to him don't you think?'

Simon was wide awake now, regarding them with his deep virtually unblinking brown eyes.

Coldly discussing a man's fate like this while the man waited patiently wasn't Cub's idea of fun. 'Well, sir the praefect said...'

Tarquin severed Simon's ankle cords with his blade. 'The magician's trying to get away. A Roman soldier who scotched such an attempt would be due for a reward.'

'If he really did try to escape, sir' mumbled Cub.

Tarquin cut the thongs holding Simon's wrists. 'I think he will, soldier. Stand ready with your weapon.'

Simon inched away from the pine log without taking his eyes off Tarquin.

The decurion-major smiled. It was going according to plan. He made his way slowly and deliberately to the temple door and, still facing inwards toward Simon, pushed it open.

'Here's freedom looking at you' he said.

Simon, Joseph and Cub saw Tarquin disappear against the intensity of light that poured in.

A rolling wave, it swept over them too. There was a high-pitched hum, a benign counterpoint to the mind-breaking, bone-creaking violence of the Roman Sound. Persuasive but gentle, it brought the air alive. Sleeping bodies were awash with light and Joseph whooped like a youngster, 'Hear 0 Israel, the Lord our God, the Lord is One'.

The soldiers started to open their eyes, but no-one seemed to know whether they should be getting up or making a challenge or running away. They waited for a sign that would clearly indicate the safest course.

Light crept up the walls, rippled over the altar. The rose colour turned into a pale green.

Legionary Kerios suddenly jumped up, dropped his sword and ran into the blinding glare that marked the doorway. The humming noise deepened and two other soldiers scrambled away in the same direction.

Barius reached to grab the arm of Demetrius, who was also on his way out of the temple. He shook the Greek roughly. 'Come to your senses.' Demetrius retaliated and the praefect, taken by surprise at this burst of strength from an injured man, was caught off balance. He toppled over and hit his unhelmeted head on the stone wall.

Cub was about to join the exodus then changed his mind and crouched down with his hands over his face. He'd had a feeling from the start that it was tempting the fates too far to make camp in this alien temple and now all he wanted was to be inconspicuous. God took on such a stern visage in this land, it was best not to antagonise Him gratuitously - especially when you were making war on His local tribe! The Hebrew deity was a real tyrant—how surprising that Nero and Caligula hadn't felt greater kinship with Him. Too much like competition, it must have been.

Cub had a theory about religion, developed during his travels as a soldier of Rome. The Great Creator was really the same the world over, no matter what name He bore. And this was plain common sense; there could only ever be one high king of a land or one emperor of the Romans. (Vitellius the pretender would soon find out about that when Vespasian landed on Italian soil.)

Yes, only One God, Cub deliberated to distract himself, but this God expressed so differently through His servants the lesser deities; the numina of wood and water and growing things; the destructive power of lightning and the winds and the sea; the men who fought and pleasured or stole pleasure from women as he did; and those who had no understanding of the way of Mars but sunk into a stupor of books or politics or became slave to other pointless habits.

No wonder men had built temples to ingratiate themselves with this strange high king of the world who gave and took away without reason or pattern. No wonder men offered ritual sacrifices to keep His wrath at bay. You could never guess what He'd do next but in a house of God surrounded by the Hebrew wilderness any unsavoury thing was possible. Instead, you needed an intermediary like Mithras the god of strength and gentleness, of courage and self-restraint. The soldiers' god. He would close eyes and call on Mithras...

The minutes passed and the caressing hum gradually faded. At last Cub dared look again. The cloud of light had gone, once again there was just the glow of the fires painting eerie shadows on the walls. Then he saw the captives sitting up; Simon having been freed from his bonds was now freeing the rest.

But not one other soldier was left! Excepting poor Varus and the praefect. Barius was lying by a brazier, his face unpleasantly pale. Cub made a move in the direction of the superior officer when he heard a footfall behind him. A woman in a white robe was walking down from the altar.

'Mighty Mithras.' Cub closed his eyes, hoping that when he reopened them, the ghostly figure would be gone. 'Save me from these Jewish apparitions' he muttered. It was no good, the woman or angel or whatever it was, kept coming onward.

Simon noticed Cub, but couldn't be bothered with him. The boy soldier obviously wasn't up to making trouble. The important thing was to collect any discarded weapons and be ready for the Romans, if - or rather when - they returned. He suspended this task just long enough to embrace Helen and be reassured that Mark was alright.

There was a noise and Tarquin reappeared at the temple door, dishevelled and with the crooked smile of a drunk who's been pushed out on the street by an impatient innkeeper. 'Great Mithras!' he shouted, looking straight at the ever-more nervous Cub. The decurion-major's eyes panned the array of faces staring at him.

'I have seen Mithras, brothers and sisters. Just as we were told, he's a god to bridge the gap between the Creator and Man, to show us the way: To overlook our madness, to soothe our self-inflicted pain.'

Tarquin's eyes filled with tears and this, more than anything, fright-ened Lydia and her daughters. They drew back, defensive but not submissive, ready for the next trick to be perpetrated by the ruthless representatives of Rome.

Mark limped down from the altar, rubbing away the cramps from his leg, once again finding it worthwhile to grip his crumpled bag and deem its contents sacred. His sick despair lifted. The Judaean looked at Simon. Ignoring his own recent wretched state, Mark spoke to him with disapproval; even authority.

'Put that sword away! You won't need it. Don't you understand? And I mean all of you. Yes, all!

'We have been graced by a visitation of the Master Jesus.'

18
POINT OF NO RETURN

A DREAM CAME TO me in that endless night when I hid from the soldiers in the Samaritan temple. It was my mother, calling, 'Menahem, Menahem, the time of Remembrance is here'. I joined my siblings and, suffering askance looks from the many Pharisee children who were our neighbours in the dyers' precinct of Jerusalem, made my way down the steps to the basement of our home. There was Uncle Barnabas, his ruddy face softened by the pale light of the olive oil lamps, and he was making ready the sacramental wine and bread. The little squares were laid out on our single, rather battered silver plate. (All mother's spare money was channelled into the movement.)

Barnabas wore such a grin of joy whenever he officiated at the love-fest and so it was that day. Mother was there, with a place left empty as usual for father so that perhaps he too could join in the celebration of our Saviour.

Mother reminded us that the bread was Christ's body and the diluted wine his blood, but of course not even we kids believed that was the literal truth. The bread was to symbolise the substance of Jesus' message and the wine meant we were invoking the flow of his life and his mighty understanding.

We joined the circle of Nazoreans, some from far parts of the city, and I could feel that old glow of belonging to a family. Then just as these things always happen without warning in dreams, a darkness swooped down and the lamps guttered out as a chill clutched at my heart. I was certain there was blood concealed by the shadows carpeting the floor and the wind that froze hearts and sucked away light carried the noise of suffering humanity like the cries of a million dying birds.

In the blackness that remained, all I was aware of was my heart jumping with fear. I may have called out, I don't know, but from somewhere there came a soothing balm - a golden honey sensation is how I would describe it - and he came and spoke to me: 'Menahem! Remember me! The bread and wine and candles don't matter. But to remember me is to remember who you are. Be not led astray by this sleeping dream or the one you experience when you believe you are awake.

'Consider the world you see', he told me. 'Would God make such a world? Full of fear and pain and eventual meaningless death? Will you tell Him that He is mistaken? Or could it be that the mistake was yours? Remember during your festival of Remembrance, which need neither begin nor end, that there is a path of service you must walk. It is a steep path that leads to knowledge. After much travail you will know disaster is not real. And reality is not a disaster.'

I was floating alone after that. No! Not alone, for I was linked by golden-threaded paths to all and everything that mattered. For a breathless moment I merged with the Answer. My task was to clear my mind of all the clutter of thoughts which I had generated when I was without knowledge of the true Self. These thoughts were a grey mist clogging the conduit of perception. Thinking separation, it was only separation I saw: War and the fearful tremors of the body; sorrow and suffering; the reaching for love becoming the clutching of dust-dry bones. With the grace of my Master's vision all this could be cleared aside - oh yes! I had it…

I expect I had only been away a few minutes, but it felt like hours… or maybe seconds. I was awakened by that heavenly blanket of light - was it pink or was it green? - signifying the end of our old lives and the start of something utterly unexpected. But I knew just as surely that this NOW, existence in the moment, could never hold without challenge or difficulty. Only by renewed effort could any of us grow into the life that was being offered. When I climbed stiff and sore from behind the altar and thought it was too late for Varus to join us in this new world, yet he could still find it his own way, I was even more certain the unknown would demand its toll.

And when Tarquin staggered back into the temple, with that look of bliss I've seen before (a disarmed, knocked-about, sometimes tearful innocence that shows up now and again when the sacrament is shared by the faithful) I was confident the Holy Spirit had done its work.

But Zadok, ravaged by guilt and old rages, could not contain his passion. His hands shook as he confronted the officer.

'It's not enough that you drag your eagle standards in a trail of gore across our country, praying to them and to your insane emperors! You would make our temple unfit for worship by bringing unclean meat and a heathen god within its walls. Out! Before I...' He hesitated, aware of his impotence when it came to revenge. And consequently, he returned to his argument, bellowing into Tarquin's face:

'Listen to me, Roman! When the Judaeans refused to let us worship in the Solomon Temple, we built our own. And when it was torn down by robber barons we built another. Yet even in this high place you can't leave us alone! You may massacre us on Gerizim, but Samaritans will live in this land when Romans are just an ancient memory. You defile our daughters in our sweet sanctuary in the name of the accursed Mithras, but you'll pay for it!'

'Quiet, old codger' said Simon. He sounded so confident (how many times have I envied that in him) and obviously thought he could afford to go slowly now, because he added; 'All in good time'. The Magus picked up the last abandoned military blade and threw it over to me while he watched Cub out of the corner of his eye. 'See that the whippersnapper takes off his sword - but gently' Simon ordered.

I laid the deserted weapon on the stone floor and told the young soldier that we didn't any of us need those things anymore. Warily, just like a nervous bear cub, he unhooked his scabbard and tossed the weapon down near my feet.

The scene in the Offering Temple was like an animated version of that game the Cathay traders invented; with a king, a queen, peasant soldiers, priests and knights arrayed upon a board. Different pieces played separate roles but a false move on the part of one could place all its comrades in danger; a single wise strike would conversely raise the hopes of the whole army.

Old merchants in cosmopolitan Tarsus, who travelled to Samarkand, became addicted to the game and I had many times seen them sitting stern as statues, only their eyes flickering from piece to piece, figuring their next move and trying simultaneously to guess what their opponent was thinking. Helen's measuring gaze strayed from place to place exactly like a chess player; I recalled that the queen was considered the most competent and powerful of all the pieces. Cub stared at her, broke off to glance at unconscious Barius, blinked at starry-eyed Tarquin, glowered briefly at Zadok and slid his guilty look past the women in the corner. Joseph seemed to peer down on the board from some remote height, I couldn't imagine what he was thinking. Even Simon, man of action, was pausing to deliberate the game-plan.

'The Anointed' said Tarquin suddenly, as though he were in a tavern talking to friends and not weighing his life in the balance. 'Not Mithras, but the Christus, d'you say? The Divine Child foreshadowed in all the mysteries.' He became thoughtful. 'Jesus sounds an unlikely vehicle, a man of the people, crucified like a common zealot...' Then that open smile crossed his face. 'What does it matter the name we put to the power of God brought to the race of men? The capacity is the same.'

The decurion-major walked down into the temple. He passed close to Simon, and of course Tarquin still had his sword swinging from his belt, but nonchalance took him past the point of peril. Simon's slitted eyes followed Tarquin to where he knelt before Barius. Tarquin cradled the praefect's head in his hands, and made sounds that compellingly suggested a half-forgotten lullaby. But sleep was not the object.

'Awake now' said Tarquin, and his gentle words contrasted strangely with his muscled, arrogant body.

Barius' eyes opened. He looked dazed and struggled to sit. 'The prisoners' he choked.

Tarquin shook his head. 'That's all over now. No prisoners. Brothers
and sisters. Just sit and rest.'

Then Tarquin moved to where Varus lay. 'May I not be too late' he
whispered as if to himself. Again, he took the head in his hands. Once
again, the crooning sounds.

A fear invaded me, as in my dream. I knew what was coming, but I
didn't want to know about it. My only consolation was that I didn't fear
alone. When Varus sighed and bent forward, we all shrank back. Even
I who proposed to teach that death was unreal, felt the awful shock of
seeing my ideas of true and false blown away on the soft wind of Truth.

A greyness began to fog my sight. I ran to the door of the temple and
the night air smelled sweet, enticing. The Saviour's words at my shoulder,
my way was clear to escape these mysteries and carry out my purpose. The
mist thickened, and it came to me that one step out of the doorway would
be the beginning and end of choice. Time weighed heavy on my soul,
centuries rather than seconds. I felt a shadow pass out into the moonlight.
I would stay, but another Mark would meet the destiny he had chosen.
The Place of Sacrifice had received its due. Without words to describe
what I had touched, but holding the pattern of it firmly like the mane of a
contrary ass, I turned and stepped inside, still afraid.

I saw the closed-over remains of the wound on Varus' neck and the
fear was overwhelmed by some other emotion which caused tears to run
down my nose as I had seen just minutes before with Tarquin. Life: not
just the physical expression we know and feel but the dance of the light
itself, the passage of time which neither begins nor ends. It mentally
shouted out to me in the silence with a message so simple, so sweet, so
sane that I went from person to person in the temple hugging them. Cub
wore a half-bemused half-horrified expression before he succumbed to the
crying, laughing hysteria of the moment and clasped my shoulders, calling me his dearest friend.

19

THE NEW PRIEST

IN THE MORNING, we awoke to find that the events of the night were no dream. The softness and magic were still in the air while the swords and a javelin remained ignored and unattended in their untidy pile where Simon had left them.

Cub went with the girls to fetch a breakfast of barley-cakes from the stone house and when we'd eaten, he and I had a more grisly proof of the previous day. With Simon, we revisited the bloodied forest to dig and fill shallow graves. Joseph stayed by the temple, talking in street Greek with Varus in a kindly way - as though acknowledging that a life saved by unknown means could help compensate for a friend's life suddenly lost. But on our return, sweaty and unclean from our work, Varus only asked after the health and whereabouts of Yigal! There was a moment of confusion and embarrassment; surely Varus realised... But I couldn't be certain Varus was even aware it was Tarquin's touch that had brought him back to life. How does a virtual resurrection feel and can it even be described?

'It was Yigal's time to leave this world' Tarquin answered Varus without emotion. I looked at Joseph who was equally expressionless. Perhaps the hermit grieved too deeply, or else shared the same opinion. In either case Varus got it this time. His voice fell to a whisper. 'I remember in the forest. We were fighting, ambushed, and you, decurion-major...'

'Don't use that title, please' said Tarquin, twisting around to rip off his Macedonian legion's shoulder-badge. 'Praefect Barius will confirm that I'm relieved of my military status.'

Barius shrugged. 'It's nothing to do with me. I'd normally report a deserter - I am, after all, a professional spy as well as a soldier - but these circumstances are hardly normal.' The praefect fingered his intact, bruise-free skull. I saw his eyes search out those of Simon, yesterday's enemy, with a look that combined weariness and wonder. 'If Tarquin is leaving the army before his period of enlistment is through, I wish him well.'

We instinctively gathered around Tarquin on the steps of the temple, shaded from the growing intensity of the late summer sun and cooled by the constant breeze. Only later did I think to wonder at Joseph's almost unbelievably speedy forgiveness of Tarquin and how easily the rest of us had laid aside our usual preoccupations; Zadok forgetting to bewail the defilement of the temple; Simon not trying to lord it over every-one; Helen not orchestrating things from the background; the exalted Barius (as you have seen) almost sweet-natured despite his military bearing complete with close-cropped silvery hair and hard-bitten features. It seemed unremarkable then, such a senior officer sitting with peasants.

The young German soldier had lost most of his defensiveness. It didn't seem so incongruous to us, as I suppose it should, that he was talking about his boyhood in the mountains, living up to his nick-name. The girls were surprisingly calm considering Rebekah's terrible, injurious treatment and their mother neither hysterical nor vengeful. (That Rebekah could hold her head up and stare down the soldiers in silent courage was almost a miracle by itself. Cub acted friendly but still avoided her direct gaze.) And I? I was somehow blessedly able to lay aside the burden of guilt that attended to my unseemly actions of the night before. I do not try to concoct an excuse; for all of us, the confusions of that night had been almost wiped away as though years separated us from it, instead of a few insubstantial hours.

Tarquin began to teach. He asked me to translate into Aramaic for those who needed it.

'The messenger of God visited me. I must spread the word while ever it is in my mind. You were right, Mark, it's the spirit of the Anointed. This spirit came from the chariot of fire, which rode from a far country where the Christus is known in splendour, a brilliance as yet too great for unshaded eyes to bear.' He looked like he was searching for that country again then returned to us. But as far as the old Tarquin was concerned, I reckoned some part of him had gone forever.

'You have questions you wish answered,' said Tarquin.

Barius finished the last cake. He had removed his heavy cuirass and a few crumbs on his face made him even more human as he joined the conversation in his own rough Aramaic, saving me some of the work of translation amongst the group. 'I've one for you all' said the praefect frowning in concentration. 'No matter what we do or the sacrifices we make in the approved manner, the gods are never appeased. Why is there an excess of pain, illness and suffering even in the most secure and wealthy parts of the Empire? Can it ever be changed? I've heard Nazorean rebels speak of their Messiah as proclaiming a loving Creator. But when you consider their actions and the rest of the Creator's handiwork, the evidence weighs against it.'

Barius cleared his throat as another aspect of the question occurred to him. 'Men developed religion to keep order in the state, that's why we must worship emperors. But this light - it was different. Things changed...' He stared at the ground. Then, 'I can see you're taking it quite seriously, Tarquin, this new power of yours. Why you of all people, and not a priest?' I started to translate this for Tarquin's benefit before he came close and calmly whispered that today he'd been granted the ability to speak and understand all of our group's conversations, no matter the language.

'I am a priest now,' said Tarquin. (Who would deny it?) 'You're not leaving the big questions to last, are you comrade? You only want me to tell you why we are born in pain, live too often in sorrow and die after a few short decades without apparent good reason.'

I might have replied that my Master had come to solve this very problem, but when it was stated baldly like that I didn't know where to begin.

Tarquin took breath. A subtle change had come over him: selfish and worldly that face had been in Gitta, whereas now it was receptive and you felt pulled by a force behind the pupils. 'Will you understand that in truth there is neither a frightening world nor, as Jesus demonstrated, any pain or suffering that we cannot overcome? But to learn that it seems we need a very long apprenticeship.'

Zadok sniffed. 'Fine words, fine words. You have shown us wonders that I never expected to see in my life, but don't get carried away! We still have to live in the real world.'

There was an enormous crash and a flicker of lightning overhead. We jumped. A looming cloud bank had darkened the sky above. Yet I would swear that only minutes before the weather had been clear. Big spots of rain splattered down on the Place of Sacrifice and another bolt of lightning heralded a second, veritable explosion of thunder. We scrambled into the temple.

Tarquin strolled in last, serene. 'The real world?' He looked at Zadok directly. 'Yes, we do have to live in the real world. But before you can live in it you have to be able to see it and I'm afraid that, along with most of your brothers and sisters, you are still quite blind.' This time, I saw Zadok clamp his jaw tight. No-one else interrupted either.

'The real world is a world of light, a world that blesses and is blessed. It's not the world you see, because the illusions you make up in your mind cloud your true vision. We each shroud ourselves in shadows and then make believe we can see straight. Before long, the lack of light makes us afraid and we attempt to strike out at these shadows, thinking to make ourselves safe.'

Tarquin shook his head in a slow, almost weary way. 'How foolish! To wish to attack and even destroy something in our mind is merely to strengthen our belief in it. All your strength is used to fight shadows. And we may continue in this fashion until the end of time but without any progress, without success. We cannot hope to triumph over what is not there! We are God's creations. God does not attack, though for our own benefit He may sorely test us. None of this means as humans we should not stand up for what we know in our souls to be correct. Sometimes that is the only way forward. The difference is this: If we are aggressive to another, it should be done only because we are a vehicle for truth and that truth does not harbour any grievance, only itself. Even when war is done away with—and it shall be one day, however unlikely that may seem—it could be necessary for us to act as a conduit for aggression in order to play our part in maintaining the cosmic balance, including our need to carry out our God-given function.'

My dream had been preparing me for this, but I was unprepared. Tarquin's words (he spoke them, but they were not his words) were both crystal clear and hard to grasp. I needed time to think about it all. If what he said was true, if there was something in it, why, it threatened to do away with most of what we believed in and acted upon - whether Jew, Nazorean or pagan.

Helen found her voice. 'Is this the teaching of the Anointed?' she demanded of Tarquin. 'Some of it is tricky, rather more like the opinions of those easterners, the Hindus and the followers of him whom they call Gautama the Buddha. How can you be sure it's Jesus you're speaking for?'

Tarquin shrugged. 'How can you be sure that you're alive? You will doubtless insist that you are. I hear the words of the Master. It is Jesus, but more than Jesus. Not Jesus the man, but Jesus the Son of God.'

Zadok stood up. He looked troubled. 'I believe now you're a good man, Tarquin - maybe even a prophet. But the minute you try to make the rabbi Jesus into a god, or even a Son of God, you're talking blasphemy as far as the Samaritans, Judaeans and Galileans are concerned. There's only one God! The Pharisees are bad enough, preaching about God's so-called intermediaries the angels. Then there's the gentiles, with their Olympians, Mithras, Isis, Zoroaster and so on. A man who suddenly becomes a Son of God - almost as good as God Himself - won't wash with me or any other self-respecting Jew.'

Tarquin touched Zadok's shoulder. 'Take it easy, old fellow. We are all God's creation, each of us a Son of God. But we do not realise our holy status, and thus we suffer in self-imposed darkness. Jesus is the Anointed because he remembered his true identity as God's Son. A worldly king accepts his kingship when he is anointed with oil. Jesus accepted his reality as God's blessed Child when he was anointed with the Holy Spirit. Man, despite all his folly, has an unquenchable instinct to shake off ignorance, and this has given rise to stories and cults such as that of Mithras, which was a forerunner or a preparation for Jesus. In the legend of Mithras, we have an echo of the Nazarene's mission.

'Don't upset yourself about that title, Son of God. God is one, as you Palestinians surely understand. We are all equally Sons of God, but to be even more accurate, God has only One Son. We who live in the world make comparisons; we judge this thing against the next; we think to love one person and hate another; but all such are illusions. There is only One Life, which has only One Source. When your eyes are open, you will see the One in the many and the many in the One. We cannot accept a part of life and reject another! The divine law rules that we either accept all of life, or we condemn the whole of it - including ourselves.

'But there is good news. The nearer we come to understanding this simple choice, and learn to choose wisely, the more we live a true life. Eventually there will be happiness, but not the happiness you have been accustomed to. That happiness was always fleeting and could swiftly turn to its opposite. The happiness I speak of rests on firmer ground. It is not found in the swing from one feeling to its converse. Rather, this happiness is real and appears when the old way is eventually dismissed and only the direct, the open and the inner quiet remains. Then happiness comes of itself and has no reason to leave.'

He sighed. 'Once achieved it is simple, but almost impossibly hard to reach without a guide. We need a friend, an elder who has fulfilled the measures, who has already walked that path. Thus, my Master speaks through me; yes, Master Jesus - who in his realised state is an embodiment of the Holy Spirit.'

Tarquin turned to Helen. 'The Buddha also came to teach this message. There is, actually, only One Teacher for the One Son, yet the illusion of time brings the illusion of different teachers. Jesus is the great teacher for our era.'

Simon came forward. 'As you doubtless know by now, I met with followers of Jesus many years ago. They told me about this Holy Spirit and I could feel it, even if that was only a degree of its full expression. '

'And you wanted it,' said Tarquin.

'I would use it only for good.'

'You still held a little too much arrogance and harboured a little too much greed, Simon. The Holy Spirit is Power. It exists in the very highest reaches of this world and may not be called upon lightly. Those who would use it must prove their fitness for such responsibility.' It was strangely surprising to see Simon not arguing or dismissive but nodding his head silently and sitting down again.

Joseph spoke then. 'Perhaps you are right, Tarquin, for I feel the power of God is near to you. But by what means do all we sinners and strivers attain to this blessed state, this happiness which you say we can reach?'

A booming roll of thunder reminded us that the storm was still in progress. The grey interior of the Offering Temple, stark but sheltering, was a sanctuary not only from the rain, but also from all the terrors and complexities of the life to be found outside. Keep talking, strange Roman rabbi, and show us our escape...

Tarquin threw up his arms. 'Sinners?' he called out to everyone's consternation. 'I don't see any sinners here. Tell me the truth' he asked, pointing a finger at Joseph, 'are you a sinner?'

The hermit scratched his head. 'Well, I have fasted many times this past month, I bowed in prayer twice a day, refrained from speaking false-hoods, kept my body clean...'

'Piffle' said Tarquin. 'Not your body. Your mind. Weren't you awake for hours last night, not just grieving for your friend Yigal, but some-times as a contrast, filled with desire?'

Joseph coloured. 'I cannot help my dreams' he said thickly and his involuntary, momentary glance at Rebekah gave the reason for his shame.

'So you meant that bit about being a sinner, after all. But I must contradict you.' Tarquin became gentle again. 'Joseph, Joseph, you are a Son of God! Don't you remember what I said a minute ago? A son inherits his birthright from his father. Your Father doesn't know what sin is. His Spirit understands our belief in sin yet never shares it. How could such a one share in such illusion? And sin is illusion, however tragic its results may appear to be. Sin is the deep belief in separation. Can you imagine it—a world of no sin or guilt, of no attack and needing no defence? It would be a world offering no retribution of any kind, a place not governed by the dark and twisted image of a God whom you suspect hates you.'

I could see Lydia was confused. 'There's not much sense in that' she said. 'Everyone sins at some time; it's human nature. And so, we need rules from God, to make sure men don't go back to behaving like animals.' She held Rebekah's hand and Rachel, who was massaging her sister's feet, nodded.

'God doesn't hate us' said Lydia carefully, in the manner of an adult explaining to a child. 'But when we disobey His covenant, he may act to punish us for our waywardness.'

I had to break in. 'That is the old way of seeing, Lydia.' I spread my hands to make the point that suddenly I found so convincing; 'Tarquin is giving us a new explanation. He didn't say God hated us; he means only that we think God is against us because of our own guilt.' I was excited as it became clear to me. 'Yes! When we are selfish and fail to love our neighbours as ourselves, we expect God to punish us for our transgressions. But the transgression is to us alone because we have forgotten that we are as one with our neighbour. We have forgotten Truth. We punish only ourselves.'

I knew what else to say. 'A few nights ago, I was telling you when, as a pimply youth in the reign of Claudius, I travelled with the apostle Paul of Tarsus. He was an unlikely missionary—a Jew who was born into the priestly caste. He came from a wealthy family, even had Roman citizenship and when he first came across Nazoreans, he persecuted them mercilessly. Paul was converted when he saw Christ in a vision.

He formulated his own ideas of what the Master was trying to say. He argued persuasively and many Nazoreans believe in Paul's Jesus. Now Tarquin it seems, has had a similar experience to that of Paul.'

'Yes, but can you answer my question?' asked Joseph. 'What must we do to see the "new world" which Tarquin speaks of? Mark, you've already explained Paul's teaching that Christians should lead a moral life and submit to the saving grace of the Father, through belief in Jesus the Anointed. But what does Tarquin say?' Joseph pushed his clammy, straggly hair free of his face. 'Mark appears to understand your doctrine of illusion. Would you clarify it for a simple man like me? Drive a sword through your belly and the pain would be real enough! Ask any Jew whether suffering is just a bad dream and he will give you a very short answer.'

Tarquin stared at his scabbard. 'I am not unfamiliar with pain, thank you.' He spoke more to himself; I had to lean forward to catch the words. 'Pain from swords is the least of it. The anxiety of unfulfilled desire; the torment of well-thought-out plans shoved aside by uncaring fate. Loneliness; being trapped in this exquisite yet pathetic little bag of bones...' He shook all over and gave a deep sigh. Then his eyes were mild and bright again. 'Withdraw allegiance to shadows. There's a light in you, find it and feed it. Don't smother it in your ignorant grievances and fear of death, which is only the sleep between night and morning. Let the light shine forth. When you meditate, reach down—or up if you prefer—for that light.

'You can only see what you believe you are, Joseph. When you understand that you are holy and you then allow yourself to be quite harmless, the world's ability to hurt you is struck a blow.' (I ought to be strictly honest and report that Tarquin spoiled the profundity of his speech by ending with one of those wonderful, silly, child-like grins.)

Rachel spoke up next, clearly and with confidence. 'If God is good and we are really all good too, and evil isn't true, why does God even allow us to think that it is true?'

'He created us like Himself' Tarquin answered, 'which means the power to create in many ways, even to make illusions, is given us'. But

Rachel persisted. 'Well then, why should we want to make illusions, if they're so horrible?'

That amused him. After a few seconds, he tilted back his head and passed a hand over his eyes. For the first time that day he seemed to be thinking before he would speak. 'If you found your mother starving and weak, Rachel, and you arrived with a big bowl of lentil broth, would you demand that she first spend an hour telling you precisely what had happened? Or would you rush to feed her?'

Following that, Simon started talking about the philosophy which his father - a believer in the Great Light Ahura Mazda - had taught him. Simon said Ahriman, the fallen angel and the adversary of the God of Light, could never triumph in the ordinary run of things but had employed cunning to establish himself as lord over the hearts of men.

'It's this way' he pronounced. 'The Jews think that their One God is the mighty Creator of all things, with no possible rival. Yet He tells the Jews He's a jealous God, so He must be insecure about His position of supremacy. Think about it! The Jewish deity, the one who's so special and ineffable that mostly He must not even be named, carries on such that you'd mistake Him for a spoiled child.' Simon had the stage, and he liked it. He fixed his eye on each of us in turn.

'If you don't believe me, read the Jewish scriptures with an unbiased eye. I'm sure that Ahriman, the great Adversary, has often pulled the wool over Jewish eyes and substituted himself for the One God.'

'So?' said Zadok belligerently. 'Simon always had a good imagination. You should stick to magic and leave religion to those who understand it.'

Simon dismissed the Samaritan with an airy wave of the hand. Arguments were patently nothing new between these men. 'To use Tarquin's vocabulary' said the Magus, 'Ahriman is the force which makes the illusions. Ahriman is the author of all things unhappy and unpleasant, the maker of the world as we see it and not of the world you would rather see.'

'Think of it that way if you like' said Tarquin, 'but never forget your part in the existence of Ahriman - and who makes the world you see. To be maker is to be master. What can be made can be undone.'

'We are told' stated Joseph, who seemed able to participate in the conversation better than anyone could expect, 'that the one they call the Christus, Jesus of Nazarus or Galilee, can lead us to bliss. I would love to believe you, Tarquin. But Jesus was no different from thousands of other Jews. He was victimised by the authorities, made a fool of and cruelly put to death. Unless he returns here in glory...'

'Was he, though?' interjected Tarquin. 'Was he killed? Mary the Magdalene would disagree with you, because she saw him walk away from his so-called grave.'

Joseph squirmed about and found himself looking at Varus, which didn't help his composure. 'I'm sorry, Tarquin, none of this is easy for me...'

'First, you have to know the difference between life and the body'. Tarquin's voice carried a clear note of authority. 'You have been sorely tested, but please listen: The body is of limited duration. Varus was healed by the Holy Spirit, I was only the helper and did not know whether he would recover, for he was very close to death. Had he not survived, his soul would have continued as expected: none of us has only a single lifetime in this world. These truths will have to be taught to those who live still in ignorance. Know for certain that Jesus continues even now, whether or not he stepped bodily from the grave.'

That was about as much as we could take for the present. Tarquin obviously realised it. He got that far-away look and wandered out of the temple and into the forest.

As so often happens when something has moved us greatly, we concentrated on the little familiar details that give comfort: tidying ourselves up and, although a change of clothes was out of the question, we directed the Romans to the mountain stream where we washed. Rebekah even asked Varus very politely about his health (amazingly, it was excellent and the wound looked much healthier than it should have done).

Ought we to have started thinking about the future? If there is a muscle that flexes so that we may plan ahead, mine at least was afflicted by a cheerful paralysis and I was content to experience events as they chose to happen. Not surprisingly perhaps, due to everything that had happened in such a short time, I began to feel an overwhelming physical and emotional exhaustion. I gratefully prepared myself for rest and a decent sleep.

If only!

20

HIS MASTER'S VOICE

IT WAS A night of horrors. Great opposing currents in the waters of Mark's consciousness met and produced towering seas, a chaotic swell that was all the more frightening because it arose from apparent calm.

All the djinns, satyrs, mischievous spirits and dark shapes of the unknown crowded about, chattering insanely, prodding, advising, offering deals, smirking, intimidating. And the reasonable voice of logic protested that Tarquin was the enemy, in no way a spiritual man but insensitive, brutish and cruel. Would God smile on such as he? Impossible! Peter and the Nazoreans of Jerusalem had warned of sin and taught repentance. How did the decurion-major's ideas fit into that? Here was a false prophet using dark magic, trying to lead the faithful astray.

Mark himself had embraced the image of a compassionate Jesus who forgave his enemies and then, burdened by the sins of the world, ascended the cross so that by his suffering, humanity's pain could be ended forever. Yet and without needing Simon's reminders, Mark was only too aware that the Persians told much the same tale about Mithras. Where, really, did his own faith stand?

Paul had spoken of the body of Christ, of which we were all members, our substance tied together, and here 'all' meant much more than the Jews but every person whose identity was willingly surrendered to the Son of God. But who indeed was this Son of God? In one of the stories Mark had copied down, Jesus told his disciples, 'I came not to bring peace, but a sword'. In other reports, his Master was the Prince of Peace. Where then did truth lie? The pressure in his head. 'Take me away, Master' he almost sobbed. 'Are you really with us always? There is so much I still don't understand. Take me away.'

More images, hallucinations, shadows of evil and damnation. But eventually, Mark felt himself rising above the mire. Beyond him stretched a broad golden band, a sort of road with gentle undulations and faint inscriptions upon it. Here, he knew, was time as the world sees it. At the beginning of the golden road were four jewels, a green for Mark, a red for Simon, a blue for Helen and a purple for Tarquin. An icy wind blew and the jewels tumbled from their golden bed, whereupon the road turned to brass and began tarnishing into dirty green with blotches of black. People climbed the hills on the road, which suddenly became steep and inhospitable. The figures fell back into pathetic heaps. Mark was sure he'd heard their calls for help somewhere before. And when he saw they were all blind, he recalled the helpless sound of new-born mice.

Then a great light burned down on the road and obliterated it. The same effect was produced on Mark's mind. Who was he? He had no history, no name, no role, no personality, no past or future. Instead of the terror of non-existence, however, the experience was of total existence.

All went quiet.

I am with you always.

Everything would be re-interpreted in the light of his being, his knowledge. And quickly, examples came:

'Sin means to "miss the mark"—literally.' (There was gentle humour there.) 'When you believe you are separate, not at one with all life, you consequently consider in your heart you have transgressed God's law. You bear the guilt of "sin". Yet you have merely missed the mark, for

God's law was not made to be broken and can never be. Sin as I describe it now, is a dream and you can choose to awaken and find it utterly without foundation.

'Repentance means to forgive your idle images of the world and replace them with God's vision. It means not to see separation where it does not exist. And it does not exist anywhere.

'Your illusions of separation are, in truth, unbearable to you. And so, you project them outside of yourself, onto others. And they, in turn, project it onto you. Your task is to let all of this go.

'I did not come to be a zealot revolutionary, a scapegoat or a sacrificial lamb. Yes, I received hatred and physical death in exchange for love and healing, yet my crucifixion demonstrated, to those who could see clearly, that the most outrageous assault as judged by men cannot change the purposes of God.

'Listen carefully, Mark, for this will be hard to understand unless you put your trust entirely in me. God is not careless of human life. Yet there must be constant change and for the required evolution to be sustained, bodies may not endure. The expressions of passing physicality, for better or worse as you think of them, are no substitute for the eternal fact of creation.'

Mark saw Tarquin then, as in a picture with a heavy, dark frame. The image wavered, became unstable, first darker then lighter, pierced with starbursts of purity and then shadowed by grimy gloom.

He knew Tarquin had done the seeming impossible, helped raise Varus from the dead, but the Judaean could see into the Roman's heart. There was darkness there still. Beyond the expected selfish passion, as Tarquin thought of possessing his concubines, there was jealousy against praefect Barius. And then his past: cruelty to slaves; malicious pleasure in putting zealots to the scourge, with its battering, pointed weights of bone, before having them crucified; drunken bouts; channelling cohort funds into grain black marketing and thence to his family in Rome; selling Jewish girls to a Syrian bordello. It was a long, albeit rather unimaginative list of crimes.

'He is your brother, Mark.' The frame changed to white and began to glow like the full moon. Tarquin's past was no longer available.

'They blamed me for forgiving sins. But I never forgave the sins of others, there being never any need. What I told them was simple truth - "You are forgiven". Yet men do need forgiveness, it is the great need of this world. To remember that you are forgiven, you must forgive your illusions about your brothers and sisters, your belief that they are full of sin and unworthy. Such beliefs are only the projections of your own guilt hidden within. If you did not ever feel guilty you would not see sin, but only mistakes that call for a corrective influence.

'You know I claimed not to bring peace, but rather a sword. This is true, but you must know *what* truth it tells. A sword may divide yet under right circumstances it unites; the weapon signifies strength. Then it can illuminate dark places that must be exposed before our planet is ready to rest in light.

'Love is a greatly prostituted word and to employ it honestly you must know its very depths. Love is not the application of sentiment or desire; love means no barriers, no exclusions; a complete acceptance. Then, the solution of forgiveness can be applied to others and self.'

Mark knew this subject was a major test. He didn't like it. 'Master, you spoke of forgiving, yet I always found that very hard to accept. The Roman is as he is. There are other Romans so much worse. Sometimes evil must be stopped the best way we know how.'

'Consider what you call evil. You will have to learn it comes not from Truth. Evil is the word you use for what is beyond your comprehension, but you are right to ask - how can you forgive? Unaided, the attempt is often an ego trap. People may seek recognition for their lofty attitude of "forgiveness", yet it is often a charade; they still harbour inner ugliness. To let it go you need a strength that is often beyond you. But be comforted. Call on the Holy Spirit's help and forgiveness will unveil your true strength. This is "a change of heart" even if you must at the same time take practical, even very stern measures as guided from within, to ensure social justice. Then, clarity is come.'

Mark saw it. What had he hated and still somewhat despised

in Tarquin, if not echoes of the darkness he was ashamed to look at within himself? Those qualities were pushed below surface because a disciple of Jesus must not covet another man's wife, impose his beliefs on others or think himself superior due to his scholarly knowledge. Tarquin did things that Mark might wish for - so secretly he would not admit it to himself. But with Tarquin proclaimed essentially at one with Mark, then...

Relax into your own innocence!

I forgive you, Tarquin, I hold you guiltless. The frame shows only light; the picture reflects it. Tarquin's past blows away, dead leaves of a bygone event. Tarquin's face shines. Two men, Mark and Tarquin. Which was which? There was difference but what about *essential* difference? There was only Light. Brotherhood. One life...

His Master's voice returned. 'When you consider the spiritual life, remember the false self that some call ego, can make anything seem fearful if you let it. But God's Holy Spirit can overlook all errors of the mind.

'The saying, "As ye sow, so shall ye reap" will be used as excuse for holy war in innumerable times and places. Yet it simply means that what you give power to will be empowered within yourself. And if you allow me, I shall help fill you with my knowledge of life that goes beyond the body. It is too easily forgotten that I only chose to go through the Palestine drama because of my love for my brothers and sisters; for the life of planet Earth.'

He would be with us always...

'When you read in the scriptures that "the wicked shall perish" it means that what is seen as wicked shall be done away, to be replaced with wholeness, the original and ultimately single truth.'

He offered a different interpretation of attack: Most importantly, to hate another would inevitably damage self.

Below, Mark saw the road again, the decrepit, tired, tarnished, cruel road. And near his right hand were the four jewels. 'Pick them up, Mark.' Carefully, he scooped them in his hand. 'Before you replace yourself and your helpmates on the ribbon of time, watch what it is that you will be helping your fellows on this planet to avoid.'

There were moving pictures in sequence, with sounds and a spoken commentary; a voice that came before him and quietly demanded he listen well. He felt as though in a dream but without the vagueness, pleasure or pain that he might have expected. It was greatly sobering for all that. Mark only knew he must attend closely like a child in school or a peasant come to listen to an ancient teacher, or a softly spoken preacher who captured attention with the clear knowledge of their subject.

'I am ready, Master.'

21

GNOSIS AND COUNTER-POLE

SCHOLARS. WRITING FURIOUSLY. An Egyptian, by the look of him, comes into focus. The man is in a fit of passion but somehow manages a careful Greek hand:

'We certainly know about others who follow the teachings of the Christ, led by men who are pleased to call themselves bishops and deacons. Anyone would think that these persons had received their authority directly from God and doubtless their intention is that people shall believe it.

'But what a poor reflection of true Christians they are! We call them lost sheep, nothing but withered fig trees.'

The man pauses to reflect on his own fellowship of believers and that calms him. His friends and colleagues in the spiritual life meet regularly as equals and draw lots. God would arrange the result according to His Will and one person would be designated to take the role of priest - perhaps his own dear wife. Another would offer the sacrament as bishop; a third would be chosen as reader of the scriptures. Several other fortunate participants would be invited to be open to the spirit and address the group as prophets offering the guidance of the moment. Ah yes! It was the right and godly way of meeting and expressing the strength within, free of interference from the spiritually uninitiated administrators of Roman Christianity.

A new scene emerges: Five great books lie on a huge plank table. Mark understands their title, *Refutation and Overthrow of Falsely So-Called Gnosis*. A tall, imposing man in rich robes speaks to an underling. The servant will arrange for the books to be copied. Their formidable author is Iraneus, a bishop of Gaul, who complains bitterly that enclaves of heretics are established across a wide area: From Gaul all the way to Rome, Greece and Asia Minor. The Gnostics are boasting that they hold the truth about Christ and to support their case insist on circulating more gospels than there really are! But only the Church of apostolic succession, the Church of Rome, may clarify and determine the words of Jesus! The servant scuttles away.

The picture re-forms to show a monk. He prepares his defence of what he calls the true Church using language reminiscent of the Essenes. 'We, the Sons of Light, have had to deal with many expressions of darkness. The pagans hated us, of course, but there was worse. We were persecuted by those who mistakenly believed they were promoting the works of Christ. But these so-called Christians don't know who they are. They have the outward form but inside they are without substance.'

For a moment, the man is cheerful. He reminds himself that the highly talented Tertullian, who defended the orthodox position in his younger days and defined the religion of Christ in concrete terms, has now changed sides.

Mark became aware that Tertullian, born in Carthage in the second century CE to a centurion in the proconsular service, was among those who believed that because Christ rose bodily from the grave so every believer should look forward to the actual resurrection of the flesh. But towards the end of his life Tertullian has altered his tack. He's seen the light now, for he has understood that the real nature of the Church and its congregation is spirit and not form. He is to become known as 'the father of Latin Christianity'.

Tertullian described the Church as a phenomenon which happens where God plans it and isn't dependent on the college of bishops.

Things are not so simple, however. Like his friends, the scribing monk faces punishment because he has dared seek liberation through gnosis, because he won't bend to the 'dealers in bodies', the literalists, the spiritually immature bureaucrats who judge belief by quantity and not quality.

He bows his head; the brief glow of optimism is gone. There will be a battle with the organised, esoteric Church and the outcome is highly uncertain.

◆

Now a palace comes into view. In a city called Byzantium—it will change its name twice in future times. Up the broad steps and past sentries dressed in the uniforms of Rome. Inside there is a wide chamber sparsely furnished but with a sumptuous chaise-longue positioned next to a tall window.

'But my lord' a man in a priest's white robe is protesting, 'I do deem this a magnificent honour. If my Lord Emperor demands, who am I to argue? Do not misunderstand my reluctance. It's only that there are plenty of gospels available despite your predecessors' ah, lack of enthusiasm for the word of God. The 50 copies which you request from me will involve major expense. I am fully aware that the imperial treasury is already greatly burdened.'

The purple-clad figure on the couch nods. 'I appreciate your honesty Eusebius. It's because I trust you that I'm giving you this commission.' Emperor Constantine fingers the small gold cross hanging from his wrist. 'Nevertheless, I see that you haven't guessed the real importance of the work. So, listen carefully.'

Constantine certainly wants to justify his formal title which is *Pontifex Maximus* (chief bridge maker). He leans forward. 'You of all citizens should be aware of the problems I faced when I gained this thankless prominence. The Empire attacked from outside by barbarians. And from within by civil strife, including the struggle involving Christians. The German borders - we can't ask for notification before they are assaulted. But there's no excuse for internal problems and thus I came down in favour of Christianity. The Christian God has protected me through many trials. Without His help my rivals would have long since trampled me down! I wished to please Him. To have Him acknowledged and loved by all. I am certain that my decision was the right one. It's surely the religion of the future with many benefits to offer both the rulers and the ruled.'

Eusebius clears his throat in acknowledgement and the Emperor continues. 'Everything looked good until I found that the practice of Christianity, like most matters, is more complicated than the first glance reveals. Complicated! As luck would have it, Christianity was worse than any other religion. You understand what I'm talking about - the damnable arguments and killings over the true nature of Christ, the meaning and historicity of the resurrection, the Gnostics...it still continues after these hundreds of years since Jesus taught, blessed and healed.' Constantine waves a hand. 'You're the historian. But I'm the ruler for better or worse. I had all you bishops meet at Nicaea to warn you that my imperial blessing was contingent upon you ending your squabbles there and then.'

Now the Emperor draws out a long sigh. 'Call themselves the Roman Church, these hair-splitters. The Roman Empire was created by piety, courage and common sense, Eusebius. The bishops had plenty of the former to survive the persecutions but precious little of the latter. Therefore, I determined to impose mine to make up for their lack.

'It was a nightmare reining your brother clerics in and saving you from their theological nit-picking, but at Nicaea I rejoiced to find in you a kindred spirit! Much was achieved at the great council with your help. Roman order won through in the end. Certain loose ends remain in Christian theology but they're as nothing compared to what went on before. We've a basis for a sensible, modern and powerful religion - appropriate for the most powerful modern state.'

The other man's face is turned away but his response is strong and sincere. 'My lord cannot ever know the gratitude I hold for you - to be hunted like a wild beast by Diocletian's officers when I was mercifully young enough to withstand those trials. And now I see the true vine grow and provide its sweet fruit across so many lands.' There is a long silence in the great chamber. 'I dearly appreciate your support and never cease my humble attempts to clarify the word of God.'

The Emperor pats the bishop's arm. 'Versatility is your strength. You can attain a harmony between conflicting viewpoints, where others stay dogmatic and fall into the stupidities of dissention. But' and Constantine's heavy features show momentary vexation at the obtuseness of humanity, 'the common citizen wants something *definite* to base his faith upon.'

Comprehension dawns on the bishop. 'The new copies of the testaments will play a part in this.'

'Exactly! Eusebius, you're a treasure. With you I never have to go over things twice. The new editions of the gospels will reflect all the decisions that the bishops voted for. I'm not going to be stingy, employ the best scholars for the necessary editing. You'll need other men as well, for an equally vital and even more demanding part of your task...'

Eusebius completes his lord's statement: 'Which is to round up all existing gospels, whether from our own Petrine Church, from the Gnostics, Jewish Nazoreans or any other supposed Christian group, and destroy the conflicting evidence.'

Emperor Constantine stands and embraces him in genuine affection.

◆

The palace is gone. Heavy-set men, their clubs and demeanour unmistakably marking them as police, burst in on an assembly of worshippers in a barn. An old man lifts his hand and comes forward as the rest of the congregation shrinks back.

'Peace, comrades, in the name of the Anointed. The Emperor Constantine has graciously granted us our freedom.'

The captain of the guard shakes his head. 'Not so, my pretty ones. The emperor blesses only the true Church of Rome with his protection. You heretics would turn folks against our sanctified religion. Gnostics, aren't you? Think you can make up your worship as you go along and call it Christian! The Bishop of Rome tells us what is Christian and it's not you. The Christ of the Romans may have no challenger. At least heathens have the excuse of ignorance.'

His speech completed; the captain signals to his platoon and well-muscled arms raise their weapons.

◆

The action shifts to pleasant woods and fields though many of the trees are unknown to Mark. There is a man called Leuthard in the picture but he, too, is of unknown origin. He stops work and lays down to rest in the shade. He dreams; a swarm of bees is entering his body and stinging him. But this is no nightmare - on the contrary it's a revelation and the man jumps awake and goes home, telling his wife that their marriage must end because he has been appointed a sacred task. And then he runs to an unusual-looking building that exudes the smell of worship, pulls down a crucifix hanging there and treads on it.

Other peasants rush to the spot in dismay - it's the cross of Jesus and a revered object in those days. But the man is unworried. Instead, he declares that God has revealed wonderful knowledge to him: no longer should they pay tithes to the clergy. And not everything in the book of Jewish and Christian scriptures was either holy or helpful. It also contained a great deal of nonsense.

There's a mystery here, because the holy book that the man Leuthard discusses with his fellow commoners is only available in Latin - a language he cannot read. (The location is some Gaulish province one thousand years after the birth of Jesus.) Perhaps he had assistance from a friendly scrivener? Unlikely that such a man would cross his path because a single Bible, painstakingly copied by Christian monks, would cost as much as a whole dairy farm complete with livestock! Such a price would be a minor consideration only for the Roman Church, a church that by this era, Mark learned with almost incredulous amazement, owned about two-thirds of the continent called Europe.

The story drew to its climax. The peasants had never heard the like of Leuthard's preaching, but they warmed to it. Increasingly large crowds listened to his ideas about 'the true Christ' and the meaning of love locked away in a book full of apparent absurdities. To reach God, there was no need for the often-self-seeking men of the cloth, nor should people ever give credence to the idea of suffering, sacrifice and holy death represented by the Cross. Mark felt himself pulled into the drama by sympathetic attraction but, sensing the unhappy end, regained his position as observer.

A bishop named Gebuin calls Leuthard in for questioning. Charismatic meets politician. By the skill of his argument the bishop succeeds in convincing the populace that Leuthard's reasoning is wrong. Abandoned by the crowd the peasant becomes despairing, throws himself into a well, and drowns.

◆

A cloying brightness this time, blue sky and hundreds upon hundreds of men, wearing white tunics with big red crosses embroidered on them. A festive air with gaily coloured flags delineating the various contingents that have arrived from several neighbouring lands. A strange chant in the Roman language fills the air.

Time moves again; the jovial army has reached its destination.

Oh! It really is an army, with its quarry Jerusalem! Not the Jerusalem Mark was familiar with yet peopled by a Semitic race like himself. It's some kind of feast day. Yes! The Passover, the time of year when Jesus was hung on the cross - of course, always it's that Cross! And these foreign warriors, suffering the unaccustomed heat of a Palestinian summer, are besieging the city of their Saviour.

A man called Laetholdous is first to scale the walls and as his well-armoured fellows climb after him with a roar of bloodlust, the defending soldiers with their curving swords are pushed back. They are chased by the Crusaders to a place that is - but no is not - the Solomon Temple.

The prophecies are proved true. The Temple of Mark's day is gone. It's still a holy venue, but the Saracens have had it rebuilt to worship God in their own fashion: the mosque of Haram-es-Sherif. Yet this is no guided tour of historical relics, the Crusaders are mowing down the

Saracens until rivers of blood flow in the places where Jesus walked. Meanwhile, unarmed citizens have climbed onto the roof and Lord Tancred of the Crusaders promises their safety. But, after a day of pillaging the city, the Christians rise early, creep secretly onto the roof of the mosque and much to Lord Tancred's subsequent annoyance, cut the heads off the Muslim men and women.

◆

The picture darkens and then, in the centre of vision, appears a young fair-haired Crusader like those Mark has just seen in Jerusalem, this time not illuminated by the Palestinian sun but by the soft flame of an oil lamp. It's inside one of the worshipping-houses they call churches. In the shadows a priest talks to the soldier:

'Your armour fits you well, my son. You are the very picture of valour, a fighter for Christ against the Islamic heretics.'

The youth bows his head. 'We march tomorrow. I know my duty.' His voice dies to a whisper. 'I am sore afraid.'

The shadowy priest lays an arm against the arm of the big scarlet cross on the boy's chest. 'Understandably. It shall be our secret. Before you go, I will cheer you with two thoughts: you will be fighting for all Christendom, which relies on you. And when you return, the Pope promises a plenary indulgence for every Crusader.'

The young man starts: 'A sure escape from hellfire?'

Now the priest's arm strokes the cross lovingly: 'Nothing less than total absolution from sin - if you draw blood on behalf of our Saviour.'

The light goes out.

◆

It is many years later. A Gaulish bishop sends out the alarm about a new sect called Cathar which is encouraging the lower classes to think beyond Roman teaching. The sect's arrogance apparently knows no bounds because its members usurp the hallowed custom of the bishops and go about laying on hands to administer the Holy Spirit. They won't eat meat, they disdain marriage and refrain from killing even the smallest creature.

Mark couldn't see that these attitudes and rules were anything to get excited about, yet a dreadful fear started to invade his belly. The knowledge seeped into him that the Roman Christian authorities weren't going to tolerate this band of ascetics - time rushed forward, he saw a fanatical new force created to deal with the Cathars and now the fear deepened as he heard the words 'Holy Inquisition'. The tortures, the lack of mercy… He wanted to squirm free of the certainty, but it clung to him like a hawk gripping its prey. Here was an institution the world would remember long after the last Cathar had been put to the sword in a civil war which would see whole towns wiped out in the name of God.

◆

'That is just a nail scratched across the surface of history.'

The words hung heavy on Mark. He had been shown that some men would take the words of his Master and turn them to unholy purposes; sometimes, in their distorted thinking believing to do good by turning their minds to hatred, to political control, to material grasping, to fear, to blame and racking guilt, all of which mocked the name of the Anointed.

Some might even go through Mark's scrolls; tearing out the pages submitted by Thomas, discarding any commentary on the status accorded to Mary the Magdalene, the companion, changing, 'interpreting'… even that.

The forces of Rome were determined to impose their religious bureaucracy across Christendom. Individual efforts towards spiritual enlightenment including whatever might be deemed as unconventional practices, were discouraged and even punished. As if it was sinful to aim too high.

Yet Mark told himself there were good and honest followers of Christ in Rome. In reply he was shown how in a hundred years' time, those who confessed their faith and refused to show piety to the emperor and the gods of Rome would be burned alive. (Yet not Roman citizens, they would 'mercifully' be decapitated.) This helped explain why, when Clement made Christianity the official state religion, the new order of

Roman bishops would so fiercely impose their rule across Christendom. It was deemed vitally important, so as to ensure survival of the new faith. But with the coming of Catholicism—the so-called 'universal' church - it also meant imposition of a schism. One side had to lose.

Mark suddenly knew what his Master had meant by saying that he was bringing a sword, bringing war. Every new and powerful impulse disturbed the social status quo. And it could be applied in more than one way. Sometimes the sword caused death and destruction, other times the blade's threat gave rise to a peace that only it and its bearers could ensure.

'This is why you have agreed to do what must be done.'

It was morning. Mark was awake and the thunder clouds gone. Having experienced a night of much darkness, he was now lifted beyond despair; feeling certain all his wrong thinking and turmoil would be overcome. The cruelty, bitterness, grasping and ignorance had to be experienced before his Master's truths could be demonstrated in their pure state, ready for a new world to emerge. How long…? Time weighed too heavily for him to know. He had accepted his function. That was enough.

22

DOUBLE DIMENSIONS

(A note from Rigorist Ardax)

AS WE ARE constantly reminding beginning students in the Alternative Histories Department, it is no less than practical to continue to be thankful for the events which took place in the Offering Temple—even if it apparently might not exist in some time-streams. Gratitude has far-reaching potential.

Our meditations, concentrated on this subject, sustain the highly fortunate matrix which was engendered in Samaria some 1,900 (Class Four) years ago. While there will be those who find the event hard to believe, experience has shown that the truth of the matter will make itself apparent, quite naturally, to those whose minds are open.

If that single incident had not occurred on the slopes of Mount Gerizim, what in Class Four is known as Christianity and that we call *Yeshua-like* could never have developed in the way it has done. Our most advanced spiritual communities most likely would never have been conceived, let alone built.

Had the historical fulcrum of Mark, Simon, Helen and Tarquin in 69 CE not been structured as it was, the possibilities for our planet would have been quite different. But as our understanding of 'time' has deepened, we recognise that in one sense, several versions of the event did, or rather *continue,* to occur.

The painstaking work of scholars under many difficult circumstances has resulted in the classification of four alternative life streams on our planet, as is now generally (if superficially) accepted. Our own habitat is Class 1. This version of humanity is still imperfect, but at least we no longer wage war on each other. The most 'degraded' version - Class Four - has attracted the greatest interest because of its strangely primitive condition. We note that the odd, the bizarre, has ever had its attraction.

As an introduction to the subject, I offer the following, presented with some approximation of Class Four speech patterns:

Surely the goal should be straightforward: peace on earth, goodwill toward men. But mankind, which has difficulty trusting itself to the essence of good, has managed to complicate the issue. We like nothing so much as to doodle on the cosmic telephone pad. Not content with a few strong lines, there have to be superfluous strands embellishing the pattern: curlicues and false starts, mazes without solutions. 'Seek' we urge ourselves, yet internally, silently, we often seem to add, 'but do not find'.

It's not hard to imagine the impact of the Anointed on the people of Israel; the galvanising of hopes and fears, ancient knowing and ego defences. Those who were temperamentally better suited to the free-flowing life of the contemplative or the charismatic took not only the Master's words but more surely, his energy as the basis for their faith. Had the world not awaited its Messiah for long years? The psychic atmosphere was highly charged with the excitement of anticipation. Even before the physical birth, Christ had already cast a light upon the planet.

The Gnostics, the Essenes, those more intuitive and less concerned with worldly status, could feel that presence illuminating their dreams. When the physical event manifested, it was only natural to continue to celebrate the Christ in one's inner life as well as by outward ritual. To look *within* for the Kingdom of Heaven.

The ancient practice of Gnosticism, faith based on personal spiritual experience, gained a new lease on life with the advent of Jesus. Yet the 'quiet believers' soon had a low profile, compared to the active, organised apostolic Church. The early clerics mainly agonised over the respective merits of Christianity according to Peter (the more or less faithful lieutenant) and Paul (mystical and radical, and but for his urgent evangelising, almost a Gnostic himself).

The politicians of religion were temperamentally of a different nature to the Gnostics. It didn't take too long for a propaganda war to fit the believers In Rome for leadership of the Christian movement; re-writing the Master's sayings, concocting things that the dead Peter and Paul 'might have said', creating a convenient 'uniformity of belief'. It was also prudent particularly for those living in the imperial Capital, to shift responsibility for Jesus' death away from the Romans.

Records were adjusted accordingly. This meant implicating the Jews to a deeper and broader degree in the tragedy, even though the Jesus movement in Palestine had remained a Jewish sect within rabbinic Judaism for many decades after the fall of Jerusalem. Already the Roman Christians were beginning to see themselves as a separate religion. For one thing, some of the newly converted pagans were starting to revert to older, more bawdy lifestyles and it was decided that a suitable theological and administrative structure had to be created to deal with the situation. The connection with Judaism became more tenuous.

By the time the Gnostics started gaining popular support especially in the eastern part of the Empire, the techniques of consolidation had been much refined. Imagine relying on one's own inner guidance to determine the meaning of Christ's message! Such matters should be left to the correct authorities. Unsurprisingly the Roman Church quickly became an authority in the upheaval and confusion that followed the Jewish War.

The Roman bishops developed a reasoning that stated as there was only one God in Heaven, so there could be only one bishop in the Church. This was the natural order of things. Only 20 or so years after the Jewish War, Bishop Clement of Rome was castigating the Christian community in Corinth for deposing certain local Church leaders. God, wrote Clement, delegated His authority of reign to rulers and leaders on earth—the bishops, priests and deacons - and whoever refused to obey these rulers was guilty of insubordination to God Himself. The malcontent should pay for this transgression with his life!

If Clement 's views were to be upheld, the democratic, mutually-supportive companies of Nazoreans who broke bread together at their Sunday love-feasts would have to be outlawed in favour of a strict hierarchy that made the concept of 'clergy' and 'laity' not only possible but mandatory. The problem of Peter versus Paul was solved (eventually) by having the Bishop of Rome carry the authority of Peter (chief amongst the apostles and putative Inheritor of Christ's mission) while the actual theory and practice of the Church was heavily Pauline, with a good leavening of pagan concepts that would make the new gentile converts feel more at home. For example the great festival celebrating the birth of Mithras and the return of light after the winter solstice was pressed into service as the date of Jesus' nativity; this symbolic parallel assured the success of Christ-mass.

If only those Byzantine reactionaries hadn't gradually alienated themselves long before they finally split off—and had the temerity to call themselves Orthodox—then all of real Christendom could have been neatly united and ready to face the stubborn Jews and the lingering heresy of Gnosticism. Ostensibly devout, Gnostics were 'wolves in sheep's clothing'. No structure to speak of, no specific creed - how could such a sect dare claim any effectiveness, let alone authority, in the matter of Christianity? Astonishingly, Gnostics did. Unfortunately, there was no other solution than to saw off this diseased branch of the true vine, burn the rotten wood and eradicate the Infection.

A justification for the anti-Gnostic pogrom went like this: had the Roman Christians survived terrible trials to be undermined by a rabble of troublemaking, free-thinking Alexandrian meditators? The Church of Rome had survived persistent persecution. For decade after bloody decade, the roll of martyrs grew as the embattled Roman Empire tried to carry out its own therapeutic pruning, murdering Christians while more converts appeared to fill the spaces left by the glorious dead.

Roman Christians were amazingly brave and dogged. They put up with this treatment literally for centuries before the faltering Empire gave in and embraced its old enemy. What a victory! The pagan title of *Pontifex Maximus* was for many years juggled between the emperor and the head of the Church. All that misery and bloodshed had not been in vain. Yet with the Church in Rome triumphant, the death-rattle was sounded for Gnostic groups. The energy of faith can be employed in more than one way, as the heretics soon discovered to their cost.

The Jews wanting to dissociate from pagan religions and not tolerating small deviations in the Hebrew law, in case their stern God - whether called Jievoaa, Yahwey, Adonai or simply the Nameless - should exact the expected punishment, was inherited and in some ways possibly extended by the Christians. A similar situation was foreseen for another child of the Old Testament—Islam.

This was the situation that we in Class One discovered. While certain religions and cultural group faiths might reasonably be expected to tolerate each other, all being aspects or interpretations of the single Truth, Class Four Christianity was poised to become yet another sect that would mostly reject any other attempts at recognising a supreme being and delivering closeness to the soul, as an aberration. We could even have the situation of a polytheistic religion, which attempted to assist humans to relate harmoniously with their eco-system through nature spirits, being condemned by a Christian theology which had lost sight of the peril that attends to a lack of eco-system harmony.

The Anointed One came to bring unity and goodwill toward men. Perhaps only the mankind of Class Four could interpret unity in terms of separation, and peace in terms of war. Two millennia ago, Jesus carried the message. That sister dimension to ours has unfortunately not yet learned its joyful meaning..

There were consequences. Our intuitives (assisted by certain technologies) uncovered a story of schism and suspicion festering down through the ages. Of Christianity grappling heroically, yet often hopelessly, for air—the clear air of truth, reverence, service, even love.

Despite many uplifting individual lives that graced the record, a fog of ignorance wreathed the years of this history, this near yet far space-time continuum of which we have recovered and painstakingly grasped an inadequate understanding.

Some of our younger rigorists found it difficult to complete their research in this consistently low frequency environment; a space I'd become somewhat accustomed to. My default solution to this problem was to recommend those students for the easier work being accomplished in Classes Two and Three.

Mostly they were happy to oblige. Bewildered by what was for them such unexpected and harsh outcomes (yet providing an excellent test of character) these interns too easily lost their inner drive. Or perhaps a better description would be a loss of 'heart' for the work. It might take a few more years to build the necessary resilience.

23

MARK 2 AWAKENS

MARK HOVERED AT the boundary of sleep and waking. He grunted in frustration. Something important, but he couldn't quite grasp it.

History. He had seen history, been history. In the Offering Temple with the smell of smoke and scorched pork. Pork? Hardly possible. Defilement. He pulled the blanket over his chin. Even more than the odours, the grey fuzz. Mist of the mind, rising from primeval depths of being and becoming. A fog of decision/indecision - and he had chosen wrongly.

Go back! Retrace steps and chose the other path. But the dream was fading, it was too late. He had taken his chance to run, scrambling down Gerizim before the nightmare soldiers could return and mock his piety with their eagle standards and thrusting swords. Leaving behind Helen and Simon and all the others. Glad to escape with his writings and his life, it seemed right and fortunate. But no, wrong! Mark surprised himself with his own certainty: this had happened so very long ago.

A figure in a tattered robe sleeping rough for fear of Romans, barely scratching enough to eat, reaching Tyre and finding himself on a ship to Egypt when he thought it was bound for Greece. Fevered and delirious.

Cared for by the friendly first mate, should have been cause for thankfulness. Yet a reproach, because of his overly simple choice. Recovered fully in Alexandria, allowing him to write his Gospel, achieve his goal. He twisted in the bed. Not the true goal. Not the right path.

He would go back to sleep and return to the temple. It was a terrible mistake to abandon them like that, the soldiers included. And Rebekah. But they were passing from him. Wait!

His muted cry was swamped by the noise of a low-flying aircraft which sent the delicate images tumbling into oblivion. Sometimes flight-paths had to be altered when the usual approaches to the city were crowded with air traffic. Anyway, it was a lucky break because he'd over-slept this morning. Yes, look at that time.

The man called Mark James thought briefly of Linda, kicked a chair and dived for the shower. There were things to be done, a big commercial demonstration this morning and they always relied on him. Especially today, the company was allowing him to suggest an internet solution. That was the World Wide Web; that was 1995 for you!

If he performed well today, it would improve his bargaining position. He was pleased with himself more as a matter of convention than from real enthusiasm. He listed mentally: petrol, yes; no milk, toast would have to do; the appropriate notes and software manuals were already in the car; watch for that treacherous loose step leading down to the street.

Soon he was driving to work, almost automatically, intimate with each part of the road and compensating for the impatience of other rush-hour drivers. He gazed at the colours unravelling across the park to his left. Delivering his demo was something to look forward to but most likely it offered no serious challenge. If instead he was to perch on one of those shaded benches at the water's edge, wagging school, he might scribble all day and produce an epic story. A story that people would remember long after his stock control system had accounted for its final circlip and roofing screw.

Problem: There was little or no meaning in the ordinary course of events. And the worst of it was that even he, who saw through the pantomime, still ached for grease paint and grand entrances. Wanted to be Principal Boy. Well, then (taking himself in hand) consider the Awful Error hypothesis; the galactic computer drops a bit when structuring planet Earth. The model called 'evolution' develops serious mathematical inconsistencies. Just when despair is maximal, a low-caste Zylaxian maintenance programmer writes a patch which activates Rescue and Repair. Bewildered green men are diverted Earthwards thanks to mass-reversal, through a black hole from regions of Nominal Ecstasy. Confused, time-warped but blissed-out. The Greening of the Planet, and everyone gets to live happy ever after. A convenient writer's dream. But *that* dream, as in this morning's weird one, surely meant, if you searched out symbols from the domain of analysts, 'face up to consequences' such as sword, such as starve - such as *brake*.

His car smacked into the silver vehicle ahead. The elderly Ford had violated the highly polished duco of an Alfa Romeo. Worst luck, it appeared to be that same year's Spider 916 convertible; certainly not a cheap repair job.

A man in a pinstriped suit got out and surveyed the damage. His mouth was a mean slit, his hair too-glossy black. 'Haven't you woken up yet - bloody negligence!'

Mark leaned out of his window. 'You ever in the army?' The other driver lost the initiative.

'No, really,' said Mark. 'You'd look very dapper as a Roman soldier with one of those leather skirts and everything.'

The Alfa driver mentally pigeon-holed Mark and produced a gold pen from his jacket. 'Just show your licence and tell me about your insurance, cowboy.' He pulled an envelope from another pocket and began copying down the number of Mark's car.

And that should have been more or less the end of it. Rear-end collisions were as common as strategies for tax evasion in that city. But Mark was worried as he nursed his slightly bent Ford into the company car park. He knew there'd been some dream about Romans during the night. What he didn't know was why the subject had assumed this degree of autonomy, why his life had so many angles, loose threads which he couldn't pull together. Why he couldn't keep a relationship alive or be content with a good job or cope with his overblown imagination. Why he found it necessary to despise a guy who drove the same kind of car which he himself could probably be driving in the next few years if all went well. And by then, he was sure technology would be so advanced he'd even have his own multifunctional mobile phone.

Mark passed a hand over his eyes. This was a waste of thinking time; he only had to keep in mind that his prospects were indeed faultless. Determined to ignore the gathering strength of the headache, he straightened his tie, lifted the software manuals and CDs from the back seat, and keeping a steady eye on the office entrance before him surrendered his unanswered questions to the panacea of Professional Progress.

◆

(an Ardax diary entry)

When Carly approached me with her first tentative findings, I had a niggling sense of *deja vu* which, because of my training, I did nothing either to encourage or discourage. Rather, I placed the report to one side; hopefully it would rate as a valuable future reference.

I took Carly's sensor-shapes home, made my own based on her results and played each one twice, applying rigour as it ought to be applied even in a situation of some excitement. I had my shower, told my wife Miriam of what was intended so her support would be available, and went into the meditation room. The subtle, friendly atmosphere instantly cheered me, as did even the appropriately timid light of the lamp.

By my very action I was giving credence to a reality-construct that I'd previously seen only as a rather unlikely possibility. I was suggesting that Class Four was 'real'. That made me chuckle. All the classes could be considered in one sense illusory, but this one where I was about to enter now was, by definition of my cross-habitation in the top and bottom Classes, more believable. Not only did I exist in Class One, but in Class

Four simultaneously when all co-ordinates were correct. Or perhaps it was only one at a time and not both together.

Part of the reason for my choosing this department had been the thrilling possibility of crossing life streams, straddling reality-patterns. (And because I could indulge in the strangeness of it all like an astronaut living on a space-station?) If we could finally carry this off, it would suggest reality had enormously increased levels of fluidity. And now, it now appeared my interest and excitement had basis in fact. I sank into my plinth, asked for the Light, invoked the colours and attained the required level of awareness.

Blackness came first, then a tinkling as of tiny bells. And small white flashes. I saw the virtual calendar we'd rigged up, a reeling clock face spinning out the digits - 1960s, 1970s, 1980s, stopping at 1995.

Full visualisations of Class Four, only partly attained before, came into view. Cities, then areas of dry and barren land covered with ugly, pathetic shanties, within which people suffered physical and emotional deprivation with only trauma-wisdom for payment. I was supposedly beyond negative emotions in that deep state, so when I saw the stick-like starving children in the waterless scrublands, I was surprised by the fist that tightened in my solar plexus.

I'd had fairly good experience of Class Four to date, but it was always as if behind a glass partition. Now thanks to Carly's work I was *right there*. My resistance was mild, but it still knocked out the co-ordinates for a short time. Vision blurred like a scratched old video. Then it returned with full sensation and this time there was no doubt. I had properly arrived, with shades of mild panic still occurring. It was the 'lowest' Class as never experienced before.

This time I breathed the raw air of Class Four and even my cells lived as Class Four cells. I had a vocation in the Department of Alternative Histories and at the same time I existed 'here'. But my body was different from when safe at home. Too bad that in Four I was fatter and flabbier than I liked...

Soon I also felt a kind of coarseness, almost a dullness that was paradoxically acute! And a thought, my thought, yes, my Class Four thought: 'Being put on this planet is the result of some dreadful error'. Oh, and such feelings of upset, annoyance!

All the co-ordinates dropped out of synch. I was back on the plinth and glad of it. Nevertheless, I'd managed contact better than ever before. Carly's work was the difference! I sent her a congratulatory message then went to bed, before deciding this success was more accurately a full group accomplishment.

In following days and weeks I returned to Class Four. Contact was not always good, but an anchor was in place that increasingly could be relied upon.

I became better acquainted with this dimension. The academic aspect was an eye-opener; research here was often erratic as one group argued with others. Many of them desired more money, prestige and power and often seemed unwilling or unable to collaborate. My training might be a hindrance, not a benefit. But I was also aware of a change in the wind. Some rigid thought-forms and philosophies were beginning to break down at the highest level, so this was heartening. The real problem was their day-to-day dealings with each other, where disharmony was often if not mostly the norm.

The Class Four 'alternate me' was a kind of doppelganger; I wondered how easily he could manage the human environment I had just become aware of. Luckily, this person had few difficulties with institutionalised society; he had the knack of working on the outside edge of it. A natural if undisciplined intellectual, he was a computer programmer and systems analyst. He also wrote science-fiction stories in his spare time. His emotional life beyond his everyday activities tended toward the chaotic. Divorced from his first wife, he'd formed a liaison with a partner such that both were very unsettled due to unaddressed difficulties going back into past time streams. They'd 'fallen in love', hit the primary reaction point (unconsciously) and had broken off the relationship in clouds of unfinished business and various subsidiary reactions, all of which had to be addressed if there was to be a better outcome there.

I started by assessing various angles to this situation. It was far from easy. Dealing with Class Four was like swimming through honey - too thick, too sense-oriented yet still unaware. Sometimes I touched this one, whose name was Mark James. (The forces of class compaction and synchronicity have a fine sense of appropriateness, and of humour.) Mostly, he would respond to me very well in subtlety, rather like a person who awakes with gratitude from a nightmare. His problem was that he inevitably returned to sleep.

Instead, I decided to concentrate on his fitness for the project, hoping to help him in other matters where and as I could. His unresolved idea of female relationship had an optimal outcome of clear-channel partnership in this lifetime. This would smooth his work considerably, but I had to confess my professional estimation that optimality here was rather a long shot.

He had good imagination - a positive factor. Additionally, his questioning of reality was at a pleasingly high level. But - and this appeared to be rather common in the 'Western' Class Four cultures - his family background had resulted in his rejection of almost any useful religious or spiritual ideas. His attitudes to the subject were clouded by childhood confusions of which he wasn't fully conscious. In short, the case wasn't at all hopeless but demanded work.

The mechanics of life-stream interaction were now highlighted. Attempting to help with Mark's relationship difficulty had already brought up the question of whether and to what extent I could make alterations. How could I ensure that any proposed changes were ultimately for the best? My training was a help, but only Assistance was certain. I continued to ask and soon it became clear that I would be able to encourage those actions and probabilities which Mark/myself had already chosen at some level of his/my Class Four being. It was an exercise in sensitivity - I probed, I nudged, I whispered to produce some response without destroying the value of the activity due to overwhelm cut-off.

The work now was slow but satisfying. Gradually, I became more acclimatised to Class Four. A wild, often unhappy and self-destructive place it was, yet oddly vibrant. Even though steeped in illusion there was still an indomitable instinct to struggle on down the dark tunnel of time, hoping for fresh air and sunlight.

Sometimes the environmental frequency was rather too much for me. I was thankful I could leave at any time and return to my own world. If only 'Class Fours' - or even just one, such as this Mark - could see that they too could become free of this place by transforming it, then changes might accelerate. Only their shared beliefs held them captive to this co-ordinate of shadows. I held fast to Truth as the whole purpose of the work and despite the many unknowns, relished it as a worthy challenge.

Keeping in mind that learning is teaching and vice-versa, Miriam, Sharnestia and I had agreed that the best course was to engage Mark with the planned project as soon as possible. If it progressed well, we believed his work would influence others, making this a node for positive Class change. Despite choosing our contact with very great care, however, there were as you might expect some stumbling-blocks.

Mark James lived on the lower north shore area of Sydney in Class Four's continent of Australasia. In many ways it was a fortunate city. The prevailing political situation was hardly innocent, but it was not unduly oppressive and certainly not openly violent as was the case in other sections of Class Four. The climate was good, the harbour beautiful; the nation wealthy enough—at least I never saw anyone starve there. The city of Sydney was a great commercial centre with thoughts of greed and the fear of loss ever-present. Success was measured quite largely in terms of income and was indicated by possession of the objects that money could buy. The very poor including many of the original inhabitants of the continent (colonised by the white races) were not nearly as desperate as in some neighbouring lands. However, this was hardly an excuse for the degree of refusal to acknowledge the widespread existence of poverty and endemic racism. The very rich were often admired as examples of what might one day be achieved by a humble but hardworking person. Yet not surprisingly the divide between rich and poor was on the increase.

Relationships, too, were seen as the getting of something desirable even though the results were often the reverse. A prevailing concern was the need to generate a greater income; this was linked with the obsession to dissipate the money through a variety of distracting activities and possessions. (Class Fours, finding it difficult to face themselves, loved distractions. As a local example, Australians often spent more on gambling per capita than any other nation.)

The desired possessions and activities were not in themselves always harmful. It was the erroneous beliefs held about these things which constituted the real difficulty. The unfortunate temptation was to believe that doing something or having something could bring happiness.

I remind myself (as I tried to remind the man Mark) that happiness is neither wrong nor impossible, but the active search for it is truly the outline of sorrow. God gives gifts of Being outside of time and space. The Almighty is beyond both and would have us accept that in essence we are also.

Mark seemed hardly aware of Sydney's dense atmosphere of confused thought-emanations, even though he lived and worked in the thick of it. (At first, I considered him courageous in dealing with this. Only later—just one of the benefits of the work—did I experience a previously unknown part of myself; that was in fact quite well able to cope with the Class Four city environment.) He was employed by a company where other young men and women waited often impatiently to secure positions offering either greater status or extra money - preferably both. During the weekend work break of two days there were frequent social gatherings where various drugs, many impure and/or dangerous, were taken to escape the perceived limitations of existence. Sometimes the events were rowdy, sometimes touching, due to the ignorance often displayed.

Mark read widely (not many of his colleagues did) so I decided to concentrate my efforts in that area. It wasn't long before I had my opportunity.

24
DECISION TIME

IT WAS IMPORTANT to find Simon. When I met him, bathing in the stream with the other men, his mood was not unexpected.

'What am I doing here?' he grumbled. 'Don't tell me the damned Italians won't come back - and in strength. I see nothing yet, but it's only a matter of time. I wouldn't like to be here when they catch old Tarquin. But I want them to catch me even less.'

'Where will you go?'

He stared into the blue sky. 'A new world - a new Promised Land. That was the voice of destiny. Helen heard it too, of course. We were to stay three nights at Gerizim and then we would be instructed. So far, nothing.'

'Look' I began. So much had happened last night. Beyond the darkness and light, the Master and the ribbon of time and the jewels revealed to me; there was more, like pure water hidden by the depth of the well. In the clarity of day, I could see the sun reflecting from the bottom of the shaft. 'Simon, we must talk.'

He threw on his clothes. 'Ah, I see. We'll find Helen.'

When we came across her, baking breakfast scones in the stone house, she told us Tarquin had gone off again, announcing his intention to spend the day in prayer. The others were suddenly unsure of their fate; Lydia was trying to get Barius to write a safe conduct for herself and the girls. Helen said Zadok had been pestering her to keep mind-watch in case the Sound returned.

'Forget about that' I said. They were surprised at my tone and paid attention. I couldn't discern my true path over the centuries, I knew the details would not be revealed to me yet, but I did know what must be done right now. There was no point in beating about the bush. 'Simon, do your abilities include seeing along the path of time?'

Helen burned her fingers; they'd touched the grate as she looked around. She waved her hand briefly to cool in the breeze as her husband locked eyes on me. 'Here a glimpse, there a hint' he said. 'What do you know of such things?'

'Last night, by the grace of the Anointed, I held time in my hands. There's not just one path, but many. Through our actions now, we decide which one we'll travel.' I took breath. 'Unless we walk the bright path that beckons today, your name will be cursed by whole nations for more than a millennium.'

They fixed me with their fiery eyes, unblinking as snakes.

'If you both stay in Samaria and teach your wisdom, it will be called a heresy against the Christ. The church leaders in Rome will spread that account of how you wanted to buy the power of the Holy Spirit. They'll see your followers persecuted, until every word you ever spoke is discredited.'

'And you?' asked Simon with a grim smile. 'Will you be scrivener to the Bishop of Rome?'

I almost felt a flush come to my cheeks. 'Never by intent, yet they might make it seem so. They'll turn my story of the Anointed to their own purposes. They'll call you a Gnostic, which will mean sooner rather than later the same to them as Ahriman means to you. You know how the Judaeans and the Samaritans fight about how many books of scripture are truly holy? The Gnostics and the Roman Christians will argue likewise - and for no better reason - except that this time the sect with fewer books will win.'

Simon and Helen were thinking together again, for they asked me almost in unison to describe the bright path.

I squatted down on the rough stone floor. 'If only I saw that path as easily as the other! There is still much travail to overcome, but the Holy Spirit's answer should bring some peace in our hearts as well as relief for thousands of souls across the Empire and beyond.'

Helen asked, 'Must we leave Samaria? What do you say will happen?'

I hung my head. 'I think it's too late to save Israel. Titus will have his way in Jerusalem and when his father grabs the laurel crown he won't forget his quarrel with the nation of the Jews. You could stay, but this fine land will become a broken backwater for more generations than I care to think of. The future eventually belongs to the North and the West - to Rome, to Gaul and to Germany.'

Their faces both reflected that fleeting, unmistakable moment of accord. 'Very well,' said the Magus. 'Rome it will be.'

I was feeling more confident than for a very long time, but I retained a desire to have all things in order - a habit developed from my earliest days with Paul, when he and Barnabas were so filled with fire that they'd invariably mislay their money and forget the shipping schedules. It had taught me caution and discipline.

'It's not that easy' I said. 'I want you to realise what is involved. Apart from the physical dangers of escaping from Palestine and then travelling into the heart of enemy territory, there's our function to consider - the very reason why we ought to be taking this course of action.'

Helen swept her ebony hair from her face. 'You're the man who's had the visions, Mark. You tell us.'

'The bright path won't eventuate unless we hearken to the teaching of the decurion-major. You have your wisdom, and powers that prove there is more to life than the peasants and the politicians have ever suspected. I have knowledge and love of the Anointed, all these stories about Jesus and his sayings which came from those who knew him. We three have our dreams of prophecy and moments when the Light dawns on our minds. But without Tarquin to guide us, we won't reach our goal.'

Simon chuckled, a harsh but honest sound. He was almost like a boy who realises his carefree days are over, because now he must shoulder the responsibilities of a man. 'The joke's on me, then. I fattened him up for the slaughter and now I'm to be his faithful follower!' The Magus leaned over to sample one of the cooling barley-cakes. 'It's fair enough, I suppose. I swindled Tarquin over his black marketing, and every time he got drunk in my dining room, I'd trick out some new military information for the local zealots. If he's got something worth telling this tired old world with its not-so-glorious Empire, he can have my help.'

Helen took a cake and passed one to me. 'Will the Roman agree to it?'

I told her we should find Tarquin and call a meeting to inform the others, but I was sure he would be willing to come. And that's how it turned out, though not because of anything I said to persuade him. Unsurprisingly, the idea had occurred to him already.

It was afternoon before we rounded up everyone and explained our decision. Tarquin was discovered deep in the forest, not near the temple at all - he said the thoughts of trees were less distracting than the emanations of men.

We sat around Tarquin on the temple steps as comfortably as if we'd been doing it for years and Helen announced that great events were in train. Each one had to choose what his or her part would be, whether to leave Samaria now or stay and accept whatever fate had in store. I suppose it sounded melodramatic, but don't overlook that the drama of hardship, displacement and death was a daily fact for the ordinary people of Palestine.

Rumour had it that there were still some lands under the sun where life was easy-going, free of suffering. I've heard Egyptian traders make extravagant claims - such places, they say, exist in the wilds of Africa, where men live close to the animals in the simplicity of their needs and the candour of their dealings with each other. Who knows? Seasoned merchants love to spin a tale.

But one thing is certain, terror of loss stalks all humanity and even emperors see the shadow of their demise from the corners of their fear-plagued eyes. We outlaws had experienced enough to understand that security in this world was akin to a child's toy, bright and attractive one moment, dashed to pieces the next. For many years I served Barnabas, Paul and Thomas because from them I caught the aroma of something sweeter than this lottery of disappointed hopes that we call living. And here on Gerizim the fragrance had grown both stronger and more delicate, more haunting yet closer to hand.

How appropriate that the downtrodden, despised Samaritans should be host to this miracle of a coarse legionary becoming a messenger of God! On the dark road of the future, the Samaritans would survive stumblingly through the centuries that followed the Jewish War, a spent force and unconsidered. Oh yes, everyone would pity the poor Samaritans, in theory at least, because of that story from my Master. But even this would be misrepresented.

Jesus had told the tale of a Samaritan traveller who is wounded and stripped on the bad stretch from Jerusalem to Jericho. A priest and then a Levite pass by on the other side, but a simple God-fearing Israelite who pays no attention to the religious feuding of the so-called wise, dresses the Samaritan's wounds and takes him to an inn. But the Roman Christians won't leave alone the power of this simple parable. They'll turn it around so that the hero of the story is a kindly Samaritan, and even though Samaritans are Jews, it will come to be agreed they are more like gentiles and so the incident becomes a not-too subtle attack on the 'heartless' Jews.

Perhaps we shouldn't blame the Christians; with the Roman police always breathing down their necks - and worse - they'll think to improve their position by disassociating from all things Jewish. It won't really help much, at least not for the first couple of centuries or so, and will create bigger problems in the future. But if we walk the bright road, something better will be in train. The Samaritan temple will become a place of pilgrimage for nations so far distant that now they don't even inhabit our dreams…

'Mark!' Someone was tugging at my clothes. It was Rebekah. 'Mark, I want to go with you and Tarquin.'

'And Simon' I said. 'He's the one who's...' I coughed to stop myself from saying it. Simon had not been very successful as her guardian, after all.

She spoke directly. 'I don't rely on Simon anymore. I've seen that even a magician can't keep everything in order. I'll try to put my trust in God, where it always should have been. I asked the Spirit of God what I must do. Up here, with Tarquin and everyone, the answers are easy to hear. Mother will go to father's family in Sebaste. Romans and Greeks run the city, but at least there's not much trouble. Rachel and mother will comfort each other while the war lasts. But after what happened to me - I can't go to Sebaste or back to Gitta, or any sort of normal life. And' her eyes dropped for a second, 'there's you. You need someone to help you on this journey. It won't be easy, will it? As a minister of God, you'll be tested in many ways. Simon has Helen. But you've travelled so long alone.'

I didn't know what to say. She was young, but beneath the childish brow her mouth was set firmly. Obviously, I wanted her to come. There had always been the feeling of something lacking in my life. But it couldn't be that easy! Consider what had happened in the temple with Helen. It was no wonder that so many religious sects forbad men to have relations with women. Your mind was distracted from its true intent; you were befuddled and weakened, tied to matter when your purpose was spirit.

I hardly had time to shake my head before she was ready with her reply.

'If you don't want me to talk about Simon and Helen, think of the rabbi Jesus. You respect his teachings above all the others, don't you? And his life was an example to us all? Well, then. His companion was a prostitute! Do I have to sell myself to qualify?'

'That's enough' I said. 'Smart remarks won't get you very far, wherever you go. What does your mother say, and Simon?' Her eyes were laughing at my parental irritation. She shrugged. 'There are no appearances left for mother to maintain. Anything that anybody does nowadays is dangerous. Simon will certainly let me come, if you agree.'

I told her that I was going for a walk and when I returned, I would tell her of my decision. Down I stepped into the welcoming gloom of the densest forest, the pine needles crunching to keep me company. It wasn't just a delaying tactic, I genuinely needed to get away and think. Think about Thomas, who'd been in my thoughts more frequently since the great light came. Think about my Master and what he wanted of me. Perhaps, like Tarquin, I would be able to apprehend his wishes better out here in the green.

I sat on a log. It was time to sort out this problem of sex as best I could. Early impressions are always powerful, so I began by recalling my original journey with Paul and Barnabas. After Antioch we boarded ship to Cyprus. That first sea voyage was a pleasant surprise: I was immune to sea-sickness and I obtained reduced rates for our baggage, which impressed Paul greatly. He in turn impressed Sergius Paulus, the hard-headed procurator of the island, by sending Sergius' pet sorcerer packing. But what interested me most was the way in which the Cypriots worshipped Aphrodite. Every woman had to submit herself to the temple at least once in her life, and by watching the entrance whenever I could steal an hour to myself, I discovered what that meant.

Any man, noble, merchant or common sailor, could walk up as bold as brass and demand the favours of the women who waited on the temple steps. Because they feared the vengeance of the goddess, even the highest-born women took their places, until some fellow came along and said in a loud voice, 'In the name of Mylitta Aphrodite, I claim you!' The money from this cultic prostitution went into the temple coffers.

Barnabas knew all about it - he was born on Cyprus. Secretly, I envied him. There was nothing titillating like that going on in Jerusalem. Outwardly we three, being good Jews, were properly scandalised. Then again, would the Master have condemned the gentile Cypriots, seeing as he was willing to befriend Mary the Magdalene along with lepers and tax collectors? If there was one thing I'd learned about my Master, it was this: he might speak forcibly to impress a point of teaching, but he never once condemned anyone.

Paul disagreed with having women involved in Nazorean worship, though he didn't mind active ladies like mother becoming the very backbone of the new movement. Ah, but Paul always found it hard to treat sex as a normal part of life, despite our mainstream Jewish outlook that marriage is a social duty. His limp, and his early absorption in the spiritual occult with its attendant asceticism, helped to make him a man apart. He always felt he had a mission, and like many of the Essenes, was determined to keep his body pure.

I could sympathise with this view, but in Cyprus my blood ran hot. I was nearly 19 years old and had never tasted the joys of a woman's caresses. Day after day they stood patiently on the steps, and some of them no ordinary females I can tell you. Notwithstanding the veils they wore.

We were nearly ready to leave the island before I plucked up courage. On the second last day, a tall stately woman walked up the steps. Rather inaccessible she seemed, but no doubt it was a way of salvaging her dignity. Quickly, so as not to think about it and become a victim of conscience - and to forestall any of the other hopefuls - I shuffled over to the temple door with my coin sweaty in my palm and in a voice cracked by shame made the required announcement.

I saw her eyes behind the grey gauze, half defiant, half defensive. She stood a forehead higher than me, but in deference to her religion she stepped over to one of the little cubicles at the side of the temple and drew open the curtain.

She knew the routine, whereas I rather dreaded what sort of stinking hole I'd walked into. However, the place was furnished with a large, tasteful couch and was sweetened by the aroma of rose and sandalwood.

Those beginning moments were dreadful, but by some stroke of luck or passion I found my confidence and when the curtains were shut, my lady abandoned herself to the occasion. It was an exciting if exhausting morning in which I made up for a lot of lost time.

Afterwards, though, I discovered how guilt works, with its attendant unspoken wish for punishment. Some Jew, who was acquainted with some other Jew who had decided upon conversion after listening to Paul, saw me. You can work out the rest. Paul got to hear about it and what was worse, the woman was the wife of a prominent member of Sergius' household, to whom Paul had recently preached Christian morality!

Paul could have learned tolerance and forbearance from that episode - the boat crew thought it a fine joke and made me their hero - but instead he became very morose. It was worse than his anger, and soon after that we parted company, not to meet up again for many a year. The quarrel was a silly one because, underneath it all, we loved each other like brothers.

More important than recalling my mixed feelings for Paul, as I sat on my log, was to decide on the deeper meaning of the incident. Sex is always concerned with bodies, at least at the beginning. Then later, if and when the true core of intimacy is approached, all awareness of the physical is stripped away, to be replaced by another sort of knowledge, soft, immediate and blissful.

Back in Jerusalem there had been a girl not unlike Rebekah.

Let me not mention her name; this is no time to over-indulge in nostalgia. We were in love and wished to marry, but she was the daughter of a haughty Sadducee who wouldn't countenance a Nazorean for a son-in-law. One evening she whispered that we should take matters into our own hands. Being summer, we found a grove of hardy shrubs outside the city, close by the needle gate. There I discovered the mystery of a woman's love salted by reciprocal tenderness. To give becomes receiving - is that why the Master said giving was the more blessed? Technically, my lovemaking was nowhere near as good as with the Cypriot woman, but who cares for technique when you're overtaken by joy?

Sex could go either way; it could trap you into the body, or it could be a stepping-stone to set you free. The distance between these two choices was short but the difference was great.

Thomas had noted the Master's opinion about this: Jesus gently mocked the belief, still common because 'obvious', that the body was the first cause and spirit or consciousness merely a phenomenal consequence of it. The Master had described the spirit as 'great wealth' and the body as poverty.

Must we then wear hair shirts and curse the body? There are monks who insist on this regime and because motive seems the most important ingredient of our actions, these strivers may yet find peace. But it's not necessary. No, my Master never promoted hatred, only love. To despise the body in a rage of frustration at its limitations is surely little different from indulging it and seeking salvation in the senses. Salvation is to be found elsewhere but why blame the body for this simple fact?

The body, I knew, was ever servant of the mind, at best a vehicle for the light of truth. Although we were all able to touch bliss in sleep or meditation—if I could, anyone could—a body was a more familiar medium; to watch gestures and listen to words, relax at the sight of another's smiling face or wonder at the marvel of sexual union, might be easier to accept than seeing a magnificent angel in a vision, even if the message and the wisdom and the upliftment were the same in both cases.

Then how to view women? Because they were the nurturers and the bearers of children, women were in many cultures associated with the earthly and merely human, while the masculine symbolised the spiritual, the divine. In Hebrew, God was always male. However, His indispensable Spirit, the intermediary through which He was able to reach the world of humans, was *Ruach*, a feminine word. Women held families together, spoke prophesies, were among the foremost Christians of the day.

Gusty weather disturbed the treetops and above the canopy a flock of geese winged past, showing themselves at the windows formed by breaks in the foliage. The pine branches, the specks of white cloud, the vibrant passage of the birds gripped me in a spell. My deliberations were fuzzy compared with that sudden celebration of life. How sadly complex we humans were, with our laws, our squabbles and our cruelties. Even such a natural business as the place of men and women and their relation to God—the ultimate law, the ultimate naturalness—was so obscured that I must needs sit here and wrestle with its meaning. How foolish the geese would think I was, if they realised what I was doing down here!

But birds and other creatures live more simply: Neither toiling nor spinning, they live in innocence straightforwardly guided by life itself. If it could happen to them, why not to me?

Then I would let life speak through me, as it had before. And I heard that desirable as companionship was, and guiltless as sexual activity might be, there would come a time when my joy was already so complete that neither of these questions could be worth bothering with; there would be no emptiness to fill because I would experience my identity as a fullness so satisfying that my only need would be to share it with my brothers and sisters.

Now was no time to feel guilty; guilt could occur only if I believed myself separate from the one stream of life, and such separation was in fact not really possible. If I let the Spirit guide me, the usual hurts almost inevitably associated with sexual relationship (along with all the other difficulties of earthly existence) would be gently transmuted into an uplifting force, pulling aside the veil and helping reveal the ever-present oneness. It was this force which had drawn me to the Master like bee to flower, for he had it in abundance. Without that kind of strength and certainty, applied with endurance and faith, neither I nor anyone else could find their way back to awareness of God.

He would take away all the fear, the possessive terror that this person was absolutely necessary to mend my broken self-image, that this prop to my play act of alienation from God was essential to my happiness, and my belief that to lose it was to descend into hell. There was another and more optimistic interpretation of relationship: Sons and daughters of God could come together to celebrate that they did not need to use each other as bandages on self-inflicted wounds; rejoicing in their knowledge of God, they would extend their fulfilment and increase their grace by sharing it with each other.

It was at this point I thought of the words of the Master as recorded by dear Thomas. Jesus taught that the seeker would find, but not without effort, and what he found would rarely be to his liking. Yet this process, honestly carried to its conclusion, proffered its own reward.

Confusion would give way to enlightenment, when a man realised the Almighty alone held rulership over destiny.

It was time to quieten down my pondering self. Standing up with a silent prayer of thanks to the forest I walked back to tell Rebekah she was most welcome to travel as my companion on our journey into the unknown.

25

MARK, THOMAS & TOLKIEN

MARK JAMES DRAGGED his heels along Pitt Street. He had just received a raise in salary and tried to convince himself that he was in a good mood. But for no apparent good reason he felt sour.

The store where he used to buy his Italian shoes had closed down. The trip uptown was a wasted lunch-hour. For some reason he was more bothered than usual by the heavy smell of leaded exhaust from the traffic and the pedestrian crowds seemed more than normally annoying in their mindless rush to go anywhere or most likely nowhere.

Hands in pockets, Mark dawdled. Even the gaily clothed and painted city girls failed to make much of an impression. A small section of shop window advertised the Adyar Bookshop on the floor above and a flight of well-used stairs offered access.

He wandered in and up. And thought about some of the unusual books he'd enjoyed in the past. There was *Zen and the Art of Motorcycle Maintenance*; and by contrast *Chariots of the Gods?*, that conversation starter if nothing else from the audacious Mr von Daniken. On a different plane was *Shikasta*, Doris Lessing's impressive, mythical thought-provoker. Then there was *Socorro Saucer*, very careful reportage by UFO researcher Ray Stanford. There might be another worthwhile title somewhere in this oddly named store.

He reached the first floor and entered the shop, noting its dignified air, like a well-established library. A stick of incense burned on the counter.

He strolled down an aisle and immediately, a small red book became caught against one of the buttons of his jacket. 'Pretty weird' he muttered, unhooking the button. The slim volume fell onto the floor. Mark picked it up with the faintest feeling of unease. How on earth could that have happened? You didn't go pulling books off shelves with your coat buttons.

It was *The Gospel According to Thomas*. Mark half nodded in approval. He had little interest in the Bible, but he'd heard that Thomas was the more or less scientific disciple, at least the one who asked questions.

Thomas was a doubter, yes, but was he a writer too? Matthew, Mark, um, Luke, John... that was the sequence his mother had taught him, while father politely declined an interest. As far as he could tell, there wasn't a Gospel of Thomas: Curious. Well then, better check it out further.

Mark, good looking, neat of frame and dress, presenting with sufficient aplomb to appear properly upwardly mobile, stood in the aisle flicking the pages of the red book. Suddenly he thought of the awkward client who'd demanded an appointment 'straight after lunch'. Mark slapped the volume down and hurried out.

That evening after work he joined the general drift to the local pub. Mark didn't really enjoy these beery excursions. However, today's sense of vague depression hadn't lifted. It was taking the line of least resistance to wander up the road with the others, talking shop and engaging in pointless political discussions. That was still much better he decided, than thinking about Linda.

'You're a richer man now than you were last week' Bruce the junior programmer reminded him when they stood against the bar (all his co-workers seemed to have heard about it). 'You'd better shout the first round.' Mark dutifully paid for the drinks but couldn't resist pointing out to Toni the receptionist, that each ounce of alcohol would destroy several thousand brain cells. Who cared if it was hyperbole.

'Oh, very impressive' she said. 'Mark, you're the new Doubting Thomas of the drinking fraternity.'

'Uh?' Some of his beer slopped over the rim of the glass. He took a swig and changed the subject. That was how Mark began his journey into Gnosticism. Next time in the city, he bought the book.

The Thomas Gospel along with many other manuscripts had been discovered near the town of Nag Hammadi, Upper Egypt, in 1945. These leather-bound papyrus documents had lain in their earthenware jar for about 1600 years, meaning that the books must have been hidden there by Coptic monks shortly after the reign of Emperor Constantine the Great. The monks' defensive action was consistent with the historical situation. By endorsing the Church of Rome, Constantine had sounded the eventual death-knell for other contemporary interpretations of Christianity.

Mark was fascinated by the Arabian Nights setting, but even more so by the documents themselves. Why hadn't he heard anything about this stuff before? Then he learned that the business of securing and transcribing the texts had been an extremely slow and fragmented process. The delay was occasioned by complex academic and political intrigue. The global interest and excitement associated with the discovery of the Dead Sea Scrolls was therefore never paralleled by the find at Nag Hammadi.

Thomas' Jesus was different from the Jesus of Sunday-school. More like a real person although an enigmatic one. He was intelligent and subtle. He offered, for example, no support to the ingenuous notion that the Kingdom of Heaven could be tied to a time or a place.

Near the end of the Thomas Gospel, it echoed the situation in Luke 17:20-21 (mother had mentioned that particular piece of scripture a few times over the years and somehow he remembered it) where Jesus was asked when the Kingdom of God would come.

Jesus told his questioners not to await signs, it wasn't a matter of saying 'here' or 'there', but of understanding that the Kingdom was within.

Thomas' Gospel went further. With him there was no sharp distinction between inner and outer. (Mark found himself speculating whether this could be because our thoughts actually did determine our external reality in everyday life and not just in Sci-Fi stories.) To Thomas' Jesus, the Kingdom was everywhere - inside, outside, spread across the earth. All that was needed was the vision to apprehend it. But humankind was a blind race.

Indeed. He closed the book. Could anyone consider honestly this polluted planet, torn with enmity and other human failings, and see evidence of heaven? Unless that person could tap into some very different dimension: a dimension which he, at least, wasn't privy to.

Edward Gibbon, the 18th Century writer, apparently achieved no such enlightened perception. But his comments on Gnosticism in his book *Decline and fall of the Roman Empire* did provide an elegant light relief. Mark enjoyed reading them:

> *From the acknowledged truth of the Jewish religion, the Ebionites had concluded that it never could be abolished. From its supposed imperfections, the Gnostics as hastily inferred that it never was instituted by the wisdom of the Deity. There are some objections against the authority of Moses and the prophets which too readily present themselves to the sceptical mind; though they can only be derived from our ignorance of remote antiquity, and from our incapacity to form an adequate judgement of the Divine economy. These objections were eagerly embraced and as petulantly urged by the vain science of the Gnostics.*

> *The God of Israel was impiously represented by the Gnostics as a being liable to passion and to error, capricious in his favour, implacable in his resentment, meanly jealous of his superstitious worship, and confining his partial providence to a single people, and to this transitory life. In such a character they could discover none of the*

Ah, yes. Heaven thought Mark. The Kingdom of God. Perfection. It was the usual problem which religion always presented. There was a good deal of interesting theory - putting the theory into practice was another matter.

And it happened that his casual investigation of the early Christian-era Gnostics was soon suspended due to an additional responsibility at work which closely followed his salary increase.

'We don't want you to get bored, Mark' explained his boss. 'These, er, stories you write - enjoy the play of imagination against fact and all that?'

Mark pointed out that as there wasn't any real money in it, enjoyment was the only benefit his science-fiction hobby could offer.

'If you were making money as well' the boss chuckled, 'we'd have no reason to pay you any increases'. The light-hearted introduction over, the boss got down to business.

'Three years is a long time in the software game. You've stuck with us. You know what we do, the strategy, the services, the products. It's time we had a higher profile in the market, old son. We could sign up a flashy PR outfit to handle a campaign in the press. However, Jack and I believe that you could do just as good a job. With your creative talents, maybe even better.'

And save the company a packet, old son, Mark's narrowed eyes intimated, while his lips formed a string of suitable acknowledgements.

Despite the knee-jerk cynicism, Mark began to enjoy the challenge of preparing press releases, reporting on successful applications of software products, and devising a brochure to advertise the company. The boss seemed to have chosen wisely. Life moved on a more even keel for Mark, his work left less time for fruitless speculations. He even met Linda at a party one Saturday night and found himself able to talk with her quite rationally.

The party hosts passed a joint around in the crowded living room and it must have been good stuff - when he walked into the dewy garden, how mellow he felt!

A few minutes later there was a familiar laugh and she walked by, arm in arm with a man. He wanted Linda's companion to be hideous, but he had soft brown eyes and his features were finely chiselled. She was looking at his face with such interest that she didn't see Mark. 'G'night' the man said in a friendly voice.

With almost skipping steps the couple left the garden and melted into roadside shadows. Another laugh. Then a car door slammed.

The garden was illuminated by nearby street lamps and moths buzzed the incandescence. Mark's attention was drawn to the chaotic movement and after a while he felt nauseous. Without saying goodbye to anyone he stepped carefully out to his car, satisfying himself that he could walk a straight line. A terrible presence, black and bony like a vulture, waited over his shoulder. He saw it out of the corner of his eye but busied himself with settling into his seat and checking that the belt was securely fastened.

The drive was easy - home without being tested for blood alcohol by the police. Up the rickety wooden steps without mishap, clothes off, into bed. Sleep came without the sickly overtones of excessive indulgence; the vulture's shadow melted into exhaustion.

Mark felt himself going down a long corridor. He had an appointment to keep. He entered a room which was startlingly foreign, being somewhat egg-shaped. There stood a portly man who invited him to sit down.

'I thought I'd catch you before things got too difficult,' said the man. He was a funny-looking fellow wearing a kind of gold-patterned tunic that stretched tightly over his generous midriff. He appeared to have a stringy rat-tail that flicked from side to side as he advanced. Mark wondered vaguely how human hair was able to get so mobile when the wearer made so little physical movement himself. The man's overall mobility was even more tantalising because it was uncertain whether his feet entirely touched the floor as he came closer.

'Difficult for whom?' asked Mark.

The plump man ignored that. 'My name is Ardax. I am a rigorist. Have a seat, Mark, and listen.'

Mark sank slowly, dream-fashion, into the cushions covering the floor.

'You've got a job to do, brother. You've already partly agreed, of course, otherwise I wouldn't trouble you. In fact, we are colleagues - actually much more than that - and the task is shared between us. Agreement is what makes these things possible. It might be as well to keep that in mind. Relax now, and we'll start. As I think you know, this obsession with Linda is misappropriating your energy.'

Mark was about to protest when he saw a shadow. The vulture cruised down from the ceiling, crying harshly, and dive-bombed his head. Terror, pain, loss! All the feeling that he'd banked at the party invaded him now with compound interest.

'That's alright' said Ardax. 'It won't come back. But you should take the lesson which is offered.' The man's rather pale face wasn't quite human - not enough lines - but it was kind.

'Linda?'

'Yes. In Class Four at this time many are being asked to refine, or completely re-assess, their appreciation of relationships.' His voice gained power. 'Life is relationship. Your difficulties are no worse than many. Your potential is high. But the possessiveness, the obsession, it has to go.'

'How?' After a moment's consideration, 'Why?'

Ardax waved his hand and a pillar of many colours grew out of the centre of the room. The colours changed in a patterned sequence that marked time with Ardax's speech. An artistic underline, thought Mark, with the clarity that may come in fragments of dreams.

'We all seek completeness' said the oddly dressed man and his colours, 'but that cannot be achieved by throwing ourselves away in favour of another. Such behaviour is only a symbol of trying to escape from the inescapable. It's darkness, Mark! You're saying she offers wholeness, but at the same time you are denying your ability to accept it.

'If wholeness *is* at all, then it includes everything real. You, too! If you're a fragment, how can you trade a fragment for the whole? You can have either fragments or wholeness - but never both. And wholeness is true, because God is. Find your own wholeness, then you can share it with Linda.'

Ardax leapt up, so high and slow he looked like an astronaut in training, and fell gently among the cushions, yet still almost knocking Mark over.

'You can't lose' he chuckled, the roll of spare flesh bouncing on his belly. This was a part Ardax enjoyed the most about Class Four. 'You're trying to win but thanks to the fact of wholeness you really can't lose.'

In that moment Mark saw the joke and joined in the laughter. 'Can't lose!' His giggles were muffled by the pillow. He saw a light-blue hint of dawn through the bedroom window and turned over.

He was sitting on a hard wooden stool at a table, and a parchment was laid out in front of him. The environment was somewhat similar to, yet at the same time very different from, the previous room. There was the same absence of 90-degree angles, but this place had dark, irregular walls. It was a cave in a high rock face and to his left was a pulley arrangement that went down through a hole in the floor. That was the only way in or out.

He knew that during this particular time and place he considered himself Gnostic. He still hadn't found out exactly what that meant; then the meaning came: 'gnosis' was Greek for awareness, knowledge. This word defined the difference between the upsurging Roman Christian churches and the individuals and groups who took a more adventurous course. Gnostics like himself leaned towards the radical. They were interested in taking individual responsibility for their own spiritual development, often following unique, creative steps that would scandalise most Christian Romans and their view of the new religion.

His clothes were of a coarse, none-too clean material; the light from a candle showed the worn sleeves as well as the written page. He was translating sacred material and the bishop mustn't find it. The others would protect his secret but even if the bishop's men sniffed out his lair as they eventually would, he'd go on until they dragged him bodily from his work. No matter the cost, people must be told the truth…

The peculiar egg-shaped room returned. This time there were just colours with Ardax's voice coming through them. 'We will concentrate on the work to be done. You enjoy writing, and you do understand that work isn't necessarily unpleasant. A good foundation.

'However, a degree of resistance is common, so let us address it now.' The colours whirled into a column. 'The only reason you would give for not carrying out your assigned task is because it detracts from what you want to do. So let us investigate what you desire; how you believe your time should be spent. Why are you alive?'

Green, purple, blue, yellow. The colours appeared to move closer. Mark wanted to get away. There was a burst of orange, and a long, sweet sound. He relaxed and stayed put.

'Your plan is to have a good time, enjoy yourself, protect your body from harm? Earn lots of money, get lots of sex, become popular and so keep misfortune at bay?' The colours smudged together. 'Hide from the insanities of the world and hope no trigger-happy politician starts World War Three?' After a pause in which the column dimmed out, the colours brightened again and blended so there was an aura of white on the perimeter.

'There's a way past this fragile truce you make with pain and sorrow. An old, straight track with the Way Shower to guide us. Which both of us see clearest in the Anointed, the Master Jesus. I am a rigorist, I have clarified your time-track tradition, traced the co-ordinates. We are brothers and more, in a manner that is not easy to explain to you. Just be aware that together we have walked the track before, Mark. And together we are choosing to return to it. Your part is just as vital as my own.

'People only accept sorrow as the natural order of things when they are mostly asleep. It's not going to be a tenable position for you much longer. I can read the psych signatures quite adequately I assure you.

Your Master is calling and we will answer. For your sake and the sake of Class Four, make it soon.'

The colours began to fade, but Mark held them in place by sheer willpower. He called out, 'Wait. Are you real? Isn't this a dream?'

Everything was hazy now, except the answer, which was clearly spoken: 'Less of a dream than you'd ever dream of. Find out for yourself. Mother used the Bible, didn't she? Any book will do.'

Mark awoke, fighting for breath because his face was in the pillow. He climbed out of bed and drank a glass of water. It was a sunny morning.

All day the events of the night oppressed him but not as nightmares do. He felt the continuing presence of the chubby man and although he lost precise recall of most of what had been said, the last words were irritatingly current, like the daily exhortation on a desk diary. Something was expected of him, and it wouldn't go away. It was also a day of rare depression, yearning for Linda. He moped around at home despite the balmy air and glistening harbour calling him out.

Monday found him just as unsettled; the internal pressure mounting rather than ebbing away. When he returned home with take-away Chinese food in the evening, he decided on an experiment. After the last plastic container was consigned to the garbage can and the television news with its tendency to pessimism was punched off, he went over to the bookshelf and pulled out his battered childhood copy of JRR Tolkien's *The Hobbit*.

Yes, mother had used the Bible when she wanted advice on some matter of domestic importance, such as whether to buy a radiogram or a new freezer. Picking passages at random used to provide some surprising and pertinent answers. But the dream (or was it a dream) had said he could use any book.

So he placed *The Hobbit* on his desk and, resigning himself to his true feelings, asked: 'What are my chances of ever getting back with Linda?' Then flipped the pages at random, stopped and placed his finger on the text. His eye travelled from there.

'...under the Master's direction they began the planning of a new town, designed more fair and large even than before, but not in the same place.'

Mark stared, immobilised, alternately reading the passage and gazing blankly out of the window at the very small triangle of Sydney harbour which showed through the trees. He felt himself to be a lonely monk peering out of a cave mouth at a bare, windy ravine. There was a sudden fullness in his chest which released in easy sobs. 'My Master.' He repeated the name as the taste of salt trickled into his mouth.

26

ARDAX GOES STARGAZING

'IT'S LIKE THIS, brother Ardax' said the Esoterics Support Chief. She had arrived at his workplace in her mottled-colour off-duty pinafore quite deliberately to create a more informal, personal setting. 'We've looked and seen our opportunity thanks to your dedicated work with Class Four. Now this is by no means a criticism, yet the present state of play is of such delicacy that it's necessary to go much further and deeper.'

Ardax's brow wrinkled just a little while he pondered the other's sincerity as well as the unusual extension of work. It was a surprising development.

Sharnestia saw the reaction and gave the briefest smile. She just as quickly patted her fine blonde hair.

'It's something we'll have to get used to. You see, as we make increasing attempts to assist Class Four, so do we find more unfamiliar clues pointing to Jesus' life and work as a solution. It must be understood and presented in very specific ways.'

'And those ways are…?'

'Some information can be shared verbally; some must be absorbed directly in energy. Come and see me tomorrow at 10am if you're free; we'll spend some time on both aspects. I am sure you're adequately primed for it thanks to your cross-class experience.'

Noting Ardax's deliberate slow nod, she continued. 'We are still at an early stage of recognising the complexity. On the positive side, we're fully aware of enhanced Assistance, giving us the opportunity for further and deeper effects than we've accomplished to date. The effects will not only be experienced by Class Four but on all levels. This change comes with great responsibility. We cannot present ourselves as superior beings reaching down to assist lesser lives. The sequence is linked; we ourselves are included.' This time her smile was almost mischievous. 'The ultimate effect cannot be estimated with any certainty.'

'And Council approves of this experiment in all aspects?' asked Ardax. He noted his own seriousness.

'Less an experiment than a methodology. This development is thrust upon us. It's not to be ignored.' She maintained her gaze a few more seconds.

The die was cast but Ardax still felt unsettled. He needed something more definite, why was she so intent on pussyfooting? 'I see. How should we proceed? As you know I am deep into the current Class Four rescue mission.'

The Chief noted her colleague's hesitation. 'We go forward in faith, now the co-ordinates are in place. Everyone involved must accept and meditate upon the change. I'll post details. It's a matter of trust in accomplishment. The process has its own momentum.'

'Very well' said Ardax. 'But can you tell me how I should work at the moment with Mark James, particularly? Contact has been made and it's solid. Hopefully we'll be able stabilise and deepen the connection. I did it using the current protocol.'

'We aren't aware of needing to make any modifications right away. Some adjustments will likely be beneficial, as we go forward. Let me know if you hit a difficulty.'

It was another week before Ardax and the Chief met again; this time it was for the required group energy initiation. This session was attended by senior rigorists in the second synthesis room with its restful, rounded edges and delicate, gradually shifting pastel perspectives. After a prolonged time of deep quiet, they moved into activity mode.

The Chief sat relaxed yet with eyes full of vigour. 'How do we start? It's simple but perhaps not easy. We must introduce some new ideas, extraordinary teachings coming from outside Earth's aura. And even to some extent from beyond the Solar System.' Sharnestia paused to let that sink in while she smoothed her hair and her eyes twinkled at the reaction. There was a stir amongst the two dozen rigorists. This ripple somehow confirmed her potency and Ardax took it as a positive sign. She continued:

'This is something imposed on us, but only because of the effort we've been making to re-establish value in the teachings of Jesus. You've been assessing and absorbing much of the result and our work has attracted an off-world response: Of almost unimaginable magnitude!

'The Master Jesus brings—has brought—an uplift designed in co-operation with the extra-planetary forces.' Her cadence slowed and deepened. 'Having reached this point, we must not isolate either knowledge system from the other. Council has made multiple forays into the connection. We conclude there is a strong dependency between them.'

Chief's intensity smoothed off a little. 'It's not my intention tonight to outline the timeline or the mechanics. This is research you each can and must do. Delve deeper into the subject matter as and when necessary for functional outcomes.'

Ardax stood up. 'We can incorporate these frequencies into our programs without delay?'

She nodded. 'The new energy-complex signature is available to everyone here in the usual way, starting tomorrow. But thanks for asking the question. Hurry slowly! This fresh knowledge is largely of a different aspect and degree compared to the methodologies you're all using now.'

Sharnestia's voice softened further. 'Approach it with diligence, allow the material sufficient time to impact and ensure you are each properly aligned. Before you apply the material, do not by-pass proper acknowledgement. Always give thanks.'

Ardax nodded, resumed his seat, not exactly excited but looking forward to the new system with curiosity. He considered his colleagues, the quiet colours, the soft angles and simple furnishings of the meeting room, the pervading sense of purpose. There were times when the job was challenging, even exhausting or rocky. But overall, he loved his profession.

◆

Ardax tripped, almost toppled over; steadied himself with hands on the corridor wall. Miriam had recently suggested he was rather overweight; losing his balance could be a consequence. Preoccupied by news of the major reset and information transfer, he had momentarily overlooked the low step to the entrance of the records department. Then, further understanding came with a degree of shock—it couldn't be, yet it was! *Overweight?* He was taking on the characteristics of his Class Four alternate self! An integration, or a collapse of necessary boundaries? He paused to spend a few minutes on Brain Gym and made a mental note to investigate later at a deeper level.

Composing himself, Ardax supposed this unusual effect on his physical body might be evidence of a gathering closeness between the Classes, whether healthy or not he wouldn't speculate now. Perhaps it was tied in with the need for absorbing the department's latest approach to its mandate. He'd always regarded himself as very open-minded—now, that self-labelling might be put to the test. He wondered whether he entirely liked the idea.

In any case he'd have to clear his head for today's task.

As an Alt. Historian it was incumbent on him to have not only a good grasp of history's mainstream but also various other dimensional quirks that had been detected and explored. Yet he'd never delved into the long and well-documented record of beliefs and practices around Sirius. All he knew, rather vaguely, was that this binary star had fascinated a wide variety of civilisations, from ancient times right up to the present.

Settling into his pod, the sensors came alive to answer the unspoken question. 'You have not needed a particular knowledge of astronomy for your work to date, so we'll start right at the beginning. Because mentions of Sirius have barely been of interest to you, we offer an overview.'

Ardax promised himself to stay alert.

Sirius was the brightest star in the sky. Then the enormous surprise: there was no chance to prepare, no preliminary to this major update: Eons before he and his colleagues had started observing Class Four and other dimensions, what was now to be known as the Sirian Authority had been and still was checking out all and everything concerning planet Earth. As well as each of the other planets in the solar system.

A binary, comprising Sirius A in company with the very much smaller white dwarf Sirius B, the system was even more important than any of the ancient texts had claimed.

Sirius was the alpha star—first or brightest—in the constellation Canis Major. (That meant 'Big Dog' or 'Greater Dog' in Latin; thus, Sirius had become well-known as the Dog Star.) Canis Major was one of the 48 visible constellations catalogued by Ptolemy the Greek astronomer in the second century CE. It represented in myth the larger of the Orion constellation's two 'hunting dogs' who accompany him as he pursues Lepus, the hare or rabbit (the brain-screen helpfully illuminated the position of Lepus, a nearby constellation in the night sky.) The name Sirius was derived from the Greek word Seirios, meaning 'glowing' or 'scorching'.

Very curiously, totally separate ancient cultures, with no apparent communication, had associated the brilliant Sirius with either a wolf or a dog. Examples: in ancient Chaldea (later known as Iraq) the star was called the 'Dog Star that Leads'; in ancient China Sirius was identified as a heavenly wolf. And it was known as the 'Dog of the Sun' in Assyria and Akkad.

Some North American indigenous tribes also referred to the star in canine terms. The Seri and Tohono O'odham tribes of the southwest described Sirius as a 'dog that follows mountain sheep', while the Cherokee paired Sirius with Antares as a dog-star guardian of the 'Path of Souls'. The Skidi tribe of Nebraska named it 'Wolf Star', and further north the Alaskan Inuit of the Bering Strait called it 'Moon Dog'.

The 'dog days' of summer for the ancient Greeks - hot sultry days associated with bad luck—coincided with the period from early July to August when Sirius rose just before the morning sun. The star was blamed for intense seasonal heat that, it was believed, could drive people and dogs to madness.

This same phenomenon, known as the heliacal rising of Sirius, was particularly important to ancient Egyptians because it marked the flooding of the Nile. This was essential to the success of their agriculture in a land that for thousands of years experienced virtually no rainfall.

To the Polynesians, mostly in the Southern Hemisphere, the star was known as 'Ka'ulua'. Nothing about dogs, but it was a marker for winter and an important reference for navigation around the Pacific Ocean.

After some more of this, the session trailed off for a scheduled pause. Ardax stretched, deliberately deciding to keep his feelings neutral as far as possible. This was basic textbook information. But where did the idea come from that Sirius was so massively important; not only to Alt. History but to everything else on planet Earth? The next section only gave historical accounts of when Sirius appeared as red in colour, compared with current observations that it obviously did not.

Ardax wasn't accustomed to feeling irritated. But he wanted the answer to his main concern without delay. Fortunately, the records department was programmed to respond to any reasonable request. He rather tersely asked for a short but pithy explanation of how Sirius could be of such extreme importance.

The system answered in a nicely modulated speech and sharpest graphics:

Much about Sirius could not be explained, only conjectured. The brilliant binary was described as two fairly young stars, only some 230-247 million years old. Technical information backed up the claim. Before Ardax could even start to get fidgety this time, there was a change of direction: the supposed age was *impossible*. Impossible because Sirius was responsible for giving birth to nine solar systems including our own, and surely each one of them was much, much older than a mere quarter of a billion years. Even planet Earth was accepted by scientists as having been around for some 18 times that length of time.

Could anyone begin to cope with the idea of a star giving birth to various solar systems? The situation made Ardax feel greater emotional kinship with the often-bewildered inhabitants of Class Four like Mark James and others whom the rigorist had approached to work with in the past. He'd had to manage those people when they were abruptly faced with the dawning reality of hitherto unknown and unimagined dimensions—now it was his turn. But after all, it was just another weird event in the life of a rigorist. He'd put uncomfortable feelings aside and immerse himself in exploration of the Sirian theme.

What followed was a few words about this supposed 'young' age of Sirius. The pleasant voice carefully intoned: 'The Sirius system could be concealing an exotic past evolutionary history involving interactions and mass transfer between the two stars. Or even one necessitating a third star that was dynamically ejected from the system while exciting the remaining binary to a higher orbital eccentricity.'

The piece ended with an admission that Sirius challenged recent theories of stellar evolution. Ardax rather enjoyed hearing that astronomers were not infallible. Coming closer to home, he wondered whether this Sirian speculation, consequential as it must be, might assist his work with Mark James. Yet how could it help clarify the teachings of Jesus?

The system caught his thought and assumed a more casual, female voice. 'Not so fast, rigorist. We must bring in quite an amount of basics before we can go there.'

He assumed there'd be a great deal of background to absorb. But Ardax wasn't optimistic about the time it would take to move from an explanation of creating entire solar systems, to practical assistance in dealing with the three 'lower' Classes of planet Earth—as well as applying it to his own dimension. Each Class had its own ideas about

Jesus' birth, his teaching and the subsequent historical developments. Synthesis didn't sound easy.

Picking up on this latest thought, AI did a personality change to The Newsreader. 'Sirius is a highly important element to be considered. But you are right to regard the situation as complex. Especially as Class Four Middle East will be the scene of much devastation and human suffering for some years in the 21st Century. Together with climate disruptions, other international disputes and wars, there is increasing possibility of widespread chaos eventually leading to global civilisation collapse.'

'Then the quicker I can absorb more essentials of those topics, reaching across all Classes, the better for everyone.' Ardax took a big breath. He was on slightly firmer ground now.

27

INNER AND
OUTER SPACES

THREE DAYS HAD gone by and everyone who knew him agreed it was a big achievement. Despite his usual so-called steady or laid-back approach, Ardax had put in 18-hour sessions, using every available technological and subtle energy aid. He was determined to crack certain barriers that had become more than evident, especially applicable to his several rescue missions. The area of Sirian knowledge that Ardax focussed on was naturally enough, planet Earth.

It energised him to learn that our world's place in the solar system, like each one of the other planets, was explicable as being in precise pattern with a particular organ of the human body. And like the organs, each was deeply necessary for the living creature's (in this case the system's) life and health. He felt very reassured that despite the drawbacks and difficulties, Earth and its occupants must be worth all his efforts. The planet performed a vital role beyond the more mundane view of little lives all too soon extinguished. Miriam found him particularly cheerful and easy to live with during this frenetic time, no matter his driven lack of sleep. He shared his thoughts with her and Sharnestia throughout. The Chief sometimes gave him a quizzical look or its equivalent in remote feedback but she never slowed in encouraging him to continue his research. She certainly wasn't going to nursemaid him.

Once or twice, without any particular goal in mind, he pondered the times when people had asked if he believed in God or if he was religious. People in Class One were less wary of the subject than their neighbours in the other Classes—as might be expected from those more degraded parallel worlds. In his world it was never a difficult or taboo line of thought and conversation, and yet still deserving of some delicacy. The religions of his Class were respected so long as they carried a central tone of sincerity. That was often as far as it went. Now, he must extend his reach.

He was dipping into something huge. If a double star could give birth to a solar system or nine, if it could eventually be responsible for this treasured world in all its layered complexities… then the new knowledge might help Mark James particularly, as stars and Sci-Fi most surely went together.

He also needed to integrate his understanding within the Christian context. The gospels of Class Four (the only place where such records had existed) were often embroidered with changes, as he knew enough from his earlier research. It was unsurprising that Jesus was at times 'verballed' in the Christian bible for what some groups would have believed to be the very best of reasons—to ensure survival and consolidation of the new religion in what had often been an ambiguous or hostile environment.

On the other hand, there was also evidence that the Jesus of the written gospels could be very short on compromise. For example, how many modern churches in *any* Class would advise the rich to sell all they owned and then tell them to distribute the proceeds to the poor? The bluntness and clarity of the messages suggested this was most likely Jesus the man, not some idealised or so-called politically correct substitute.

Ardax's musings were interrupted by a thought message from his leader. 'Have you meditated deeply on how to conduct your next stage?'

He hadn't. No need to reply, the Chief would have noted his instant response.

Meditation gave reward, more so with an advanced technique just released. It was brilliant, a gestalt, all the lines and forces whirling into a pattern. He sat quietly to hear/see/feel it resolve into an understanding of the next step. Sharnestia sent quiet applause.

As a result, new information and ideas started to become available.

For example, he was given the statement that, whichever was their home Class, *all humans were inconsistent* in thought, attitude and behaviour. The reason was bound up in the universal duality of forces. Ardax rather easily acknowledged this conclusion. If he honestly scanned his own actions, let alone those of others, he could only accept human inconsistency to be true. Another, almost incidental idea translated to his list of practising essentials: Don't be too quick to decide that you have the measure of whoever or whatever it is you want to pin down. Particularly at this early stage, proceed with caution.

Next, what about the current crop of rescue missions? Self-interrogation led Ardax to the sudden memory of an early lesson as a small boy: *Computers don't think for themselves; they do only as they're told.* So, no matter how cleverly the AI works, everything depends on the quality of the feed. Mostly, how do we ask for its help. Do we have the intelligence? Do we have the wisdom?

Even Class Four placed some importance on the spiritual element. That was cause for optimism, even if many of the results there were confused, mangled, perilous or utterly twisted interpretations.

For Ardax's purpose the nub of the matter soon became: Who was the man Jesus? Did or does anyone really know? How and from whence did he arrive? What stories did we tell ourselves and were they really adequate?

And shouldn't we re-think the ideas of our own Class just as we'd attempted to ameliorate the difficulties of the other three? Here was another admission of uncertainty, a step back into humility.

Ardax posted these thoughts to Sharnestia. Asking her permission to continue was no part of it. He wasn't seeking direction; she'd surely know direction had landed on him. There were two pressing goals, neither of them easy: To clarify the role of Jesus (Yeshua) across the Classes and to gain a far better grasp of the Sirian system, its nature and powers. Then, these two would need considerable integration.

Any rigorist worth the name needed to search for useful techniques and be able to apply them as appropriate. Still refreshed by the morning's meditation, Ardax came up with one deceptively simple, yet highly effective practice often mentioned in Christian teaching. It was the power of forgiveness.

Physics wasn't his strongest suit, but he could hardly forget that throughout Class Four, misdirected megajoules of energy, due to the endless expression of human grievances world-wide, were massive. (A monthly estimate equated it to a small-sized hydrogen bomb.) There was only one upside to this: should lack of forgiveness be a major factor in any Class, the continuing interplay of forces disturbed the status quo, thus ensuring change would occur over time. But it was far slower in producing beneficial effects compared to true forgiveness.

In trying to shine a light on Jesus, Ardax noted differences between what the Nazorean taught and demonstrated compared with, for example, the practices that grew up around the Greek gods in their various guises.

Greece gave birth to the first true nation. It still held mysteries, including Plato's description of the ancient war with Atlantis (enough to start its own believers vs unbelievers culture war). The Greek deities were archetypes, personifications of how universal planetary forces were believed to act, bringing blessing or misfortune, and giving humans clues as how best to cope with them. The Roman gods were similar. By contrast, Christianity was about accepting values endorsed by Jesus and according to him, imposed by the One God. His standout command was: 'Love one another'.

That exhortation made a big difference. History gave an early example:

There were an estimated 150,000 Christians scattered across the Roman Empire in CE 200. Yet in another hundred years this total had apparently increased some 20 times to around three million. A very likely reason was that a pandemic - the Plague of Cyprian, possibly as terrible as Ebola - spread across the Empire starting around CE 250. St. Cyprian, then Bishop of Carthage, kept the record. The plague was so ferocious that the population of Alexandria was estimated to have fallen from about 500,000 to 190,000. Yet a very likely benefit was that people's attitudes to such disasters went through a significant change. Christians were expected to show their love for God and their neighbours through acts of kindness to the sick and needy. The evidence suggested this had its effects during the pandemic; there was an attitude of community service that was hardly evident in earlier times. Another change was the significant Christian belief in the promise of life after death. Suffering on Earth was widely considered a test that helped believers reach heaven when they died. Together these two perspectives caused a difference. The pandemic encouraged these ideas to spread; it became more certain the new religion was here to stay.

Ardax shook his head, flicking his rat-tail. He found it strangely reassuring, especially whenever facing an inescapable negative. It was too obvious these Christian benefits were not destined to endure in their purity. Especially in Class Four; corruption of Christ's mission would eventually become widespread. Horrific things would be done in the name of the churches.

Yet there was at least one positive. Thanks to his focus on Class Four, Ardax remembered reading the Gospel of Matthew's teaching when Peter asked Jesus how often he should forgive a brother—seven times? And Jesus replied: 'Not up to seven but seventy times seven'. Even if not a totally genuine saying (there are echoes of Genesis 4:24 in the statement yet in that case applied to revenge not forgiveness) it was surely an honest attempt to present an essence of the Master's teachings. Most significantly, it was *people* who were being asked to forgive rather than putting responsibility for forgiveness on God. Ardax couldn't find mention of forgiveness being important when Cyprian was writing about the plague; but the adversary in that case was pestilence not humankind.

Grasping this insight cheered him for a while—although ongoing research and everyday experience pointed out that human forgiveness was an action or even only an ideal too easily ignored, passed over, left behind. (Especially in Class Four, even though that is where the Christian scriptures were located.) Also, who had ever properly defined *a sin?* While it was something that no-one wanted to be the injured party of, the perpetrator could be just as unhappy with the emergence of this event as the so-called victim.

Forgiveness as a value was rarely promoted or even spoken of publicly in Class Four. The term too easily became associated with weakness, a lack of resolve, perhaps an impractical ideal. For many, if one 'knew' the other party was guilty, to forgive that person was a retreat from the truth. To 'maintain the rage' was often considered acceptable. This was despite one recent Class Four Christian teaching focussing strongly on forgiveness. Comprehensive research by fellow rigorists had concluded that *A Course in Miracles* offered teachings worthy of deep consideration, reminiscent as it was of some Gnostic ideas along with its own brand of spiritual psychology.

Working his way through the subject, Ardax awoke after a somewhat disturbed night with these words in his head: 'Unforgiveness blocks self-knowledge.' His subconscious was getting involved, and he needed to upend a general unwillingness to delve into the Class Four Bible. (This was an old prejudice, based on his distaste for a bunch of books that he'd regarded as of dubious authenticity. There were historical spiritual records in Class One but because religion had developed differently here, the Christian bible remained an outlier.)

And so Ardax deliberately set aside time to ponder the many gospel teachings about forgiveness. The more he thought about it the more valuable the practice, stripped of all dogma, presented.

It wasn't too difficult, he decided: if I have negative emotions toward another, I cannot partition myself from those emotions. They impinge on me in direct proportion to what I have projected onto others. As an exercise, he decided to encapsulate this by setting out some clear principles.

Quite soon he had his list: (1) Forgiveness is in essence an internal act. It doesn't require any spoken or written confirmation. Therefore, each instance had a good chance of avoiding external interference or criticism. (2) There was benefit to both the forgiven person and the forgiver, because the act of forgiveness readjusts an error in perception. (3) This error is the persistent belief that we are all totally separate beings, due to our different physical appearances, personalities, actions, ethnicities, goals, needs and so on. (4) By contrast, a theme discernible across a swathe of religious and spiritual teachings, both ancient and modern, places focus on our essential, spiritual oneness. A person who chose to forgive would silently (and perhaps unknowingly) be affirming the fact of *a single, unifying living principle* without having to explain or convince anyone else. It could be seen as a healthy subtraction, divesting us of something intrinsically inaccurate and unworthy.

Ardax knew quite well that humans could and very often would be in opposition to each other, as would even souls. But the interactions of opposing attitudes, beliefs, feelings, was not in itself the problem. It was what we did with them.

Any policing action or other sanction taken against 'the perpetrator' need not rule out the benefit of genuine forgiveness. The real problem was the all-too frequent condemnations, the projections of guilt against the 'evildoer'. Such projection onto others could never rid us of our own turmoil, however deeply hidden. And from there, especially if not acknowledged, it must fester.

If I retain ongoing negative emotions toward another, Ardax decided, I cannot partition myself from those emotions—they impinge on me in direct proportion to what I've projected.

As he sat in the meditation room something shifted. A mental/emotional platform began dissolving, actually flaking away and he knew why. Could there be any real benefit in typecasting others as either 'good' or 'bad'? That old platform of belief drifted, scattered and could not re-assemble.

Yet there was still some push-back. Looking and feeling scratchy to him like a rusty chunk of wire mesh, the opposing view demanded to know if this forgiveness solution was not too 'soft', too impractical. He was weary of the argument and thankfully an answer appeared: there was support for that solution based on a sound scientific principle.

The principle was Bell's Theorem, Dr John Stewart Bell's seminal work applying to quantum mechanics. It told us that any two or more particles, whether separated by millimetres or even megaparsecs (an unimaginably long distance), can be associated or 'entangled'. Measurements performed on one particle instantaneously affect the state of the others. An inference might even be made that this says something about the connection between oneself and one's neighbour.

Bell's work had never been disproved despite numerous attempts and was described in 1975 by fellow physicist Henry Stapp, 11 years after Bell came up with his theorem, as 'The most profound discovery of science'. There it was, physics chasing Ardax again. (Mightn't there be a better description, a better word than 'physics' to encompass this wonderful, overarching way of explaining the universe?)

After an hour or two of pondering these ideas, Ardax felt a delicate sense of mental breeze brushing and integrating his brain; he'd had it before when experiencing new knowledge and understanding. Rather than write up yet another time-consuming report, he'd continue to act as his own guinea pig. With the suite of technologies at his disposal, all results would be recorded anyway. Game on, maintain the edge!

◆

Despite her cheerful personality, attractive appearance and penetrating mind, Carly had a rather ambiguous idea of herself. These plusses had never overcome some feelings of inferiority and an unwillingness to throw herself into quite the same mould as her peers. Beneath the happy exterior was a belief that she had yet to express something extraordinary, something that justified a dramatic feeling of self-worth. Now, left for a while to her own devices with some basic administrative work while her colleagues pursued their own lines of enquiry, Carly speculated on something that grew increasingly obvious: Alt. Histories was not exactly the tight professional group she had first thought! It was more like a bunch of enthusiasts where each struck out independently, yet ever willing to assist a comrade. And then from time to time, in response to some silent call, they'd all come together to correlate and celebrate their findings. This camaraderie only worked because everyone was individually driven to replace ignorance with knowledge. It helped ensure that the delicate seedlings of scholarship and intuition would not get trampled by bureaucracy before they could produce a worthwhile harvest.

It dawned on her: You didn't ask permission to probe what you knew begged for explanation; you simply stuck to the unwritten rules. *That's why she'd been so attracted to this career path.* Ardax was finding out about forgiveness and Carly was suddenly certain, without giving herself airs, that by taking a slightly different approach she'd soon be able to add another insight to his.

It wasn't long before she discovered the thing she hadn't known she'd been looking for.

The Sirian viewpoint was key: not some strange collection of 'off-world' ideas but a system of universal principles sustaining themselves by intricate interaction. Yet access to the Sirian knowledge could not be forced. One had to be humble, await instruction. Carly remembered having briefly studied Sufi practice and the phrase; 'Stand tall in this world, bow in the next' resonated with her. The 'next world' did not mean a dimension beyond the grave but rather a more subtle, spiritual realm. And for that, humility was always and completely appropriate.

Having applied the correct attitude, she discovered Sirius taught that Free Will was all but impossible! Humans were each born with a certain pre-programming that drove them on a specific path through life. On the other hand, that person's own efforts could then help to round out the soul's more creative and wholesome proclivities.

There was supporting evidence from Bell's Theorem: If as it suggested, there could be no such things as 'separate parts', then it also infers that events being autonomous happenings is an illusion.

Finally, after a good deal of studying the transcripts, meditating and awaiting answers, Carly was rewarded with this Sirian statement: *'We trust that you will see the non-imputation of any blame or any stigma, no matter what activity a human being is indulging in. No-one may criticise...'*

Galactic wisdom! She noticed the warm connection in her chest. It spread around her body and at the same time, rippled throughout her inner sense of self. It settled something that had needed settling. Feeling relieved without knowing why, she loudly asked herself and the rest of the world in general: if that very clear statement wasn't promoting forgiveness, what the heck else would you call it?

28

ANSWERS AND QUESTIONS

SIMON WAS ITCHING to be off and his impatience was contagious. There was, I reasoned, nothing to keep me in Samaria. If we were to run the gauntlet of the Galilee, where Roman garrisons were tougher on Jews because resistance to General Vespasian had been a messier and far more bitter affair than in Samaria, I wanted to get the ordeal over with as soon as possible.

Varus and Cub spent their last day at the Place of Sacrifice in carving wooden toys for the timid cow-herd children who brought cheeses for Helen to distribute among us. Painstakingly, the two soldiers shaped dolls with the points of military knives. It was a suitably ironical comment on the importance of weaponry.

Not for the first time, I was aware of a sense of unreality up on Gerizim. We literally lived above the tension and misery of the rest of Israel. I didn't want a privileged position. Something within me said that I should be suffering or fighting along with my countrymen, even though the thought scared me.

'You don't really believe that you aren't making a contribution?' Tarquin chided me. 'Fighting isn't difficult. I've done enough of it myself—decurions can rarely stay in the rear. Soldiering becomes a job like any other. When your blood boils, or even if you only think of next pay-day, of staying alive or maintaining the honour of the legion, it's not hard to kill and keep on killing. Men have been doing it since time began.'

We were engaged in packing baskets with a few provisions for our journey; cheese and barley cakes, a little fruit and some groats. (The Master had sent out his disciples to preach with nothing but their faith and the clothes they stood up in; but Tarquin felt that a secret mission in wartime allowed for a little more preparation.) We squatted against a rough-hewn stone column at the entrance to the Offering Temple - not nearly as gracious as Greek architecture or as imposing as that of the Romans, but honest enough in its intention of honouring the One God.

Tarquin's big nostrils dilated as he drew in a long, slow breath. He spoke in a quieter, clearer voice. 'To hate and kill a body, even in defence of your nation, is to believe that bodies determine the extent of victory and defeat. Can life be contained by these little forms of arms and legs, wondrous as they may be?

'Attacking an army is a kind of compliment in that you acknowledge its power.' He shook his head, almost impatiently. 'Power has never ultimately rested in the armies of this world, or in anything else physically present. Life isn't troubled by appearances; however grandiose they may seem. The Unspeakable alone empowers life. It gives rise to Light, and Light is the true strength.'

He gave me a piercing look. 'You have seen too much, and understood too much, to go back to the dimmed vision that substitutes for seeing! When we dismiss our certainty of evil, we see a very different world. Yet there must always be difficulties to overcome. At the right time, sickness is correct, insanity is a required state, death of a newborn should be an important step forward for the baby's parents. Pain and difficulty are powerful teachers; only thus can spirit grow and temper itself.'

I prepared myself for more discussion. 'I think I know why my

Master told us to turn the other cheek. He didn't mean we should be weak-kneed pacifists. If we did not fight to resist evil, we might prove to ourselves that belief in evil is powerlessness, not strength.' I regarded the Roman, my thoughts confused. 'But I'm a Jew and I take no pleasure in my country being torn to pieces by armies that manage a very good appearance of power, even if in truth they don't actually wield any.'

Then Tarquin laid his hands on my shoulders. 'Don't distress yourself with these matters. If you would help your nation, we'll take the swiftest passage out of Israel to the sea and bring the teachings of the Anointed to Italy, power centre of the Empire. That's where they will do the most good, because from there they'll spread across the civilised world.'

That was what we decided. We left at sundown. I was surprised at how my heart wrenched to leave the Place of Sacrifice. I somehow loved that mountain-top and its sad old temple with the mixed memories of conflict, death, pain, fear and enlightenment.

Lydia and Rachel gave Rebekah a subdued farewell, but I saw the tears in all their eyes. Praefect Barius made Varus and Cub tidy up their gear and polish their armour in readiness for the long walk back to barracks. Varus found Tarquin and, stammering, thanked the decurion-major for saving his life. Later, Tarquin said Varus had promised he would make sure that the troops heard about how he'd cheated death - dangerous as the undertaking might prove - because he was convinced that such was the will of the Gods. 'But don't forget the real lesson' Tarquin impressed on him. 'The body of the strongest soldier is at the mercy of a dozen forms of death. Comfort your comrades not with tales of apparent sorcery, but with the knowledge that life and the body are not the same.'

Tarquin showed concern as the soldiers adjusted their sandalled footwear. He went over to Barius and spoke bluntly. 'How will you explain yourselves?'

The praefect regarded him with steady grey eyes as though this was some camp parade-ground and none of the events at Gerizim had ever occurred. 'If the security boss of Samaria can't cook up a believable story, then no-one can' said Barius. 'But I will expect your co-operation in not getting detained, because I'll report that John Mark the Nazorean and Simon the Magus committed suicide by throwing themselves into a ravine when trapped by my special unit near the Offering Temple.'

'With God's help, we'll do what we can,' said Tarquin. Barius lowered his voice. 'I can't cover for you, Tarquin. That's stretching it too far. If you'd been killed, thcy would cxpect your body. I'll say you were lost in the skirmish - just don't expect them to be taken in by that explanation.' Tarquin understood, very clearly, how the Romans treated deserting legionaries in wartime. Barius continued, and now he lost the easy confidence that goes with command: 'Stay out of sight, lie low for a few weeks at least; look, be very careful...' Tarquin silenced him with an embrace; the praefect in his imperial uniform succumbing to his subordinate who was now wearing only a simple garment purchased from the cow-herds.

Joseph decided to join forces with old Zadok. They would strike east in search of a suitable community of believers. 'This land has gone crazy' Zadok replied when I asked how a Samaritan could leave his traditions behind. 'I don't go easily' he growled, and I could see he spoke the truth, 'but I've watched enough goings-on in Gitta to see how the old ways are being turned inside out. We've more chance of peace in the clean air of the desert.'

The last meal on the mountain was a quiet one. We nursed our own thoughts, while at the same time there was a feeling of great kinship and the shy smiles of those who carry a richer complement of emotion than they care to express.

Tarquin led us in a prayer - Romans, Samaritans, Judaean, German and Persian - in this fashion: '0 God, the One God who is God of all life, keep us in mind of our true identity. We may believe we are either free to do whatever we wish, or we are weak, fallible and full of sin. But we cannot change our reality or yours. We made up a dream in a futile attempt to prove we were separate from you and each other. We give thanks that your Spirit (here Tarquin used the word *Ruach*) was sent to awaken us and lovingly teach us to lay aside such foolishness. We give thanks for the time we have spent together here, and the miracles which you expressed through us to show us what is true. We ask your grace to bless us with Truth as we travel; and we seek your guidance always.'

We sat in silence until Rachel went and knelt at Tarquin's feet. She asked him to tell us about the rabbi Jesus' resurrection - 'before you go away and we can't get any more questions answered'.

The light of the setting sun struck Tarquin's very Roman nose, his thick eyebrows and big forehead. He was so still that after a while, Rachel repeated her question. He reached down and took her hands. 'I heard you. You might think that being a Roman soldier, I wouldn't know about Jewish beliefs. But I had to learn something of the local religion to carry out my duties. I had heard, Rachel, how the people wondered whether Jesus' much-reported resurrection could possibly be true. The hopeful said yes, whereas those who were too burdened by the war and the world believed it was only a fairy-tale. Then there are the Sadducees who don't believe there is such a thing as resurrection anyway'. His glance flashed over us. 'Not so?'

Rachel nodded. 'But you know the truth, don't you?'

He laughed. 'The truth is in *you*, otherwise you could never hear it from me, or anyone else. So, listen to me, and hear your own inner knowledge. The resurrection never happened.'

My jaw tightened. What did this mean?

'Don't play with us, Tarquin.' It was Helen speaking.

'Aha. Then I throw the ball to you, wise lady. Be so kind as to share your insights with us.'

Simon went back on his heels as Helen sat up straighter. Something went between Helen and Tarquin as used to go between her and Simon.

Helen hesitated, but only at first. 'Well, perhaps what Tarquin says is true. There wasn't a resurrection really. It was a powerful event, but symbolic...'

'Helen!' I couldn't contain myself. 'You don't know what you're saying. The whole of Christianity rests on the foundation of the resurrection.'

Tarquin held up his hand. 'Let her finish.'

'Relax, brother' Helen said with surprising warmth. 'We two have several times found it hard to successfully blend our purposes' - here she smiled knowingly - 'but I see your worth and I am your friend.'

'Then explain what you mean' I replied, still a little embarrassed.

She stood up. 'Listen to this, everyone, it's important. It depends on how we define resurrection.'

'Hmmp, that's how your get around it' said Zadok. 'This is simple wordplay! Don't waste our time with such cleverness.'

Tarquin answered him. 'It goes well beyond words. For example, I did *not* resurrect Varus. He was very close to death, yet I was just in time to assist the living spark of life to regain his body. Once the vehicle is gone it is truly gone and no miracle will assist or change that. Be aware in this situation we are talking only of the flesh, not the spirit.

'Jesus was not resurrected, and for a very good reason. What we call death couldn't touch the Anointed and he came to demonstrate that we cannot die either. There must come a time for each of us when bodies stop working and fall into decay, but life itself never ends. His body hung on a Roman cross for a while, but that ultimately had no effect on *Ruach*'.

Rachel asked timidly, 'And what is the resurrection, then?'

Tarquin bent his head toward hers. 'In a different sense, and not wanting to muddle you, Jesus *was* resurrected. We achieve a resurrection when we awaken to our real nature. Rabbi Jesus came to know himself and thus he was reawakened or resurrected as God's Son. To be fully resurrected is to become Anointed as Jesus was.'

This sounded better to me. 'Oh yes' I said. 'Thomas told me, the Master promised that when we came into an understanding of our true nature, we would know - a glory of surprise within our heart of hearts - that we are indeed the Sons of the Living Father.'

'Are you resurrected, Tarquin?' Rachel asked shyly, squeezing his knees with her fingers.

He shook his head. 'I am still in the tomb.' He stroked her hair. 'Yet I hear the angel knocking for us all to arise. Once resurrection or awakening has occurred, there's not much reason for a person to remain in this world, although his presence will continue to be felt by those who stay behind.'

'There's one more point I'd like to clarify' said Zadok, 'and then we should leave before we're stuck on the mountain when the light fails. There was a persistent rumour - you'll have come across it, Simon - that Jesus was born of a virgin. What's the meaning of such superstitious nonsense?'

'I can answer that one' I said. 'Sometimes, when we have a feeling that were near to something miraculous, something holy, we can lose the miracle by being led astray into the merely sensational.'

Zadok pulled at his beard. 'You've certainly lost me, Judaean.'

'It's like this' I said. 'In the Book of Isaiah, as all Judaeans know, there are prophesies about the Messiah. One says: "Therefore the Lord Himself shall give you a sign, behold, an *almah* shall conceive and bear a son and shall call his name Immanuel." The problem arose when a Greek translator wanted to use the passage on behalf of Christianity. *Almah* means a woman whose womb has not yet born fruit but there is no Greek equivalent for the word. So *parthenos* was used as the closest approximation. And that means the same as the Hebrew *bethulah* - literally a virgin.

'It shouldn't have confused people, but many wanted to believe, in a time of trouble and approaching war, that the Messiah was as supernatural as possible. The whole story was helped along by the idea that on attaining the Christ nature, the Master was no longer tainted by the world, not doomed to the wheel of rebirth. Innocence is a characteristic of the mind, but the common error is to ignore the mind and concentrate on the body.

'Paul tried to set his followers straight when he said not to give heed to fables' I added. 'Yet the virgin birth story seems to have taken root, no matter how hard I've worked to eradicate it.'

Tarquin shrugged. 'If we are to be gardeners of the spirit, we must not use our energy in trying to pull out weeds. We should cultivate the soil properly, then the true crops will flourish and the rest will die out of its own accord. In any case' he gave me a questioning look, 'who's to say that a virgin did not give birth? With God, most things are possible. And now' he said, gently setting Rachel aside, 'we will do as Zadok says. Rebekah, Helen, Simon, Mark, step this way! We travel according to how the Spirit leads us. As the rest of you leave, be mindful that distance cannot stand between the Sons of God.'

I walked quickly then slowed at the edge of the clearing and looked back. The other participants in the greatest drama of my life were only silhouettes. Here was evidence of my physical eyes; inner vision had quite another story to tell. And even that was bound to be far from complete.

29

CLASS ONE BRAINS TRUST

ARDAX CONTINUED HIS investigation still enthused. Coinciding with his interest in forgiveness, the associated concept of sin wouldn't leave him alone. Supposedly simple, there was something 'sticky' about it. Delving into that little-used three-letter word might unwrap into something important. He needed to find the starting point, the right access.

He began by taking note of what he considered a typically ponderous definition: 'Sin: an <u>immoral</u> act considered to be a transgression against divine law'. It was a word not often heard in general conversation, no matter which Class you looked at. (Reacting against the solemnity of dictionaries, he personalised his investigation by nicknaming it 'my sin*full* project'.)

Then Sharnestia came up with something helpful from her early studies into Sirian science. Much of the material had seemed obscure to her but she wouldn't let any part go unheeded. Apparently bland or obvious statements could suddenly take on a depth of meaning. Using the clearest energy connection she'd attained so far, she discovered that sin was described by Sirius as a constant in the human world, yet not exactly as the churches would describe it.

Ardax followed his own route: Start with the obvious. The word 'sin' if used at all nowadays mostly applied to 'shameful wrongdoing' associated with Christian confessional practice. In such cases sin required penance.

He'd previously spent time reviewing the Sirian concept of duality and perhaps like others before him, assumed sinful acts might be explained as a negative energy polarity in a person's life. But he felt immediately uncomfortable: the straightforward description wouldn't do. Miriam came to his rescue.

They were seated at their favourite garden table drinking juice made from their own plums; the weather was good, butterflies coming in mini swarms around the shrubbery. Miriam, keen gardener, was able to report that her green vegetables and berry patch were doing particularly well this year. Ardax however was regretting the way he'd loudly failed two of his first-year students that day; having taken them to task about their slackness in studies. He'd never done it before! Perhaps he was working too hard, overstretching himself, not enough sleep? Now he was feeling guilty. Miriam quizzed him: 'I thought you had full authority. You didn't have to pass them.'

'I remember very much like the same thing happening to me some 40 years ago. I flunked an important exam, and the drubbing down wasn't pleasant. How did I manage to lose my composure so easily?' He had the feeling of being adrift.

'Just take a minute, drop down in energy; breathe slow and deep'. Still in her old gardening clothes she adjusted her floppy hat, closed eyes and bent her head. He watched the butterflies keep coming. The atmosphere in the garden began to soften. He sighed and let some of his tension drain. Miriam quite soon had an answer.

'Of course Ardie, you're aware you've sinned. But here's the point I don't think we've ever noticed before; *you* feel it even if your students didn't or don't. The nub of the thing is that when we are in that fragile state, *that* dislocation is sin, it's *our* sin even if we manage to cover it up and forget it, even if we project it onto others, and even if no-one else knows anything about it. Sin hangs on you—or me or anyone who gets to that point. So many spiritual paths are involved in trying to overcome the self-harm, the loss of peace. There's a lot on the subject to be found in that teaching called *A Course in Miracles* we were looking into a couple of months ago.' She called it up on her communicator:

And read it out: 'This world is an attempt to prove your innocence, while cherishing attack. Its failure lies in that you STILL feel guilty, though without understanding WHY. Effects are seen as separate from their source and seem to be beyond you to control or to prevent. What is thus KEPT apart can never join.' Miriam wrinkled her brows in concentration. There was something else, if only she could catch and clarify it…

'And…Oh yes, I have to be ready for more while the energy's still with me.' She moved faster than might have been expected for her 73 years; Miriam vanished into the house and entered the meditation room. Ardax sat on the garden bench and waited while the butterfly clouds reduced then faded. At the same time the weight in him seemed ready to lift, so he sent it on its way.

He was almost asleep when she returned, serene. 'I was given an understanding Ardie, there may be more but here's what I found out: No-one has to tell us about sin, we know it all quite intimately whether we are actually conscious of that or not. It all fits rather neatly with what you were feeling and the passage I read out to you just before. There really is *no such thing* as sin despite our universal belief in it.' Miriam almost looked pleased with herself. Then let it drop as she continued.

'I was informed about that, as well as why we experience this malaise, where it comes from. Because we are incomplete in ourselves! Each human and their soul are to some degree separated in 99.99 per cent of the population and this sense of sin is the unfortunate result. It takes place in all Classes, though as we might expect it is more worrying the further you move away from Class One. To experience that separation from one's soul further implies a sense of separateness from our fellow humans. An important part of our task will be to help others bridge the gap. I was also told this cannot be fully achieved without the help of extra-terrestrial sources; solar and even pure Sirian energy. Heaven knows—I believe that's a precise statement by the way—how big a task lies ahead and how long it will take.'

◆

Ardax knew he'd been on a tiring run. Yet uplifted by progress made, he put in another eight-hour day at the Institute. When he'd finally had enough, rather than go straight home he decided to take a break at the rigorist lounge where you could fix a drink of your choice. It was definitely a hot chocolate moment.

Getting all the ingredients right, including the cinnamon and honey, he sat down in the corner where colourful bird holograms floated near the ceiling. Minutes later his old friend Roberto came by. Both preferred their own space over gossipy socialising so for a while they sat together in comfortable near silence. But it didn't last. Roberto had just checked out his colleague's most recent conclusions that were now available on the distribution system and was keen to ask what might be an awkward question.

'What struck me, Ardie' he said, 'is your conclusion: that forgiveness is of such great importance. Therefore, we wouldn't want Jesus to contradict it, would we? But if we reference the Class Four bible and accept Luke 14:26 was an accurate report, where Jesus insisted that any would-be followers had to hate their family, how could such a statement be justified?'

Ardax nodded and gave a somewhat weary smile. 'On the surface it sounds pretty tetchy. But it depends on your interpretation.' He brought up the biblical reference on his device. 'Here's a reasonably accurate translation: "If anyone comes to me and does not hate his own father and mother and wife and children and brothers and sisters, yes, and even his own life, he cannot be my disciple."' Robbo nodded. 'Pretty clear, isn't it?'

'Yes Robbo, I'll give you my understanding. We shouldn't take those words too literally. But families always *do* create their own thought-forms. Those thought-forms might be supposedly helpful or unhelpful, yet inevitably they're disrupters to the individual's unique path through life.'

Roberto sat back, tugged his neat white beard. 'That's right, the *thought-form*—haven't heard that term mentioned in a long while. Came across it working in Class Two; always considered it apposite. Their science community and our intervention resulted in the expression being accepted as a good label for when a mental creation grows powerful enough to generate a life of its own.'

'Quite so' said Ardax. 'Families create their unique, living psychological profiles. A disciple, especially a follower of one as powerfully spiritual as Jesus, cannot afford to hang onto these very strong if subtle impressions. Perhaps "hate" is an unfortunate label. Yet one way or another, the psychology of the past - of one's upbringing - must be disposed of. To serve a Master may be superficially appealing; nevertheless, it comes with a price. Think of the apostle Peter who according to the Class Four biblical record considered himself utterly faithful only until his life was on the line. He couldn't manage to pull together full commitment when Jesus was arrested. True spirituality is mostly the toughest game in town.' He sighed and turned to his friend with a rueful smile. 'Under similar circumstances, I wonder whether we would do any better.'

◆

Having offered silent thanks for the latest door opening onto knowledge, Ardax was sure he could keep up momentum with what he was privately willing, for the sake of a little extra light-heartedness, to call the most profound angle of his mission The Sirian *Dog's Breakfast*. (A popular saying in Class One proclaimed that levity was to research, as yeast was to baked goods.)

Sharnestia too, was on a roll. Her latest revelation about the Sirian teaching meant that before Ardax could continue any further with his researches, she'd called a meeting that all Alt. Historians were required to attend, once more, *in person*.

'This Sirian knowledge needs to be studied and internalised with the benefit of group intensity and synchronisation' she explained in her call-out. 'There is a great deal for us to understand, and we will be much more effective if we can imbibe and use this knowledge on a group basis, as well as individually. The very fact of us all holding the awareness of this body of work in solidarity, is designed to ensure greater effectiveness.

'As you know, we are engaged in an attempt to better understand and applicate the teachings of Yeshua, Jesus the Christ, the Anointed One. This had for a long time been left out of our most serious studies into spiritual practice, partly because we did not have the biblical record that remained with Class Four. We always have to re-boot our willingness to look at anything from any source that may genuinely assist in developing better social outcomes. Recently we have been particularly inspired to seek more from our growing understanding of Sirius including the double star's broader systemic range.'

Having decided that most of the wider astronomical information had already been adequately dealt with, Sharnestia explained how ongoing sessions would concentrate more closely around the effects on Earth and its sister planets in the solar system, due to the undoubted influence and overlordship of the Sirian star system.

For this latest meeting, the Chief wore her favourite if well-worn indigo trouser-suit—never keen on acting the glamour queen. As the rigorists arrived and settled in, the meeting room sported soothing 3D visuals floating around, the kind you might find in a dental surgery or an eye clinic. Ardax suspected Sharnestia had decided to get things started in an unusual manner—that quirky sense of humour. Soon everyone invited was settled, and private discussions had more or less petered out. Not saying anything but giving the briefest of smiles, the Chief mentally initiated the session then sat down in a corner.

There was, very unusually, a voice broadcast. It started with a careful explanation that all science must rest, or would hope to rest, on certain fundamental axioms upon which later, extended propositions could and would be founded. From the streams of accepted knowledge, one or more compatible resulting ideas, or even completely new ones, could well be added, taking their results into various fields of human interest and endeavour.

With the application of some ingenuity including further development of existing technologies, there might well be any number of new accomplishments resulting from these theories.

Science acted in the belief or at least the hope that its conclusions would remain stable and results continue to prove workable. The voice-over noted that despite difficulties, the rollout of new ideas and applications was generally considered 'so far, so good', although in continuing practice things were bound to get more complicated.

The voice became more sombre. It pointed out one or two examples of a single great benefit that introduced one or more negative results. These somewhat or greatly outweighed the original positive.

A few more instances of all the above were then delivered and commented upon.

By this time, a good deal of discomfort was evidenced in the room. Increasingly, the shuffling of sitting positions: The quizzical looks: The whispered comments. Why were we going into this time-wasting kindergarten stuff? And only using audio? Two of the younger Alt. Historians, Rolleston and Imohere, were trying out their newly acquired telepath ability: 'Wot No Great Graphics?' was Imo's attempt at a critical review; by default it was broadcast to anyone in the room who happened to be on receive.

Sharnestia waited a few more minutes. She nodded to herself. A suitable tension embraced the room. The Esoterics Chief stood, walked slowly to the front. For barely a second her fingers brushed her golden hair. She put that hand down again quickly as though it had acted without the proper permission, looked around the room and drew breath.

'Rigorists!' she beamed. 'Thank you for your patience! I want to bring your attention to something—a belief we have laboured under for a very long time. Now we have the opportunity to accept our error and in doing so, we'll gain the benefit of an important new perspective.

'We go back to ancient understandings, poetic ideas. That's because despite our best efforts, science still faces the problem of reductionism.

There is we should also admit, the stumbling block of our belief in the possession of a superior science. Don't we think we are all so much wiser, better off than those of the *higher* Classes?' A pause (yes, it seemed they'd somewhat appreciated her little joke.)

'I do hope you'll pardon me for that brief audio presentation—for trying to teach you, my dear group of grandmothers (and grandfathers) to suck eggs. What we just heard was simply a quick reminder of how our sciences have done so much good while still producing various levels of difficulty. Now we stand at the beginning of something different. Nevertheless, it doesn't diminish what we and our predecessors were able to achieve. We will of course continue our attempts to maintain the well-established goal of advancing our knowledge and promoting a more fulfilling existence for everyone.

'Yet it is particularly exciting to become aware that now we must move in a mostly unexplored direction, to include a more accurate perspective.' She gave a soft cough, angling for the take-off.

'The magicians, the poets and pixies, those who stood outside of our science—use whatever labels you prefer—nevertheless have something important to teach us. And now we've broken through the veil. Or better, we've had the veil dispersed for us by our Sirian guides. Our understanding has moved quickly as a result. I remind you that everything we know, however unlikely it may seem as well as challenging to internalise, is totally dependent on Sirius, the double star and its complex of nine solar systems. Which of course includes all the energies and lifeforms on planet Earth.

'But even this can be broken down further to its most essential point, the very start of everything everywhere. We can go there now.'

She had followed Ardax's research virtually in real time and was aware of his conclusion about the value of forgiveness resting on the One Life, with Miriam's high-grade help and Carly's brilliantly intuitive grasp adding to the mix. It was pleasing to experience their enthusiasm, their mental and spiritual reach. And in understanding his decision to go under the radar of strict officialdom, she'd cover for Ardax; his conclusions were dovetailed into much the same place she herself had reached.

Her latest announcement would only go a little further down the same track. Yet it was highly significant. She knew now, with fullness of heart and mind that reality was more *one* than even Ardax had grasped. The Chief hesitated, looked around again. As if including the room in an idea that might almost go beyond the reach of words, she gathered herself and in doing so crouched down ever so slightly. Then gave a clear stage-whisper: 'The entire universe, every galaxy, every star, every planet, every cell and protoplasm of course, every molecule, every atom is *alive*.'

30

A MOST LIVELY DEBATE

THERE WAS TROUBLE in paradise.

A delegation of rigorists covering each of the four Classes had successfully applied for Council's blessing to discuss their concerns with the Chief. Tireless research was one thing, the building of creative new perspectives was laudable, but expecting instant acceptance for the concept of a 'living universe' was a tad too far. Many contrary arguments were assembled, and several had already been agreed to by a majority of the dissidents. A subsidiary complaint was that the intentions, methodology and findings of rigorist Ardax had not been disseminated on a regular basis according to Institute guidelines; thus impeding proper overview and feedback.

Sharnestia was surprised to hear she would have to explain herself. But on reflection, what she'd said - without argument or evidence - did justify a considered response. 'Slow ahead' she told herself.

A new meeting took place in one of the outdoor pond rooms, adorned with ferns and fragrantly ventilated while protected from the weather by the energy equivalent of tough UV-sensitive plexiglass. Council would often commission this holiday environment for the more robust sessions. Each delegate would choose a floater with adjustable environmental controls; discussion could be verbal or telepathic depending on the focaliser's choice of meeting dynamics. Even though unruly behaviour was strictly off-limits, honesty and openness were expected. Yet only one person could speak at a time, enforced by discrete technology.

Prior to the meeting the Chief called in help from Miriam and Ardax. The three of them agreed that her task was to better explain her personal acceptance of a living universe. After all, Sharnestia's field was where all manner of once-fringe ideas had become more or less mainstream. Miriam said it would be easier for the Chief to convince her peers—since 'exact science' was now often tied to intuition—if she could find the words to express her genuine sense of inner knowing, as much as by any cerebral argument.

The cerebral arguments came first, as no doubt they should. Several people lined up to make their points, have their say. Although many theories existed, all the early speakers had to accept that scientists were unable to agree on how life began. Several competing hypotheses had been proposed over many years, yet nothing stood out. Scientists not only disagreed about which chemical components of life came first, but even where on Earth life first arose.

One of the younger rigorists (yes it was Imohere) pointed out the accepted foundation of life was matter showing certain attributes including responsiveness, growth, metabolism, energy transformation and reproduction. The next speaker posed the difficult question: which of these many processes that take place in living organisms had emerged first? After this there were a range of opinions about how life appeared. There was something of a consensus among the dissidents that material life most likely got started being powered by currents of electrically charged protons within alkaline vents on the planet's seabed. But none of this was near the crux of the matter, nothing specifically dealing with Sharnestia's claim of universal life. It had to be dealt with.

Luckily when the time came, she was able to stand up in the floater without losing her balance.

'Thank you ladies and gentlemen for your contributions to this discussion. I see that we are still at the very early stages of our adventure into the extent of life. Because as you might recall, I am talking about it as a principle that extends *infinitely*, which of course includes everything beyond our small planet.

'Then let us go back to basic physics. The good work done concerning all Classes by rigorists Carly and Ardax encouraged me to turn my (and your) attention to Bell's Theorem, it's a typical piece of algebraic complexity. As you may recall, Dr John Bell proposed that either the statistical predictions of quantum theory are false or the principle of local causes is false. A few years after his claim was published, Clauser and Freedman were able to validate the relevant statistical predictions of quantum mechanics. (We should remind ourselves that decades of research and application in more than one Class have shown that such statistical predictions applying to quantum mechanics are *always* correct.) And some years after that, Alain Aspect refined our understanding of the importance of these findings. He conducted an experiment to determine action and consequent reaction between two events and to test for local hidden variables. Aspect was able to demonstrate that even though the settings of the measuring devices could be changed faster than any information could be transmitted from one device to the other, including even at the fastest possible speed—the speed of light—it had no effect on the results. Simply put, local causes made no difference. Or in other words, we can quite legitimately use the delightful phrase that "locality fails".

'Bell's Theorem showed us a world we might never have thought possible, a continuum of connectedness in which we are forced very seriously to consider there are no such things as "separate parts" anywhere. Instead, all is a holism, a oneness. From there we can investigate further, though most of that is beyond my intention today.

'However, another physicist, Henry Stapp, had some pertinent remarks to make following the result of Aspect's experiment.

'You might remember Stapps' quite brilliant assertion that "Everything we know about Nature is in accord with the idea that the fundamental process of Nature lies *outside* of space-time…but generates events that can be located *in* space-time." I very much like that word, Nature. For our purposes it is highly appropriate, perhaps even more apposite than that other word Universe. Because after all, what could be more natural than All That Is? This Nature has its own methods of achievement and as long as we don't try to interfere too much with it, we should be able to improve many of the things we do now; as well as accomplish many more things that so far, we haven't been able to manage at all. The word Nature gives the perfectly normal impression of something alive. And as you all know by now,' she gave a broad grin, 'I say that it most certainly *is* alive.

'You may recall if you have studied the implications of Bell's work, one likely consequence of his Theorem is that what we call Free Will as we define it does not—cannot—exist. These are the deep waters we are navigating now.

'Another point I should make, concerns the reference above to the speed of light. Those of you accustomed to communicating telepathically, including right here and now, will know that superluminal (faster than light) speeds are nothing special or extraordinary with this particular comms modality. We are normalising higher physics sometimes without necessarily recognising it!

'In an attempt to popularise science, we have the classical step-by-step explanations of various phenomena beloved of schoolteachers. But this won't work easily for quantum mechanics because classical logic frequently doesn't apply. We need to develop different ways of thinking—or unthinking—that by-bypasses those mental methods that are so useful to us in other situations. Here lies our challenge as we move forward.

'It is but a short path from what I've been talking about here, to understand that no matter what discrete events, forces and/or bodies one might identify as belonging to this Nature - this universe - they together are the expression of one limitless organism that commands, creates and is fully aware of whatever occurs. No doubt you recall Einstein's dislike of non-deterministic aspects of quantum mechanics which he expressed with his heartfelt statement: "God doesn't play dice with the universe". But what if the universe is simply *the complete*, the total idea and manifestation of God? Then no-one plays dice with anyone. The infinite universe is awareness, embodied and unembodied. Seeing it from that viewpoint, the drama and conflict we experience everywhere is perhaps real in essence but not necessarily real in experience—or maybe it's the other way around? Not permitting those two polarities of existence and thus of consciousness to collapse, is the most vital requirement. Here is a road less travelled but we are being given an opportunity to walk down it now.'

The Chief stopped for only a moment or two. Then: 'Another important comment, if I may.' She looked around and saw she retained the room's attention. Only the soothing low hiss of the pond's reticulation system and some very gentle lapping of the pond water could be heard.

'A major difficulty with our standard scientific definitions of "life" that some of you started describing today, is that this so-called singular life has not appeared anywhere except on Earth. The many attempts to find living matter in other parts of the solar system or in the greater cosmos, unfailingly get caught up in the expectation that any such must manifest identically to our local Earthly life, the specific phenomenon that some of you have so carefully described. But shouldn't we rather and more logically anticipate discovering life which is concordant with the particular environment, especially its range of wavelength that we happen to be observing? By not doing so, we have searched but most unsurprisingly, we have not found.

'Such elementary lack of discrimination on our part is simply an inability to recognise for example, that while all of our sister planets in the solar system are by design closely-interacting neighbours of Earth, their versions of "life" cannot and will not present identically to ours. The Sirian teachers are explaining many things we did not earlier understand, including that each of the nine planets are in pattern with our human major organs. Do our lungs look or operate like our liver? Should we expect the thyroid to be the same as the thymus? The life forms in and on the other planets will be as uniquely different and diverse as the many organs, hormones and energy pathways that can be found in various parts of our own bodies. I understand it's a very bold idea to many of us, but please don't think this relationship between body parts and processes that I've just introduced to the discussion was given only for some kind of whimsical or dramatic effect.' She paused again, for a few seconds as if consulting a hidden map. 'And the same principle of relating life to environment should apply to any other extra-terrestrial territory.

'Fellow rigorists, all of you here have done the work, contributed the input that has led to the unfolding understanding of patterning on a scale never considered before. It's been my pleasure to bring forward our best, our latest understanding of this remarkable relationship.

'The planets of our system are indeed in pattern with humanity and with each other. So, I'm going to repeat myself. Every one of the nine planets is equivalent in its energy function—I emphasise that description—to one specific organ of a human being. This beautifully illustrates the precise design that is inherent here and, I believe we will discover, everywhere.

'People have different viewpoints as to what constitutes an organ. For our purposes we have ascertained the following, based on the principal of those organs being essential to bodily existence: these are the blood, kidneys, liver, lungs, digestive system, heart, marrow, skin and finally, flesh and muscles. Therefore, nine distinct organs represented by nine planets. What we don't yet know is which planet corresponds to which specific organ. That knowledge may or may not be made available.

'We cannot say how life will present itself outside of this solar system. Yet I remain convinced that there *is* life everywhere because our work points to a living universe being the fundamental reality. Our current responsibility is humble acceptance. The rest is for the future.

'And why would we not suppose "life" exists elsewhere (everywhere) when we currently have intelligent communications coming from a place as distant and as enormously different to our planetary home, as the star Sirius?'

She could sense gaining plenty of traction so far, but it was important to address that problem of keeping people up to date. This time, she was sure she'd been right to let Ardax plough ahead, against needing to maintain the protocol for sharing each individual step, a rule she'd actually helped create. Sharnestia took a big breath. 'Now, for an apology. Some of you have felt excluded from the processes and results of our work. The conclusions I've outlined here are my own, although I've had plenty of help from several of you and I'll specifically acknowledge those people in further follow-ups.

'A wise teacher of meditation once said if you plant a seed, you don't want to keep digging it up to see how it's developing. And that seems to work best for us in this Department. We prefer not to release our findings until we are pretty sure the seedling has properly germinated.

'I knew Ardax was on a roll and needing clear air to put his thoughts together. His recent work didn't specifically address what I've been talking about today, it was more to do with spiritual ideas coming from the Yeshua/Christian background. I assure you we shall soon have much more to report on that topic and when we do, I hope it will be sufficient for you all to see the connection between those two zones of knowledge.'

She sat down in the floater, a bit wobbly in more ways than one but satisfied. After a few more questions, answers and discussion there were no more objections. Less a win than a teaching triumph.

Viewing from his office Ardax sent congratulations, knowing her position had come from the heart; and well beyond political motivation. Now they could hopefully focus on the work still to be done.

31

MR JAMES JOINS UP

I T WAS SUNDAY. Mark James would be happy to do most anything or nothing. The weather was pleasant enough. He could go for a swim or a long walk along the harbour; he could swot up for his work tomorrow, or he could turn into a slob and watch TV. One day he would get around to something a little more structured, how about having a go at abseiling from the cliffs dropping to the water's edge not so far from here? But that would take him away from his main interests, even if he couldn't properly or fully express what those interests were. He could call up a friend but going to the pub didn't excite and that's what Ted would probably want to do. After a beer or two Ted was entertaining, but if he kept on drinking, he became a garrulous bore.

Meanwhile, Mark did know about an immediate challenge, and it was this: an itch that could only be scratched by sitting down and writing. Yet he wondered as usual about his ability to turn out anything worthwhile. It went together with that constant niggle: the one called Linda. He had felt something deep down move decisively during the strange experience with the funny fat fellow and getting such a pertinent if not quite shocking message from *The Hobbit*, but it wasn't something he could tell anyone about. The weirdness probably had to work itself out further, but how and when?

So it was a straightforward walk, after which something might present itself. Sydney in autumn was probably as good a city as you could have for such a simple recreation. The harbour's clean colours, a gentle breeze, various sail craft and a ferry or three, constant road traffic looking like toys running across the iconic coat hanger bridge; his round trip was a modest six or seven kilometres, but it brightened him up. Climbing the stairs to his front door again he thought about making a snack and then he hoped he'd be ready to scratch that itch.

'Take some quiet time first' was a whisper from nowhere, but he wasn't so surprised that he didn't immediately know it was Ardax. 'Remember that weekend when you went to the meditation seminar?' continued the whisper. Mark wondered if the whole thing was getting too serious. But it was also rather interesting, maybe even exciting. 'I'm making myself a sandwich' he said to the wall where the voice seemed to have come from. 'And then I'll try it.'

◆

'We are going to start you off with an experimental change' said Ardax. 'This is in the nature of a new development that may or may not be available more generally within a particular group of people.' Mark waited but nothing happened. Surely something or someone was trying to pull the wool over his eyes. How could he go along with it? Does Mr Golden Uniform with the odd little rat-tail think I'm so totally naïve?

That inner dialogue ran out of steam when he noted the sliding, slipping change in his view of the well-worn though still serviceable kitchen-dining area that badly needed a tidy-up, a thorough clean, a new coat of paint but was unlikely to get any of it soon. The dowdy old room quickly grew sharp with a cold light. He was sure it was too artificial, like a picture composed of bright primary-coloured blocks. He somehow knew it was a kind of wrapping and should that wrapping be torn away, the real room would be revealed.

It took a few bouts of this over several days; he quickly became accustomed to Ardax purely in energy, not in physical form, turning up and working with him. He forgot or just didn't want to remember how odd he'd at first found these sessions. And there were rewards: he would surely never forget that first astonishing experience of the kitchen changing from its unexciting older self into a place of magical translucent colour and shadow like a hologram. It was bright, light and no longer appearing irreducibly solid as it always had been. Instead of the area appearing no different to thousands or millions of similar rooms across the country and the planet, his kitchen actually glowed. 'What happened?' he demanded of his tubby teacher.

'You see things as they are when fresh, when NOW—as is—and not concretised by the actions of the lower mind' Ardax replied. 'It means you are in the moment, where you ought to be, not dredging up the remembered past with all its time-fixed perceptions; and when I say perceptions, they are not limited to what you see.' This hardly seemed a final or even a utilitarian explanation that Mark could benefit from of or explain to others. 'Don't be too hasty to judge' Ardax replied with irritating insight when he pointed this out. He tried a different approach. 'How did you do that?' Mark demanded.

'You did it' said Ardax. 'I only prepared the groundwork. This exercise is known to a few of your spiritual teachers; you can read about it in a book called *The Unfolding Now.*'

After that everything started to regularise. There was a program that more or less fitted in with Mark's work schedule. First the quiet time; then the instruction. Ardax explained that he was going to be helped to understand and internalise a degree of suitably advanced knowledge about the universe—knowledge currently either unknown or restricted to a tiny percentage of the population. This was an irresistible drawcard as no doubt it was intended to be. What better way for Mark to write science fiction, if the science was not simply unusual and fascinating but neither was it totally fictitious? That paradox made him chuckle; it was a gift he couldn't turn down.

Should he then start writing his latest novel or short story? 'Not yet' said Ardax, 'although it would help greatly if you kept a thorough record of your new findings. And when you eventually use those notes, do it wisely. These ideas are not to be bandied about willy-nilly or they will likely follow the fate of seeds thrown into rocky ground, as told by your great spiritual master Jesus of Nazareth. As you gain in wisdom you will doubtless become aware of how you are to treat the very rare knowledge you're being permitted to learn.'

So it began: Two men of different eras, different Classes, different viewpoints yet still somehow as close to each other as a heartbeat. Even in strictly personality terms they could appreciate similarities; neither was noisy in his ambition to know but both were insistent in the pursuit. Were they really two and not simply two sides of one? It probably didn't matter.

Mark had scaled surprising heights with his experience of a new world in an old, rented room. The 'hologram' sight hadn't continued beyond an hour or two but in the next few days he would occasionally see little edges of light appearing around familiar objects. This was surprising enough, especially when he learned from Ardax that the triple-volume teaching called *A Course In Miracles* described this very same phenomenon as a positive sign of progress.

Returning from the event that he had already mentally labelled 'the kitchen cabinet' the rigorist showered, ate a quick meal, brought Miriam up to speed and listened to her news and comments 'Don't try to overstep your capacity!' she suggested. 'Both of you need to develop carefully to get the best advantage out of this process.' He valued her feminine energy more deeply at that point. Yes, he carried nurturing genes without which he'd never have qualified for his position, yet was all too aware he had to give that side of himself more attention to benefit from these new subtleties.

Then it was back to work in the meditation room. While there, Ardax was made very aware of the urgency in addressing *forgiveness* with his new student. It was understood that conditions in Class Four were going to deteriorate quicker than expected and would sink lower than most could ever have imagined. He considered his best line of approach.

'You are reasonably happy with life because you can manage your current means of earning a living and you sometimes enjoy the challenges the work brings' Ardax pointed out. 'You can identify with the internet and all that it offers now, including being able to keep abreast of developments and gain acceptance from your business clients. What you don't know is this: how savagely things will move into the negative and the way that these technologies can be employed to undermine the social structure, often while supposedly attempting to improve it.

'The problem is happening even now although few in your world have yet noticed or grasped the implications. Be sure the new ways of improving communications, transactions and lifestyles will have their corresponding downsides, and this is beyond anything you would have come across so far. The fault lies not in the technology of course, but in Mankind itself.' (He wasn't going to mention the obvious disadvantages of Class Four.) 'The desire for public recognition, for fame to be obtained at almost any cost, for viciously demeaning certain types of people and beliefs, for ingeniously but ruthlessly stealing money and goods; these and more will show the dark side of the latest electronic innovations. Because of certain defects inherent in your world, the anti-social traits will multiply in many ways, very quickly! A situation will develop in novel directions that hardly anyone here would envisage at the moment.

'Forgiveness might not be the expected remedy, but the opposite of forgiveness is attack and that is a perfect short description of the anarchic forces building up right now; getting ready to unleash. Are you willing to assist?'

Mark hardly needed to think about it. The fat man believed in him! He had no idea of the work he'd be expected to carry out and refused to be concerned about it. Feeling more at ease than for a long time, he nodded.

32

THE NEW TRINITY

'IT'S A LITTLE too early to invite Mark James into our full confidence, but I'm looking forward to the day when he and me—call us the two in one - will be working very closely together'. Ardax was sitting on a wooden bench with the Chief, Miriam and Carly.

They were enjoying the garden, unwilling to waste the warm weather with its light airs, pleasant outlooks of fruit trees and lower down, vegetable beds haphazardly populated with clumps of vigorous plants.

Carly, invited at the last minute, was still getting up to speed with the latest developments. Her green eyes in a face full of lively intelligence, were corralled by a mass of ginger curls. Having unlocked the better access to Class Four that had been so significant for Ardax, together with recently reaching the powerful, additional understanding of forgiveness, Carly's attendance was regarded as essential.

'Can you tell me what's so important about this whole idea?' she wanted to know. Carly had never thought about the word 'redemption' before. It sounded somewhat archaic, yet she'd been a rigorist for long enough to know almost nothing was to be dismissed lightly.

Sharnestia nodded. 'As you know, we've been working on certain themes from Class Four Christianity. That's their equivalent to our *Yeshua-Like* practice. In Alt. Histories we don't have any religious preference of course, but our research in the last months have pointed us mostly in that direction, so I've placed more resources into following that path. We've come up with three particular ideas that don't get much airplay in general religious or spiritual discourse. We've been working on the deeper meanings of forgiveness and also sin; and now the latest factor needing to be better understood is redemption.'

'The idea of redemption is actually much older than any Christian teaching,' said Miriam. 'We are talking about something going far back into the history of every Class. You can find it in Class Four's Old Testament and there are some similarities in other teachings such as Hinduism, Jainism and Islam.'

'But what does the word redemption exactly mean in our context?' Carly wanted to know. 'It's hardly part of our everyday language, is it?'

'No, and I think we all have to be careful about the meaning' said Ardax. 'It's both precise and at the same time, has quite a wide application. Redemption means returning a situation to its former and preferred state, frequently requiring and expecting that payment be made.'

'There appear to be a number of elements associated' added the Chief.' We don't believe redemptive events or sequences are simple folklore, they're vital to Earth's cyclic existence. To create renewed life, there must be the so-called payment of an emblematic death and then comes the reward of a consequent resurrection, which we can expect will also be demonstrated in symbol. This naturally makes us think about the various stories of Christ's death and his miraculous return, the details of which remain more or less enigmatic to us just as they would have been to many followers of Jesus at the time.'

'I for one would like to know a lot more about these "events" or "sequences" said Carly. 'Is there anything we can look up or otherwise investigate?'

'Not a simple exercise' said Ardax, flipping his rat-tail. 'They're matters still cloaked in mystery.'

'Not entirely,' said the Chief. 'We know this much, redemption is specifically for this planet and this planet alone. We have challenges on Earth not known across the rest of the Solar System. The Sirian forces are fully aware and will lay down a path for initiates. Following their precise training, we will be required to build the systems and processes to assist those who are ready into awareness and function.'

Sharnestia patted her hair. 'This subject has been written about in earlier days and can be located even now by those who wish to find it. A source of many esoteric teachings was transcribed during the early to mid-twentieth century by a dedicated Class Four woman and mother named Alice Bailey. She heard and wrote down words spoken to her tele-pathically by a senior Tibetan monk, resulting in a large body of knowl-edge that was eventually published as a series of books. One of these was titled *Discipleship in The New Age*.' She took out her communicator. 'In volume two, page 385, it states that the theme of redemption "underlies all the initiatory processes". Initiation is a word used to describe the several discrete upward steps resulting eventually in a life of service and enlightenment. We here are all walking that same path in our own way. Or at least we aspire to it.'

Ardax swivelled to face the Chief. 'Something new, of spiritually high intelligence and life has come to and from Class Four!?' Then he looked down, in admission of his inadvertent discrimination.

Sharnestia checked her screen. 'I'll read you the extract: Here it is:

"Stage by stage, initiation by initiation, the disciple arrives at an understanding of redemption …later, he shares the redemptive work connected with all true hierarchical endeavour …after the fifth initiation of Revelation, he sees with a new clarity some of the karmic liabilities which have led the Planetary Logos to create this planet of suffering, sorrow, pain and struggle; he realises then (and with joy) that this little planet is essentially unique in its purpose and its techniques, and that on it and within it (if you could but penetrate below the surface) a great redemptive experiment is going forward…"

'So the answer is yes, Ardax, it's another piece of the puzzle.' The Chief nodded as much to herself as to him and put the communicator away.

'And the word *karmic?*' queried Carly. 'I'm not familiar with it.'

'Karma is a term used mostly in Class Four, coming from the Hindu teaching' said Sharnestia. 'It is not so likely to be used in our Class, although some rigorists feel the word is quite suitable. It describes the need for a suitable balance between the twin forces which must obtain in order for the universe to operate correctly. A more archaic belief was that personal karma, whether so-called good or bad, was the result of our earlier actions; typically arising from behaviours in a former life—a former incarnation. For example, a person who did good deeds this time would gain benefits next time. And vice-versa: negative traits like cruelty or selfish violent behaviour would attract difficult conditions in a following lifetime.' She hesitated, hoping she was getting through. 'It's understandable how these ideas arose; they suited humanity's concepts of morality. However, karma is more accurately an aspect of the universal balancing mechanism where one condition tends to be offset by another that opposes it and, in this way, ensures the required universal unfoldment.'

Mostly measured in her speech, Sharnestia grew suddenly intense. 'Once again, we must tone down or discount the good/bad dichotomy! This topic will be included in one or more of our new explanatory media being produced to update our understanding of Sirian genesis and identity, including far greater knowledge of the solar system. Obviously, this is massive subject-matter and Carly' she gave a reassuring nod, 'like the rest of us, you'll need to check out and study these subjects once we've completed the necessary research edits.'

Carly nodded in acknowledgement but wasn't about to stop asking questions. 'And in practical terms, with this redemption idea… is there good evidence we can help humanity?'

'I believe we can', said Sharnestia. 'The most intriguing point about redemption is that it's for planet Earth alone. We've challenges here not known across the rest of the solar system. The Sirian forces are aware of our efforts and have laid down a path for those who are dedicated. It appears the Earth's unique difficulties allow for a unique solution. We'll employ a standard development sequence—confirm adequate knowledge, build appropriate systems and procedures and then assist the ready ones on their journey of enlightenment.'

'Have we any idea of timing for a result?' Carly wanted to know. 'I mean, do we believe it's something we can work on right away, or are there more steps we should take first?'

'Timing is little known as yet,' said Miriam. 'We go forward in faith - as usual. But here is an interesting aside. We know Earth in its internal energy function is governed by the number three—as in for example Father, Son and Holy Spirit, or in the Hindu tradition Brahma, Vishnu and Shiva—and these elements we're now working with are another three: forgiveness, sin and redemption. The pattern of this new-found trinity looks and feels supportive. I expect the timing will unfold as appropriate.'

Miriam smiled softly, moving into a space where others might not follow. 'My name comes from ancient Israel so I've looked into redemption there and found it could be expressed in various ways, including even political or martial. But redemption is much more significant than that. It's the stuff of mythos—the return to a Golden Age, the putting to rights of ancient wrongs…' Then she corrected herself. 'Not wrongs, but misalignments. Truthfully, we just don't know how far it can reach. Or even how to best embrace it. Faith then becomes essential.'

'I really had no idea of *what* I was getting into with Alt. Histories' Carly pointed out with an expansive grin. 'Especially the really super surprising reach of Class Repair - where we're taking paths into several directions at once'. Her grin actually broadened. 'And now I'd say that my complete ignorance was just as well…'

33

OLIVE'S FORGIVENESS LESSON

BY THE TIME we had negotiated the most difficult part of the descent, it was quite dark. Helen lit a torch and we continued for another hour before Simon called a halt. 'Well, are we going to try skirting Sebaste tonight, or shall we hole up somewhere?' he demanded. 'It's a tricky business passing so close to military HQ. I'd rather get some sleep soon and move at first light.' He sniffed the air. 'I doubt there are any soldiers hereabouts, but to be on the safe side I'll wrap a screen around us while we camp.'

Tarquin agreed that we should settle in a copse a little way off the road. 'But before we bed down for the night, I must clarify certain things about our journey.' We made ourselves comfortable and Tarquin addressed us.

'No-one is here for his or her own benefit. We are on our Father's business, but don't worry, for you will eventually learn that truly complete fulfilment comes from doing God's Will. Dismiss all your preconceptions as to how your lives are to be lived. The practical effect is that we who are dedicated to this mission won't make any decisions by ourselves anymore.'

'We've always taken notice of the signs,' said Helen. 'Nevertheless, the knowledge and the judgement of the decision-maker is vital if we are not to be at the whim of every superstition.'

'You are a clever woman' replied Tarquin. (The statement was in no way patronising.) 'Then grow in wisdom. The judgement of the little self is what we must learn to avoid. We seek the true judgement of our Source. How can we be sure what actions will be in our own best interests? Or in the best interests of our shared goal? We may be full of facts, we may be able to throw our minds to the far corners of the Empire' (here he paused, significantly) 'but we can never have enough information to match the decision-making ability of the Holy Spirit. His decisions for us are always perfect. Perfect for our past, our present and our future. Not only for us, but for all other living things, too.'

Simon fidgeted in the dark. 'Now hold on' he said. 'I've spent many years of self-discipline developing the powers of my mind. In Gitta, they showered me with gifts and queued up for my advice. And even I'm not such a fool as to think that I can always get the right answer, all the time. We're not gods, but men.'

Tarquin said 'Yes, we *are*-men. And who, out of all mankind or womankind for that matter, understands the real meaning of peace and happiness? Pain comes, then there's some passing pleasure, but no certainty to rest upon in the shifting sands of illusion. Even the "Great Power" of Gitta has suffered, at times, the raucous voice of madness in his skull - I've heard it!'

The Roman's voice hushed. 'God wouldn't change us from caterpillars into butterflies in the space of just one summer, lest the sudden onset of Truth scare us. But He does ask us to be led that way as soon as possible. How many thousands of years will we choose to suffer? How many lifetimes of ignorance, picking up a lesson here, climbing a step there? The Nazarene came to speed our escape. Why should we drag our heels when freedom beckons?'

After a long minute had passed, Helen said, 'Perhaps you'll explain what we must do to find this perfect answer?'

'It is simple. The Anointed has told us how. We ask our questions and listen to the answers. Only don't forget that we must first refuse to hear the noisy advice of the false self, otherwise the clear yet gentle wisdom of the Holy Spirit will be obliterated. The Word may not always be in words. God needs no symbols with which to communicate, even though we have taught ourselves to believe in them. The message may come in many different forms, or in no form at all. What's of paramount importance is our willingness to hear.'

'I'm glad you're with us,' said Rebekah. 'You will surely teach us to listen well. There's still one thing I can't understand, though. If Jesus could hear God's Word, as the prophets of old did, then why wasn't he able to escape the cruelty of the Sanhedrists and that nasty Pilate?'

Ignited by new-found revelation, I joined in. 'Jesus chose - it was his reason for being here - to go through the crucifixion for our benefit. What you must realise, Rebekah, is that all the cruelty was aimed at a mortal form. If a person believes he or she is nothing but a body, the body's weakness will likely have a stronger hold. But try as we might, we can't be just a body, and our ultimate self can't ever be in danger. To one who knows the truth, pain and death become increasingly meaningless. Jesus went through the drama of the cross to show us this. He never cursed his captors. And he promised that we would be like him.'

Tarquin added, 'We are like him already, if we'd only wish to see it.'

Rebekah took my hand. Holding her was luxury despite the hard, stony soil.

'Take first watch, Simon,' said Tarquin. I felt certain this was done to keep the Magus occupied, and not because Tarquin considered it essential. When Simon said he would scan the countryside, Tarquin joked that he wasn't to scare us by reporting on owls or foxes. (The next day Tarquin took Simon aside and told him that his powers were not to be used any longer for selfish purposes and not even to help others, if it was done only upon the Magus' own initiative. 'Release all of your attributes, both those you think of as beneficial and those you believe are bad, to the Holy Spirit' he advised. 'Only He is competent to direct you always for the highest good.')

We travelled for two days without incident, accepting Tarquin's leadership, buying or being given handfuls of food from villagers, growing ever more travel stained as we followed goat tracks across the central highlands toward the Galilee. We kept away from garrisoned towns and met no patrols, although we heard of troop movements around Caesarea which suggested they were the preliminaries to the campaign against Jerusalem.

Only in our holy city, as well as in the zealot stronghold of Masada on the heights above the Dead Sea, were the Jews still openly in revolt against the might of the Empire. The Romans and the Jews, best of enemies, shared a common enthusiasm for civic duty and industriousness, with the result that in many conquered areas of Palestine, life had returned to something like normal. The drowsy warmth of late summer, with its fields of swollen corn, commented uneasily on the brooding peace that lay across the land, while the Romans waited for their darling Flavian generals to orchestrate the final thrust that would eclipse, perhaps for centuries, all hope of Jewish national independence.

In numerous small unspoken ways we communicated our awareness of the dismal political situation. Rebekah avoided all mention of her father. Simon and Helen never spoke as if they'd owned a fine house and a high position in society. Perhaps even more to the point, neither did Tarquin.

I still couldn't quite forget that Tarquin was nominally the enemy. This was heavily underscored when we made camp in the afternoon amongst a jumble of boulders on the slopes overlooking the Qishon River. We were drinking a little wine to reward ourselves for reaching the Galilean border. Tarquin began regaling us with tales of Roman army life. It seems that in an earlier posting he'd seen service in the Rhinelands.

'The barbarians never stopped making forays across the river. It was bad news if they broke through into civilian areas. They had a habit of scalping any girl-children they captured, then making wigs of the hair.' He passed the wineskin to Simon. 'As if that wasn't enough, their religious practices were bestial. I've seen nasty sacrificial rites in my time, but these were the most imaginative.'

'Should a man of God be talking like this?' asked Helen, but she stretched her legs and watched him with new interest.

'We had our own methods of imposing the *Pax Romana*' continued Tarquin, turning in my direction. 'You Jews say an eye should pay for an eye, or a tooth for-a tooth. We decided that a child was worth a child. Once, after a particularly messy mopping-up operation, we rounded up half a village's complement of charming little healthy, blue-eyed Germans.

'I'm from a poor family, but I had contacts at the Capital in those days - wealthy knights and senators who cultivated an aesthetic appreciation for young males. We got more from selling *them*; but we did alright out of the little she-wolves. What a night! Celebrated with a cask of pricey honey wine from Britain. It was being held at barracks for just such a happy occasion, and we used no water! We considered trying out the merchandise there and then, and in gratitude for my assistance, the Century voted that I might have first choice. There's a lot to be said for the comradeship of a good legion.'

Sickly shock…and unmoving silence.

We had been eating a meagre meal at the time, the usual bread and olives, but this stopped us. I couldn't help recalling the night when I'd seen into Tarquin's soul. The avarice and boorish cruelty of his story was scribing the very same signature as before.

'Don't look at me like that,' said Tarquin. 'Jews, and especially Nazoreans, are too damned self-righteous. What about that Josephus? A cunning little crook who sold his country down the drain; had Jews put to death to save his own skin.'

I felt the heat rise in my face.

Tarquin nodded slowly, as much to himself because we all knew about Josephus. 'Yes, he undermined the revolt when he was supposed to be revolutionary governor of the Galilee. And now he's the principal Jewish military advisor to Titus. A Jew from the priestly caste, and he's only helping to plan the destruction of the very centre of Jewish religion.

Huh! Josephus hides behind a smokescreen of sanctity, making out what he's doing is divinely inspired. And you'd dare look down your nose on Roman soldiers who are honest about grabbing what we can?'

After the rush of blood, I was chilled. I felt the sweat icy in my armpits, though the day was still warm. 'Roman soldier? You said you were finished with all that.' It was the best I could manage.

'Once a soldier, always a soldier' said Simon all too quietly. I noticed him playing with a little dagger. He was scratching the word 'Mars' in the dirt.

'You're not at it again, you men?' said Helen.

Tarquin told her: 'I need no mothering to save me from this one, he's not dangerous.'

Simon lifted his knife and held it, relaxed, in his lap. The warrior had surfaced, eyes slitted, muscles ready. Rebekah assumed a wild expression. Her short life had taught her to sense death in the air.

Seconds passed. No-one moved or spoke. We were taut metal of a coiled spring. Tarquin regarded each of us in turn. I saw the wineskin at my left where Simon had dropped it and tried desperately to formulate a plan - squirt someone's face, anything.

Time moved uncaringly on its appointed course, mocking my feebleness as a man of action. But that role belonged to others, while I... everyone knew I was the secretary, keeper of accounts and diaries, recorder of holy words; but Father, what words could possibly explain this madness, a man of God gloating over profit from cruelty and boasting of his licentiousness?

There is no sin. Even now in this situation, I heard it within. But rampant sin vomited from Tarquin's anecdotes. I saw sin too in Simon's skillfully handled dagger, felt sin growing from the fearful set of Rebekah's mouth.

There is no sin. How could it be? How could it not be?

Again the opposing forces of ideas; Tarquin was staring straight at me. His pale eyes grew ever harder. My worst fears were confirmed. Slowly and deliberately, and more shocking than I could ever imagine, he winked.

'There is no sin' I said, hearing the words come out with the surprise I should no longer have felt. 'Evil is not real as we think of real. It's the balancing effect; destined to evolve into a purer expression.'

'Thank you, Mark' said Tarquin, 'you've introduced the subject I wanted to talk about before we crossed the river into the Galilee. The all-important subject of forgiveness.'

Trying to be unobtrusive, Simon slipped the knife back into his robe. Helen coughed and rearranged the bowl of olives. Rebekah said she was looking forward to hearing more about forgiveness.

Tarquin grinned like an urchin, an expression I'd never seen from him before. 'A little demonstration is sometimes worth a thousand words. You will perhaps accept that it's so very easy for a stick to be poked into the pot of guilt we carry. Stir the pot, the guilt is dislodged and immediately that becomes very uncomfortable for us.'

He reached for an olive and bit into it. 'It's as though we had suddenly tasted a poisonous fruit. What is our reaction? To place as much distance between the offending guilt and us.' Tarquin spat the olive morsel onto a flat stone and pointed at it. 'Now that it seems safely outside of us, we can say the guilt has really nothing to do with us at all. Unfortunately, something still nags at us within. Being God's children, we cannot really fail to understand the tricks we play upon ourselves. At that point, if we are still determined not to learn the truth, we may conveniently translate our discomfort into a feeling of rage or fear.'

Tarquin reached out with his foot and ground the black flesh into a smudge on the surface of the rock. Slowly, he pulled back his leg. The piece of olive had spread over an area several times its original size. He shook his head. 'It never works, though. All that our fine display of righteous indignation will do is increase our inner distress.' In his hand he now cupped two olives. 'And however loud we shout or however hard we tremble, we serve only to increase the darkness in which we dwell.' He scooped a handful of the dark, glistening olives.

Rebekah was following the dissertation with a studious frown. Tarquin threw her an olive, and she jerked out of her reverie to catch it. The Roman said, 'You were about to ask a question, my dear. Yes, it's an important one, isn't it? Where does the guilt come from in the first instance? How does the needless pain begin? Your sister taxed me on it before. All I can say is that God wanted us to accept by our own choice that we were His children. Thus, we might learn to create through closeness to Him - or, if we choose, to miscreate, which is only an illusory activity. In miscreating, we cannot experience God's reality. When Sons of God—and Daughters—take the shadowed path away from wholeness, we experience a deep feeling of guilt, believing that we have 'wronged' our Creator by pretending we are unlike Him.'

Tarquin was in one of his wonderfully light-hearted moods. He plucked up the wineskin, sent a stream of purple into the air and caught it in his open mouth as it fell. 'Yet here's the lesson' he continued, wiping the liquid from his lips. 'God sees no shadows. His world is only Light. He knows we were never wrong because illusions are not real and therefore, we need no forgiveness from Him. He knows we are whole.

'But, while we still dwell in the illusion of illusions, forgiveness is our way out of the deadly maze in which we surely think we are trapped.'

Helen said, 'You mean we have to forgive ourselves.'

'Certainly, although the easiest way to do that is to forgive our neighbours' said Tarquin. 'It goes like this: We think we have transgressed God's laws. Impossible, of course, but our belief inevitably leads to guilt. We think we have snatched autonomy from God. Just like in the story of Prometheus, who stole fire from the gods. We believe we are usurping God's authority. In our guilt and terror at this "sin", we mostly prefer to punish and destroy ourselves, rather than wait for the sword of Damoclese to fall from on high.'

'Why?' asked Rebekah. 'Our instinct is to survive, not die.'

'Not necessarily, Rebekah. Don't forget, we too easily believe ourselves to be autonomous, not part of the one indivisible Life. If you could truly read them, you would find many people believe we created ourselves and thus we must walk our own lonely road, menaced by God and relying only on our own pitiful resources. If we can punish ourselves by generating supposed sickness and death, we are somehow victorious. This reasoning is insane and could be seen as such, if only we were awake.'

'We forgive ourselves and then everything's alright?' demanded Helen. 'It's too simple. If salvation is as straightforward as that, why don't people do it and live their lives in seventh heaven?'

'Sadly' said Tarquin, 'we have a habit of teaching ourselves only to do those things which are complex and difficult. We are at one with all life - now, what could be simpler than that? Our inability to accept the truth of oneness is the very specific reason why forgiving ourselves is hard. Cast your minds back to my little play-act with the olives. We experience the guilt within us as unbearable, so we naturally contrive to see it outside of ourselves. We paint a world that reflects our opinion of ourselves - a world full of threats, a world that is cruel and makes no sense. When we forgive that world—or rather, when we forgive our false images of our brothers and sisters who seem to be outside us—then we find ourselves forgiven.'

'You're saying that I should smile sweetly at every murderer and ignore every injustice' Simon said. 'I don't want to live like that, even in exchange for heavenly rewards.'

'Listen very carefully,' said Tarquin. 'The only reason why forgiveness is not only possible, but also essential, is that we are never forgiving what is real. We're not taking something that's true and trying to convince ourselves that it's false. Instead, we are taking an illusion, a wrong perception, a false belief, and letting it go. Letting it be obliterated by Truth. In essence, no-one is guilty, so to forgive them is merely to re-establish that Truth.'

Simon grunted. 'Murderers are not murderers?'

'Not even you, brother' said Tarquin, and for a second Simon looked at the ground. 'Murderers may kill bodies and the Holy Spirit may direct that they cease or be restrained from their unrewarding activities, but they have not violated, nor can they violate, the Law of Oneness. They may be temporarily lost in illusion, but for us to condemn them is only to join them in ignorance. Bodies, as we all know, are not eternal. What is not eternal is unlike God and therefore not in any ultimate sense, real.

However, bodies are not evil either and the belief that they are is just another concept requiring forgiveness.'

It was Helen's turn. 'What practical methods can be used to bring about this miraculous phenomenon? This forgiveness? Is it worth a try?'

'Call it a habit, the habit of seeing through the eyes of the Holy Spirit and not the limited eyes of the ego' Tarquin replied. 'You need call upon that power of clear seeing, for only when you are "in the spirit" will you be "inspired" In your right mind and capable of real forgiveness.'

He took one of the olives from the bowl and polished it carefully, stroking it with his little finger. 'Consider your brother—or sister - when you feel anger towards that person. Think about their crime for a fleeting moment, how they've wronged you. Then place yourself in their position, stand in their sandals. Would you condemn yourself for doing the same thing? Maybe you'd see your "sin" differently - perhaps a simple mistake, a misunderstanding, or the consequence of pressure, fear, upset. If you'd done what that person did, wouldn't it almost always be explicable - forgivable. Or at least, some part of you would say so. Why then do we not apply such generosity to the actions of others? We don't do it because it would rob us of our excuse to project our guilt to those "others" without.

'We think that if we didn't use projection to send it away, this guilt would crush us, but faith shows a different result. Refuse to see evil in others; see rather a mistake, an error, a confusion perhaps. Then we'll discover the lack of evil in ourselves. And what is that realisation, if not Heavenly?'

I could never again look at an olive without thinking of Tarquin's words. I suppose that was his intention. As every day went by and another bowl of olives was emptied, we'd understand better the deep meaning behind his words. Because what he spoke of was the beginning of a revolution more powerful, more sweeping in its scope, than anything the zealots had conceived of.

We waded across the shallow, swampy Qishon and made our way up the northern side of the valley toward Nazareth, the place where the Master had grown to manhood. Centre of the Lower Galilee, home of the fiercest nationalists and hardiest fighters. Massacres had taken place in this province, and bitter reprisals. Not only Roman against Jew, but Greek and Syrian against Jew, Jewish moderate against Jewish extremist. Brother against brother.

For us Jews, proud of our heritage and our destiny in the world - trying to give more than lip service to the concept of solidarity as the Chosen People of God - internecine strife was possibly the cruelest aspect of this war. But Paul and Thomas and Tarquin were bringing the message of inclusion. To hate others reflected our deep discomfort with ourselves. There was—greatly difficult as it might be to believe—no substantive enemy 'out there'. If we could practise forgiveness as the Anointed One prescribed it and as Tarquin explained it, legions might someday beat their swords into ploughshares, children would no longer be dragged off to the slave market and there would be no more war widows begging for alms on street corners. The dove of peace would spread its soft wings over the noisy confusions of the world, even though life remained an enduring challenge. It was more than possible that neither life nor its challenges would ever end.

34

A CLASSY OCCASION

IT WAS CONSIDERED entirely fitting, from the earliest discussions, that Alt. Histories should invite Mark James to the Department's evening celebration. Ardax knew the task of getting him there was not an easy one, but the motivation wasn't lacking; everyone came together and helped. It was agreed that parachuting Mark into Class One for a few hours must be possible. If Ardax was able to invade Mark's dreams and visit him in Class Four, then the opposite could not be an insurmountable task. And after some furious work, that's how it turned out.

Following Alt. Histories' usual custom, the party was held at the home of the project's most senior rigorists. Ardax prepared most of the food and Miriam spent diligent days in composing a hologram devoted to contemplation of the project.

The Chief came along and was willing to sit on the periphery of the event. She didn't need praise and only wanted to see and feel the general contentment with the work on Class Four as exemplified by Mark's surprisingly effective understanding and development, thanks to his time with Ardax.

It was inappropriate for the party-goers to consider the positive result in terms of personal triumph - not only would this be inaccurate but it would fail to uphold departmental practice - yet Ardax was willing enough to treat the gathering as one of his life's true high points. The department would receive tremendous benefits, naturally. There had been the ongoing minor problem with public appreciation of Alt. Histories' true worth, but all attendees were confident most of that would drop away now.

Ardax concluded that in some ways the work of class repair had barely begun. He started to see his department's task as the process of leaving a curated range of key Class One thoughts with each of the other Classes. Carried out by his group of colleagues, the delivery of such thoughts to Class Four would help improve the energy bandwidth and as a result, act to lift its ingrained patterns of suspicion, sadness and competitiveness. These qualities had served to make the dimension so very serious beneath the often-false veneer of jollity the inhabitants assumed. All Classes were inextricably bound as they always had been, but Mark's appearance at the party became the certain evidence that they might even meet face to face and consciously do the work of reaching towards amalgamation.

The hologram flared up, scintillated gently, muted itself subtly, burst into ecstatic movement against the background of the night. It was getting late and people were starting to leave. The dispenser provided them with 3-D copies of the report while Ardax rested in the garden, savouring again the major findings.

Mark experienced the event as even stranger for having been so brief. He managed not to get overwhelmed even though arrival into Class One felt rather like psychedelic dreaming. Nevertheless, he'd adjusted himself to the new dimension more easily than either he or any of the rigorists expected. He was almost fully engaged in relating to his Class One peers, clearly grateful at having been chosen for the highly peculiar transition from one world to another.

In following days he noticed some differences. His everyday IT work was much the same—quite okay at keeping his brain alive but still somewhat tedious. His feelings about it hardly mattered now; he had other fish to fry. Talk about surprise, he'd received a birthday card from Linda! Then when he called her to say thanks, she acted in a friendly manner, almost as if much of their more difficult history had never occurred.

Recently Ardax had helped Mark buy himself a few more books, including *The Sirius Mystery* by Robert Temple and the effect of the party was to give him more reason to study them. These were only supports to the real work and none of them were entirely necessary, but Ardax understood his student quite well by now. Mr James appreciated a wide-spread context.

Class Four 'reality' was much less alien now. The rigorist saw through most of its frantic activities, with the eyes of compassion that Assistance offered. Their courage, their vigour even in the face of the oncoming chaos of their world, warmed him.

Still dozing at the party's fringes, Ardax noticed the family's favourite peacock appear at his side. The bird's brilliant colours were picked out and contrasted by the illumination of the hologram as the system displayed its final sequence.

He whistled and the peacock bobbed over to him. Ardax held out his hand, and it pecked some crumbs from his fingers. He loved this house, this garden, this village-group, this dimension. But all things are joined, meaning that he couldn't afford the ignorance of smugness. The brothers and sisters of all Classes had to share in the same good fortune, otherwise it had no real foundation.

His race was on the brink of accepting this truth in large measure as it related to overall planetary conditions. A later challenge on the horizon was to include other dimensions starting with a refreshed and deepened solar perspective. Life's responsibility to life was ever ongoing, and by no means was that an impossible burden.

All the resources were available for Mankind to fulfil its cosmic obligations no matter the various inbuilt difficulties. We had earned some measure of peace and wheels were set in motion for this peace to spread eventually to Class Four. Our contribution to the saving action would energise, not exhaust. The Anointed One had surely taught us that. To give was ever to receive.

He winked at the peacock and drained his glass.

35

THE HOLLOW STAFF

WE TOOK REST above the Qishon and watched the sun dip beneath the land into the Great Sea. When it was dark, barely discernible flickering lights showed amongst the hills on the opposite side of the valley, some way to the west of the track which we'd taken earlier that day from Samaria.

'I can tell you the story of those lamps,' said Simon. 'In those rocky places surrounding Mount Carmel there are devotional communities. They hold similar ideas to the Essenes of the Dead Sea, but they also have a big temple up there. The Essenes would never go along with that because simplicity of worship is one of their major tenets.'

He told us that for decades the Carmelites had applied themselves entirely to aiding the advent of the Messiah into Israel. 'It's said in the Galilee that Mary, mother of Jesus, was specially chosen and trained, in order that she might be made suitably pure to act as vessel for the entry of the Anointed.'

'And perhaps she was' commented Tarquin. 'There are stranger things happening all around us than we'll ever discover in a lifetime's search.'

Rebekah peered out at the tiny points of light, turning back to face us with an expression hidden by the night. Her voice, though, was queer… and excited. 'How many lifetimes shall we need?' She took my hand and squeezed it. 'I've started my journey with you all - and Mark has chosen me as his partner. Make a pact with me, dearest! Say that you'll travel the centuries with me until all secrets are laid bare to us!'

I tried to laugh at her girlishness. 'It's an easy wager that you would give up on me rather sooner than that' I said ponderously, half-aware of needing to stall for time. 'For my part, I'll be grateful to reach Rome in one piece.'

'No, Mark.' She put her arms around me. 'I'm not playing games with you. Look! Across the valley there is Carmel, where generations of men and women have given their lives to God. And beyond us' she swung her arm in the opposite direction, 'is Nazareth, where the Master came from. We're in the middle, between two holy places. We're dedicated to the same service of what is true. We chose this work because it's the only thing that can satisfy the longings of our hearts. How can we hope to do it all in the span of a single life? Let's pledge ourselves to meet again each time as the wheel turns and keep the work progressing.'

I loved her with the love of a man for a woman, but that couldn't blind me to the significance of what she'd said. Yes, I desired the soft warmth of her in my arms, the tingle in my body, the brush of her hair against my face, but I heard a deeper message, too. Unembarrassed in front of the others, we made our solemn pledge.

Tarquin stayed silent until we had finished, when he blessed us. My heart felt large. It expanded, encompassing my friends, the hills of the Galilee, the Roman supply camp at Ptolemais on the coast, the brow-beaten people of Samaria, the Christians sheltering with mother in Pella, the invasion headquarters with its thousands of soldiers and auxiliaries amassing at Caesarea, the zealots in Jerusalem… and then I searched Rebekah's face.

For a second, I knew her as someone else. This wasn't Rebekah at all, but a woman called Linda. Linda? The moment passed, but the unwanted name unsettled me. I had never heard of such a name before. The incident was at the same time trivial and oddly important.

Helen interrupted my disjointed thoughts. 'These two lovers deserve a proper bed for the night, Tarquin' she said. 'Come to think of it...' and Simon completed her sentence, 'so do we '.

'Yes said Tarquin. 'This is the proper time to seek for an inn.'

'Choose the right place' emphasised Simon. 'I want rest tonight, not a fight with half the Fretensis legion—that's the Tenth by the way. It may no longer be in Israel, but I hear it's never been beaten.'

'You'll sleep well' Tarquin promised, 'and awake to a fresh chapter in our journey. I can recommend a friendly little establishment on the outskirts of Nazareth. The road's just over there.'

Perhaps I should have taken better notice of the finality in his voice, but I was too relieved at the prospect of returning to the trappings of civilisation. We made good time on the road, and the inn was everything Tarquin had led us to expect. It was clean and airy with a cheery host who didn't ask awkward questions. I wondered, vaguely, how Tarquin had discovered the place - a minor mystery which was of course only one of the surprising things about our former decurion-major.

'A nourishing meal!' Tarquin ordered in street Greek and the inn-keeper showed his understanding with smiles and bows and soon after, with steaming bowls of boiled fish, bread and leeks. We relaxed, unwound, enjoyed the simple pleasures of food, wine and good company. It felt as though God had given us a 'night off', a time to forget the rigors of our sacred duty, a time when we could just be little and human.

I savoured the sight of Tarquin, tall and chunky with his short brown hair and typically Roman features. By contrast, Rebekah was so small and dark, yet she held a strength no less. I considered Simon, vigorous in movement and thought, always outspoken - a rare kind of honesty - and Helen, my brief lover who had never seriously pitted her considerable woman's wiles against me, though God knew I had been vulnerable enough.

They were my true friends, our differences seemed trifling enough in this safe, cheerful environment. I smiled to myself; I had already failed in my attempt at 'time off from spiritual matters' because I was thinking of how we were indeed just one being, the single body of Christ. To be at peace with our fellow humans was the only way to gain the peace which everyone sought, whether tax collector, tiller of land or tribune. Could it really be true? It had to be, and yet...

My brother is myself. Once again, I smiled and refused more wine. I was already happy.

I suppose I expected a peaceful night, washed and fed, holding Rebekah until we drifted into sleep on the soft lamb's wool mattress. But my tendency to vivid and disturbing dreams had not disappeared. This time, I saw Tarquin whispering to the innkeeper - hadn't he been a little too friendly? - and I heard the chink of money. Coldness like a bolt of iron pressed against my belly.

'Why?' I demanded of Tarquin. 'What's it all for? I thought you were one of us.'

The innkeeper vanished, swallowed by the dark. Tarquin's face filled my vision. 'See broader, Mark' he said. 'See wider. There are matters you have missed. Now take note! An army courier was knifed by Simon near Gitta - remember the blood on the Magus' blade? Simon was a most audacious guerrilla, but in his haste, he neglected to check the dead man's hollow staff.' Tarquin held a wooden rod and tapped my head with it. 'The next day my men recovered this important item.'

The tapping continued and I awoke to a soft knocking on the door. Rebekah stirred at my side. 'What is it?' she whispered.

My heart bolted when I saw the innkeeper standing there in the dawn shadows and were I not surprised in my nakedness, my body might have followed.

'Peace' breathed the man at the doorway. 'Not a sound! Dress quickly and come to the stables.'

Rebekah appealed to me with frightened eyes. Her anxiety was not reassuring. I rubbed my eyes to convince myself I was awake. 'Explain yourself' I demanded of the innkeeper.

He didn't answer at once but thrust forward a staff and twisted the top. This came off to reveal a hollow interior. 'Tarquin told me to show you the message cavity' he explained impatiently. 'Heaven knows why.'

If this was supposed to answer my fears, it was hardly successful. Yes, the waking experience matched my dream, but what did it signify?

The innkeeper reacted to my confusion. He pulled the light blanket from the bed, making Rebekah clutch for her robe.

'Come on!' he said waving toward the door. 'Before it's too late.'

Was it a trap? I didn't need to understand it all, if only the Holy Spirit would give me guidance. But there was little hope of hearing the still, small voice at a time like this, with my pulse racing. I began to pray silently when a small hand grabbed my arm and with her other hand, Rebekah threw my clothes and shoulder-bag at my face. (Our prayers are seldom answered in the way we'd like them to be.)

When the three of us reached the stables, Helen and Simon were there in the company of four hardy desert horses that stood fully saddled, stamping the straw and champing at their bits.

'Tarquin?' I questioned the innkeeper. He handed me a letter. 'Simon's seen this' he said. It was written in a hasty script: 'Message in the staff gave a warning, situation now deteriorated. General orders to units across Palestine imperil your lives. Suspected followers of Jesus will be detained to comply with non-aggression treaty ratified by Nazorean nationalists. Nazareth a prime, symbolic target. In saddle bags military passes to Tyre may help. Make haste for Rome. Our Master is with you.'

I asked after Tarquin again, though I hardly needed to be told. 'He's helping evacuate Yeshuas from the town,' said Helen. 'A full cohort's marching from Tiberias.'

'Yeshuas?'

Helen nodded. 'Tarquin came to us - in a dream. That is the word we are to use now.' The innkeeper fussed with the horses, constantly checking the road with bird-like movements of his head. Helen spoke rapidly. 'All true religions were one, he kept telling us. "But if you must have a name, call yourselves Yeshuas." He said he mightn't get another chance to speak with us, even though he'd always be at our side.'

'Will you stop jawing!' The innkeeper's voice was insistent. 'Mount up and go while you still can.'

We did as he told us and the man calmed down. Just as we were clearing the courtyard he called softly, 'There's a cold breakfast in your bags'. Then he disappeared inside.

I lifted the leather flap and my fingers closed around a small wineskin, cool and dewy. The vintage was well watered, with a hint of sweetness. Rebekah sat uneasily astride her mount while I tied her rein to my saddle. Of course, I had told Tarquin that I'd learned to ride while travelling Asia Minor, and luckily Helen and Simon could handle their horses well enough. I sipped the wine. Our remarkable Roman friend seemed to have thought of everything.

'He planned all along to go away and leave us' said Rebekah, echoing my thoughts. The sun was just up and the soothing, rhythmic sound of hooves on the road was carried by the still bright air that betokened a hot day.

'Yes' I replied. 'He had his task and we have ours. First Rome and after that, who can say?'

She looked into my eyes and I was glad to see innocence and wisdom mirrored in hers. 'Mark, we'll never see him again.' It was a statement of acceptance. No-one commented. There would be time enough on the road to catch up with my deep feelings. It was sufficient now to know - even if I still didn't quite believe it - that fear and death were not in complete command and as Paul had explained, all things worked together for good to those who loved God and are called according to His purpose. The actuality of this truth would eventually come to me and to all my siblings in Christ.

I urged the horses to walk faster and took a long drink from the wineskin.

36

OF SCIENTISTS AND WRITERS

MARK JAMES SAT down at his desk. He'd just finished a session with Ardax and there was a lot to take in. Events were speeding up. Much as he was enjoying this new secret life, there were inevitable downsides. It was all very well, having a professional relationship with a supposedly non-existent scientist from another dimension, including occasional entry into that scientist's home dimension that didn't even have the beginning of a description according to any science he knew of. His life was somewhat akin to that of an indigenous stowaway from the South Pacific islands in the eighteenth century: Who after becoming more or less accustomed to ship, sailors and rum, had to deal with the shock of coming ashore in a major European city teeming with even stranger people, objects and events.

This comparison was more accurately a mild one. Mark could hardly grasp the enormity of his changed existence; he was even pleased that Linda hadn't contacted him for a while. Much as he'd warmed to her last call, he needed more personal space now than ever. Yet he wasn't lukewarm about this relationship. After so much upset and anguish, he felt surprisingly calm in anticipation of getting together again. Rushing it wouldn't work anyway.

There'd been several discussions about how he and the rigorist should collaborate for the best mutual result—considering the inevitable differences in knowledge, experience and expectation. Yet Mark was more or less ready to accept that he and Ardax were in some way, on some level, *the same*. The rigorist suggested this intimate connection was best described as due to them both being projections from the same soul. Mark didn't feel obliged to reply. He'd leave that one for later.

It was agreed Mark should get organised for his new book. It was a task closer to his normal routine, although one of Ardax's explanations was seriously chilling: Class Four was going to experience the most appalling upheavals in the not-too-distant future; the birth pangs of a new era. It was explained that Mankind's global civilisation must splinter and fail due to sickness both physical and mental. Instead of trade, industry and service mankind would increasingly fall into predation: a situation where society would become increasingly *catabolic*—the living entity devours itself.

Catabolism meant a turnaround in the capitalistic model of humanity that had mostly held sway around the globe. Cybercrime, predatory lending and financial fraud would be added to increasing corruption, rampant drug dealing, racketeering and human trafficking. International affairs would get—here the AI system seemed to hesitate, then used the unexpected word *dicey*. Wars would flourish. These harms would be exacerbated by events in the natural world where thousands of animal and plant species would continue to become extinct while weather patterns went even more haywire, delivering destruction, deluge and despair. The term 'Christian' would become so rubbery that anyone might take it proudly for their own, no matter how unhelpful their preferred interpretation might be. (Christianity wouldn't be the only religion to suffer like this.) The great need was for renewal of first principles.

And so, to work.

The sense of being the writer was mostly a calming one, slipping into a world where at least in theory he was in charge. Yet there were many times recently when he'd experienced that feeling of being 'written through', rather than recognising himself as the creator. Just to sit there quietly before working was luxurious, but it was no longer enough. There were added responsibilities now; he must spend some time every day in meditation. He felt the benefit of this; it wasn't a chore. Life had changed—there was no going back.

Today the book project had been cleared by the Council and Class One rigorists! It was patently a goal meatier than his usual short stories. Not that there was anything wrong with science fiction as a genre, especially remembering the powerful accomplishments in this field by Arthur C. Clarke, Brian Aldiss, Frank Herbert, Ray Bradbury and other Sci-Fi heroes. But Mark knew that his own stories, despite their moderate success, rarely reached the kind of heights he was aiming for. That was all the more reason for his determination to do better. He'd concluded it was the effort that mattered, effort was the thing that would help move evolution on its commanded course.

He began to understand why there had been an undefined lack in his earlier work. One editor mistook the fault for a virtue and called it Mark's 'haunting' quality. The simple fact was that the most extravagant plot, the cleverest extrapolation of some scientific theory, often didn't deliver the guts of what Mark angled for.

Meaning was the elven bread he'd always sought, very aware that Sci-Fi was an excellent creative medium for this. Despite his previous best attempts, he had often felt they were little more than playing with toys. Now, he had a real theme, a chance of putting it right.

◆

He switched on his PC and connected the printer, skimmed his eyes over the view of the grey and white clouded harbour, listened to the small, homely noises of the family in the flat below and considered the line of well-thumbed paperbacks straggling across the shelf within reach of his right hand. There were a few new additions to his reading collection now: *The Dancing Wu Li Masters* by Gary Zukav, *Journey Without Distance* by

Robert Skutch, *Synchronicity* by Carl Jung, *The Tibetan Book of Living and Dying* by Sogyal Rinpoche.

Was all this preparation a delaying tactic? Writing could be a conveniently uncommitted activity. It was easy enough to change your mind without anyone being the wiser. You could press delete and screw up the sheet you'd just printed and within a minute or two, change direction entirely.

But not this time. There was inner pressure just as it was also his free choice. This book would be about Jesus, but neither the Jesus he had met in Sunday-school, nor the Jesus whose gospels helped mother in the purchase of new household equipment. It must be the Jesus who had proclaimed, by his courage, by his plain speaking, his humility, his practical works, his compassionate dispassion, his down-to-earth yet transcendental reality. It had to be a Jesus who inspired us to reach for that same reality.

Interwoven with this had to be the bigger picture of the Sirian presence that watched over Earth and helped underpin the entire solar system as well as many more such systems in our galactic neighbourhood.

He pondered the seemingly imponderable: was Jesus a direct projection from Sirius? But shouldn't we have our own teacher who could bring us to the point of accepting our planetary responsibilities? Immediately after that thought launched, he knew Jesus came from Earth's own energy environment. The Master's mission was to sow seeds helping humanity pull ourselves up by our bootstraps, while the high extra-terrestrials lent a subtle yet vital guiding hand.

Mark had a growing sense that very influential spiritual teachers like Jesus, like the Buddha, like Mohammed and perhaps others less known like Mithras, had the imprimatur of our Sirian guardians. These guardians would rarely if ever present themselves directly even as they had assisted the planetary teachers to infuse greater knowledge and understanding into our world.

Recently, in brief multidimensional flashes - impossible to describe - he had sensed that the ethos of Sirius and the Anointed would claim him entirely. Looked at from the standpoint of base ego-awareness, a sacrificial act might be demanded of him by spiritual tyrants. Within the currency of the flashes, however, such a sombre, dramatic view was utterly out of place, laughable.

Yet even as he considered this the shadow arrived:

Where was his confirmation?

Did he really know anything? After so much certainty and without warning he suddenly felt horribly exposed. Was he kidding himself? Was he a little unhinged?

Tumult.

There was a chasm opening. It must be resolved quickly or remain unresolved for who knew how long.

Without conscious thought, Mark reached out a hand for his Bible, shiny in its recent acquisition. His apostolic namesake had reported something appropriate on the subject of spontaneity and action. In chapter 13, verse 11, Jesus was extolling a principle that Gnostics later tried to live by:

'And when they arrest you and deliver you up, do not be anxious beforehand about what you are to say, but say whatever is given you in that hour, for it is not you who speak, but it is the Holy Spirit.'

He must ever go within and ask what to do, say, write. It was what many an author longed for; to be lifted above the restrictions of style and plot and have another self—wiser, more creative, better disciplined —pick up the pen or take over the keys.

And while he waited for that other self who more readily approx-imated the higher Self he both wanted to be and knew somehow he already was; perhaps there were sub-selves who could help? Not just the plump man with the funny rat-tail, but also a monk, face creased with care and the burden of forbidden knowledge, yet so certain of his mission that he was willing to sit writing, cramped and isolated in a draughty cave?

Certainly his ancient namesake had worked hard to tell the world about Jesus, the Anointed One, and did so despite the likely distortions of his own personality and the editing of future generations. John Mark of Judaea might be able to speak across the years, whisper into the ear of

Mark from Neutral Bay. Somehow, he knew the two were one, just as he and Ardax were one. He didn't know how he knew.

The coffee was half cold. He was calmer now. There was no need to inflate the balloon of emotion. Opposites could be reconciled. Mysteries could be lived with. He would continue. Once again, he considered physics.

Scientists had proven to their own satisfaction at least, the fluidity of what we call time and space. Mark remembered when the Sydney nuclear physicist, Charles Brian McCusker, who was Professor of High Energy Nuclear Physics at the University of Sydney from 1961 to 1985, had said on the radio that our belief in a three-dimensional space, extending off equally to infinity in the three directions and a linearly flowing, irreversible time, was a quite incorrect description of reality. McCusker had published in the fields of cosmic radiation, particle physics and transpersonal psychology.

There was the mysterious reality of quantum mechanics. You could hardly be considered strange due to holding unusual spiritual ideas when you knew quantum mechanics was a collection of understandings amongst the very strange - yet at the same time, wholly practical in application. There were many unanswered questions about these new discoveries; they often made no 'common sense'.

As recognised by Heisenberg's uncertainty principle, some measurements were impossible, yet the new physics was successfully used every day to construct much of our modern technology like computers, global positioning systems, fibre optics, medical imaging and lasers. And the physicist John Wheeler had written back in the seventies: 'May the universe in some strange sense be "brought into being" by the participation of those who participate? … "Participator" is the incontrovertible new concept given by quantum mechanics. It strikes down the term "observer" of classical theory, the man who stands safely behind the thick glass wall and watches what goes on without taking part. It can't be done, quantum mechanics says.'

Recalling these exciting ideas, Mark began to feel less marginal—or perhaps he never really had been on the margins after all.

There was the anticipation of navigating through this playground of fact and inspiration. And why not as a result arriving at a hitherto barely noticed secret garden? It wasn't hard to believe in this possibility, considering the amazing events that had occurred recently. And now his active involvement was necessary. He was more than a participator, he was *called*.

The blank paper still challenged him. He typed the words The Anointing. It looked right. Yes. In our own ways, we might all aspire to and attain some measure of that uplift. He emptied his coffee cup.

The name of Jesus is the name of one who was a man but saw the face of Christ in all his brothers and remembered God. So he became identified with Christ, a man no longer, but at one with God.

In his complete identification with the Christ - the perfect Son of God, His one creation and His happiness, forever like Himself and one with Him - Jesus became what all of you must be.

Walking with him is just as natural as walking with a brother whom you knew since you were born, for such indeed he is. Some bitter idols have been made of him who would be only brother to the world. Forgive him your illusions and behold how dear a brother he would be to you.

From *A Course in Miracles*, Foundation for Inner Peace 1975.